Problems and Issues of Diversity in the United States

Problems and Issues of Diversity in the United States

Edited by
Larry L. Naylor

BERGIN & GARVEY
Westport, Connecticut • London

Library of Congress Cataloging-in-Publication Data

Problems and issues of diversity in the United States / edited by
   Larry L. Naylor.
      p.   cm.
   Includes bibliographical references and index.
      ISBN 0–89789–615–7 (alk. paper).—ISBN 0–89789–616–5 (pbk. :
   alk. paper)
      1. Pluralism (Social sciences)—United States.   2. United States—
   Race relations.   3. United States—Ethnic relations.   I. Naylor,
   Larry L.
   E184.A1P76   1999
   305.8′00973—dc21   98–41383

British Library Cataloguing in Publication Data is available.

Library of Congress Catalog Card Number: 98–41383
ISBN: 0–89789–615–7
      0–89789–616–5 (pbk.)

First published in 1999

Bergin & Garvey, 88 Post Road West, Westport, CT 06881
An imprint of Greenwood Publishing Group, Inc.

Printed in the United States of America

The paper used in this book complies with the
Permanent Paper Standard issued by the National
Information Standards Organization (Z39.48–1984).

10 9 8 7 6 5 4 3 2 1

Contents

Contents

Preface

Cultural diversity is perhaps one of the most discussed topics in the world today, perhaps even more so in the United States, since it represents the most culturally diverse nation-state in the world. The significance of this topic gained considerable importance when the world began to see example after example of what can happen when the conflicts that accompany the cultural diversity that characterizes all modern nation-states reaches the critical point. With the break-up of the former Soviet Union and as newly created nations of Africa attempt to find their way in the world of nations, constituent cultural groups have surfaced to affirm their legitimacy and identities. Each has asserted their primacy/prominence in the social and power structures. The inevitable conflicts resulting from competition with other constituent cultural groups have been taken to the extreme—the attempted genocide of entire groups of people. That this could happen in any nation-state has become quite clear to everyone, even Americans who take great pride in their diversity. Cultural diversity (multiculturalism) has characterized the American culture since its very inception. Many Americans have begun to seriously consider the idea that if Americans cannot come to grips with their own national diversity—confront and adequately deal with the many social and cultural issues and problems of that diversity—they, too, could find themselves in circumstances and in levels of cultural conflict similar to those being seen in Europe and Africa. Because of these cultural clashes, cultural diversity has become the "buzzword" of the 1990s. Proposed solutions to many of its accompanying social problems, while popular with the general public searching for easy solutions, are all too often simplistic and naive, reflecting the rather skewed perceptions of cultural diversity shared by most Americans.

Most of the discussions and books that have recently appeared on the topic of cultural diversity in America focus on such things as race, ethnicity, sex, or gender. For most Americans, this is what cultural diversity is all about. Up until the mid-

1980s, most diversity presentations focused on the specific concerns and interests of particular groups represented in the generally cultural diversity of America (women, black Americans, and so forth). Those presentations were more focused on advocating the special interests and ideas of the particular group than conveying knowledge about the group. The commentaries were argumentative, self-serving, and did nothing to help Americans confront their cultural diversity as a nation. This was a period in which the cultural groups found in the United States pursued their own agendas and strategies, advocating what the group wanted everybody else to think and/or do. At the very least, groups were involved in "bashing" those who did not agree with them. In the 1990s, there was a perceptual shift in the discussions toward developing a better understanding and awareness of cultural diversity as it had come to be understood in America. Unfortunately, this means Americans have not really come very far, for the topic continues to generate images of little more than black, white, and brown based on the rather skewed perception of race held by most Americans, their grossly overgeneralized perception of ethnicity, and a recognition of the gender differences. What this means is that most people continue to speak of stereotyped and arbitrary social categories and overgeneralized "ethnic groups." Most Americans do not address the actual cultural diversity of America. They conjure up social categories and aggregates of people that are not cultural groups at all. Unfortunately, government decisions and policy reflect the broad generalizations and stereotypes that underlie this view of cultural diversity. Just as unfortunate, the efforts to deal with diversity are doomed to failure because of it. The desire to find quick and simple answers to the complex problems and issues of diversity only seems to make matters worse.

Despite the tendency for just about every American to believe that they know what the issues are, what the problems are, and what the solution should be, serious questions about the cultural diversity of America remain unanswered, and a great many issues have yet to be resolved, many of which are still being debated among scholars, politicians, between different cultural groups, and even within cultural groups. Increasingly, it appears that a number of the social problems created by diversity seem to defy resolution. This collection of readings addresses some of these issues and problems and is designed to initiate serious dialogue on some of the most serious questions.

Some of the most important issues and problems of cultural diversity are a direct consequence of Americans not understanding what culture actually is and the role it plays in their lives. Other issues and problems are a consequence of the inability of Americans to distinguish between ideal culture and real culture, and still others result from the contradictions or paradoxes that characterize the nation-state cultures, themselves arbitrary and artificial to a large degree as they attempt to bring large and fragmented populations together. American culture does exist, but in that existence, there are many contradictions and conflicts that originate from the core ideas that bring them together as a society or group. Americans are pre-occupied with race, and the persistence of racism continues to fuel the inequalities evidenced in minority status, group stratifications, prejudice, and discrimination.

Such things are not limited to "racial groups" alone, but are experienced by nearly every cultural group of America, and this fact raises serious questions and issues. The widely misused concept of ethnic or ethnicity, a product of the development of civilizations and the territorially based nation-state, plays a significant role in cultural diversity, but the term is not an easy one to define. The meaning of *ethnic* (*ethnicity*) has shifted over the years, and currently, there is little agreement as to its exact meaning or the purpose it serves. While America is multicultural, so, too, is every individual American who must create his or her own cultural constructs within which to live, given whatever limitations he or she is born with or comes up against later as additional limitations are imposed by others. Given the vast number of constituent cultural groups in America and the generally unrecognized cultural variations within them (the unrecognized hidden cultural diversity of America), resolving the many political, economic, educational, and social problems posed by, and in, cultural diversity will not be easy.

The basic difficulties associated with America's cultural diversity are laid out in chapter 1. The reader is introduced to the first problem of cultural diversity, the concept of culture in both its ideal and real forms, and in terms of its relationship to the problems and issues of cultural diversity. The natural and inevitable conflicts created when people representing different cultures come together are addressed. The idea of social categories as compared to cultural groupings is discussed, along with how this affects the actual cultural diversity of American society and culture. The context of cultural diversity in America is examined and outlined, setting the backdrop for the remaining chapters of the volume.

One of the most serious problems to be assessed has to do with the conflicts, contradictions, and issues that come with America's core ideas and values. The reality of such things as social stratification, prejudice, and discrimination actually prohibit many cultural groups from fully participating in the American Dream. This is discussed in chapter 2 by Danny M. Wilcox. Wilcox addresses some of the most obvious contradictions that exist in the United States between the orienting ideas of America (its core or primary values), some other less agreed upon values, and the social behaviors generated by them. Wilcox suggests that people need to have a more realistic view of their culture—distinguish the ideal from the real. Many of these contradictions point to the difference between ideal culture and real culture, which is the subject matter of chapter 3. In this chapter, which focuses on the U.S. Navy, Clementine K. Fujimura confronts the issue of ideal and real culture, which is crucial to the real understanding of cultural groups and the pursuit of realistic solutions to the problems of diversity. Solutions must address what actually exists, not simply what people want to think exists. It is important that people distinguish between official (ideal) and unofficial (real) cultures if they hope to develop the awareness and understanding necessary to confront the problems of diversity. To be able to propose more realistic solutions to the problems, Americans have to begin where they actually are on these issues, not simply where they think they are. It is rare that the ideal and real cultures of America go together on a one-to-one basis. In addition, Fujimura demonstrates that the military cultures of America are very different from every other kind of culture that makes up America. Military groups function according to very different ideas and behaviors than most other Americans, even different from those characterizing the nation-state culture—in essence, making the United States a pluralistic society.

There is little doubt that race persists as one of the most pressing problems to be faced in the context of American cultural diversity. Despite all the evidence to the contrary, Americans are steadfast in their belief in the reality of different races. They are equally convinced such groups are characterized by the things they learn about them and that some are superior to others. The persistence of this racist thinking introduces some interesting dilemmas into the topic of diversity and the social and cultural reality of the diverse nation-state. In chapter 4, Erma Jean Lawson and Vijayan Pillai examine the persistence of racism in America and what it contributes to the discussion of cultural diversity. The persistence of race and racism raises serious questions about this nation's ability to ever resolve some of the most perplexing social problems accompanying the cultural diversity that so characterizes America. In a nation so pre-occupied with race, such problems may even appear to be insurmountable. The persistence of race naturally leads one to a discussion of prejudice and discrimination, the subject matter of Debra A. Harley et al., in chapter 5. The authors compare discrimination and prejudice to a powerful machine that is running out of control, destroying everything in its path. Despite their suggestion that knowing what to do is not the same thing as knowing how to do it, the authors offer a startling suggestion for how to do it.

In chapter 6, Tyson Gibbs focuses on the problems of variation with cultural groups. He specifically focuses on African-Americans, making it clear that not all blacks are culturally the same, even within such a well-defined and established cultural group as that of the African-American. Gibbs also makes a good case for not overgeneralizing and stereotyping people simply because someone might share some physical or cultural characteristic. The fact that even within such a grouping as African-American there is variation demonstrates that there is a significant hidden cultural diversity that goes largely unrecognized and unaddressed in the normal discussion aimed at finding solutions to diversity's problems. If left untreated, it is this hidden diversity that will undermine most efforts to find adequate solutions. Currently, most proposed solutions or responses to diversity problems aim solely at the overgeneralized cultural groups.

The problems with ethnic and ethnicity are the focus of chapter 7 by Kimberly Porter Martin. Ethnicity has lost much of its original meaning over time, but there is no doubt that it continues to play a significant role in the lives of individuals and groups of Americans and in the many discussions of diversity. Some have argued that it is no longer appropriate in the modern world. Some would suggest that it is only appropriate in the context of modern nation-states, important because of the increasing movement of people from nation to nation. Others argue that ethnicity serves in the self-identification of specific groups of Americans and their cultures. It plays significantly in the ongoing debates about affirmative action in America and whether or not the continuation of bilingual programs originally designed to help people integrate into the American cultural context, will be continued. In this chapter, Martin considers the many definitions, issues, and debates associated with the terms *ethnic* and *ethnicity*.

Some social categories consist of cultural groups extremely difficult to define, for they rarely bring their members together as a group, despite the fact that their members share core beliefs and behaviors. Socioeconomic classes and generational groups represent such cultural groups. Sometimes they may be better seen as cultural scenes, for they exist with a fluid membership and only function at very specific times and places (within severe time and space limitations). In chapter 8, Norma Williams focuses her attention on one such socioeconomic grouping, the poor. She points to the variations within this socioeconomic class and relates them to the ideas of minority, prejudice, and discrimination. In chapter 9, Beth Kaminow shows the difficulties in defining age groups or scenes. She argues that such terms as "Generation X" can describe a significant segment of America's youth, but it cannot describe all of America's youth. Such identifying terms simply represent gross generalizations on the part of different generations to understand one another. Kaminow's chapter also leads the reader to think about the individual within the context of cultural diversity. While nation-states are multicultural, the individual members of them are multicultural as well. Individual cultural constructs make the vast majority of individual Americans multicultural. Patrick James McQuillan discusses the individual within the context of cultural diversity in chapter 10, particularly the conflict between the strongly held belief in individualism and equality. McQuillan points to the power of cultural beliefs to hide and distort, as exemplified in the structure of school systems to work to the advantage of the upper classes and to the disadvantage of diverse student bodies. He argues that equal educational opportunities are closely tied to the social fabric that holds the nation together to make it what it is.

1

Introduction to American Cultural Diversity: Unresolved Questions, Issues, and Problems

Larry L. Naylor

American culture exists by virtue of the ideas, behaviors, and products shared by all Americans, regardless of other cultural identities that may also characterize them (Naylor 1997, 1998). Culture is the learned patterns of beliefs, behaviors, and the products of these shared by, and in, groups of people. But saying that America has a culture, that Americans share ideas, behaviors, and the products of these is not meant to suggest that all Americans share everything or even a whole lot. It would be incorrect to assume an American homogeneity simply because Americans share beliefs (particularly in such things as the orienting ideas of America), behaviors (in the sense that there are prerequisite behaviors that must be adhered to by all Americans), and the products of ideas translated by, or through, behavior into something (they all participate in the same enculturation, economic, and political systems). Because of the origins of this modern nation-state, its history, and the fact that it is a nation-state with all the complexity and fragmentation of such territorially based states that came with the advent of civilization, American society is also culturally diverse, perhaps the most culturally diverse of all modern nation-states. American society encompasses a large number of constituent cultural groupings, each of which play a significant role in the social fabric of American society. Together, they determine what is American culture and society. Cultural diversity is both a strength and a curse for America. Its strength comes from the many rich and varied cultures that contribute to what the country is all about. Diversity is a curse because of the constant conflicts and seemingly unresolvable problems it creates. Despite all the increased attention that cultural diversity has received in recent years, a number of serious questions do remain unanswered. Scholars continue to be embroiled in a number of serious debates and there is anything but agreement even within specific constituent cultural groups regarding the many issues associated with diversity. Despite all the recent efforts to come to grips with cultural diversity, many of its accompanying social problems seem to defy resolution. This volume is intended to consider some of these issues and problems, discuss our progress, or lack thereof, on some of the important questions and debates, and suggest where we might have to go from here.

When Americans think about cultural diversity, they inevitably conjure up images of broad social categories of people whereby differences focus on race, ethnicity, and sometimes even sex and gender. They think of "white Americans" and "black Americans," and sometimes even "brown Americans" (although the thinking of "brown Americans" tends to be isolated to regions of the country where the numbers of such people tend to be substantial). The same can be said for the group that Americans refer to as "yellow Americans." Of course, they think of such racial groups in whatever terminology represents the current designation for each of these racial groupings. To do otherwise is politically dangerous and incorrect according to someone. Ethnically, they think of Hispanics (Latin Americans, Latinos, Chicanos, or whatever the current designation for this group might be). They might think of Asian Americans, Middle Eastern Americans, South Asians, and so on, or they might think about groupings based on age, sex, gender, or any number of other special interest groups. With cultural diversity represented in such groups, Americans are lulled into the belief that they have a fairly good grasp of the cultural diversity that characterizes their society and culture. Unfortunately, this is not the case, for these widely recognized groupings are not really cultural groups at all (at least not yet), but social categories that people create for other people for social purposes, usually to distinguish "them" from "us." They represent ways people group other people in order to interact with them—a product of the increasing numbers of different people attempting to live together. Because Americans tend to interact with those groups as if they are in fact cultural groups only leads to more problems and difficulties than might come from cultural differences alone. Social groupings are not always cultural groups, and it is in the interactions of cultural groups that the problems of cultural diversity come into focus.

CULTURE

The first problem of cultural diversity that needs to be confronted is the idea of culture. Most people do not have a good grasp of what culture is or the role it plays in their lives. Based on a review of popular and scholarly journals, one can only conclude that Americans are uncertain about their culture. Most residents of the United States identify themselves as Americans, but when pressed, they do not have any real sense of what that means. Some of this can be seen as a legacy of history and some of it can be attributed to the composite population that makes up the United States. Both of these things have led to the widespread popularity of the "melting pot" metaphor most often used to characterize American society and culture both at home and abroad. It is very tempting to conclude that the United States has no culture of its own, or that it consists of the commutative contributions of all those people, from all over the world, who came together to make up the

American population. Of course, the definition of American culture depends upon how culture is defined, and even here there does not seem to be much agreement among the recognized cultural experts of anthropology.

Despite their differences, most anthropologists agree that culture is learned and not acquired as part of one's genetic inheritance or place of birth. They agree that culture is something that is shared within groups of people who are differentiated from others in that sharing. Of course, how much needs to be shared occasions much debate. There is agreement that culture is based on symbols or the utterances to which some cultural meaning has been attributed, and there is also agreement on the proposition that all the parts of culture are interrelated. Culture is not simply a haphazard assemblage of customs or traditions that accumulated over time. Culture is a coherent whole in which the parts are integrated and interrelated. There is also agreement that culture is not the same thing as society, although most Americans tend to use the terms interchangeably. Society represents an aggregate of people who share social relations—have claims and obligations to one another. Culture is the thing (the glue) that binds the people together in the human society. While some anthropologists would suggest that they see culture as only ideas—rules for behavior—others see it simply as behavior (what can be seen, felt, or tasted); still others see culture as the products of ideas and behaviors (as translated into material or social products). Despite their particular individual preferences in definition, most anthropologists do consider that ideas, behaviors, and products are somehow involved with culture. I see ideas, behaviors, and products as simply different aspects of culture.

AMERICAN CULTURE

In the final analysis, it really does not matter whether one defines culture using all three of these elements or whether one prefers a more narrow definition that limits it to just ideas or behavior. Based on any approach to the definition of culture, an American culture does exist and the existence of it accounts for the shape and form of American society. As already pointed out, there are things all Americans share, despite the presence of apparent differences. All Americans are the same by virtue of the cultural patterns they share; on the other hand, Americans are also differentiated into other cultural groupings that are distinguishable, one from another. This makes for the existence of an American culture and, at the same time, it makes for a culture characterized by its cultural diversity. Most Americans do not understand (nor do they want to see) their sharing of many different cultural patterns with other Americans, or that their national culture is directly tied to their preoccupation with individualism, or their lack of understanding of culture itself and the role it plays in their lives.

American culture is not a melting pot. It is a society and culture that from its very beginnings has been characterized by diversity. But herein lies much of the difficulty in defining American culture, a difficulty shared by every other nation-state within our modern world. The origins of nation-states or modern societies and cultures are quite different from those of societies and cultures before the onset of domestication and the development of so-called civilizations, with their territorially based existence and centralized political systems. Modern societies and cultures are characterized by large and fragmented populations, complexity, and superimposed national cultures—in other words, their cultural diversity. The nation-state culture is artificial and arbitrary, a culture created out of conscious decisions on the part of their founders.

American culture is the result of large numbers of people being brought together under one centralized political authority (territorially based unit). These peoples came to the United States with a learned culture already well in hand, but they also were given a new nation-state culture to learn if they were to survive in the new context. The people brought together represented (and still do represent) all manner of cultures brought with them from all over the world (specific and distinguishing ideas, behaviors, and products). The nation-state culture that these people had to learn was a consciously created one designed to bring together the diverse groups and establish a national consciousness and unity (shared beliefs and behaviors). Without some shared national consciousness and unity, there is simply no hope for the continued survival of any nation-state society, and by extension, its culture. The needs of a nation-state society and culture are no different from those of any other cultural group, it is only made more difficult because of the complexity and fragmentation that characterizes it. Even at the beginning of the American state, there was no suggestion that Americans would share everything, but there was the suggestion that all Americans must share some things.

All Americans share the orienting ideas of the culture (Naylor 1997, 1998). This would seem to meet the criteria of those emphasizing culture as shared ideas. Laid out in the founding documents of the nation are ideas on which everyone can and does agree. Freedom, individualism, diversity, and conformity are the dominant orienting ideas of America that are shared by every American, irrespective of any other identification they might also claim. These orienting ideas of America lie at the very heart of the American Dream to which all Americans aspire and which continues to bring still more people to the United States. Beyond these orienting ideas, there are few other ideas, usually spoken of as values, that are shared by all Americans. In fact, the conflict in these other ideas as one moves from group to group is one of the most serious problems of cultural diversity. The so-called mainstream culture, viewed by some as reflecting the shared values of Americans, is something altogether different. For some, mainstream culture simply reflects idealized culture; to others it is the specific ideas and values popular at any given time that reflect the ideas and values of those in the power positions of the society. One of the most serious problems of cultural diversity has to do with the conflicts, contradictions, and issues that come with America's core values (the orienting ideas), and the actual reality of class stratification, minority status, prejudice and discrimination, and strategies developed by cultural groups to achieve their objectives and participate fully in the American Dream. This is discussed more fully by Danny M. Wilcox in chapter 2. Wilcox focuses on the many and obvious contradictions that exist in America between its orienting ideas (its core values) and the social behaviors that are generated based on them.

From the shared orienting ideas come most, if not all, of the values usually proposed for Americans. Depending on a person's constituent group affiliation or affiliations, one's perspective on these other values can differ substantially. More importantly, the values represented in the orienting ideas of Americans are in conflict with one another. In other words, conflicts were obviously structured into the ideal pattern set out for American culture right from the start. Individualism and freedom are harmonious with the idea of diversity and the high value placed on it but are clearly at odds with the idea of conformity, which is also structured into the culture and society. While the orienting ideas of America have generated other values that have waxed and waned over the years, different perspectives on these other values do reflect the interests and/or circumstances of the various constituent cultural groups of the country. There is little doubt that Americans want members of their group to act like Americans. This leads to looking at these particular beliefs or behaviors as the basis of defining American culture. As with the orienting ideas, there are clearly behaviors that all Americans share as well. Part of establishing unity among Americans and social order within such a large and diversified population involves the establishment of behaviors expected of all Americans. All Americans must adhere to certain rules, behave in particular ways, or they will face some form of punishment from the state. This ensures that minimal behavioral expectations will be met by everyone. For example, all Americans must follow rules of the road, and while these can vary from state to state, there are minimums to be met. Driving requires a license, as does marriage or operating a business. All Americans are required to pay taxes. Americans are not told whom they must marry, only whom they cannot. Americans cannot advocate the violent overthrow of the government, but they are guaranteed freedom of speech (within limits). They have other guaranteed rights, but also the responsibility to respect the rights of others. All Americans know what behavior is expected of them. They all learn the rules, and they know the consequences of violating the rules. There can be no dispute that Americans share behaviors.

If products (both material and/or sociocultural) are made part of the definition of culture or are the focus of definition, again it is clear that there is an American culture. Certainly, Americans share all the same material items of life (or at least those they can afford), and they share the same sociocultural products created to respond to the needs of the society at large. All Americans must function within the economic system created to handle the resources available to meet the needs of Americans. While a person's ability to participate in that system depends on their socioeconomic status, everyone must meet their own needs through the established system (the money-dominated market exchange economic system).The political system of America is another sociocultural product shared by Americans. One can disagree with the system or what it should do or should not do, but everyone must operate within it. All cultures must teach future generations the ideas and behaviors required for group membership. America ensures that the American culture will be learned (including the organizational systems within which Americans will operate on a day-to-day basis and the behaviors expected of everyone) by requiring that all members or aspiring members of the group pass through the same educational system in which minimal curriculum requirements have to be met.

The American culture that was created over 200 years ago was a unique nation-state culture that responded to the wishes and desires of the people who came to America for their own reasons and consciously created it. Neither American culture or society is based on Americans sharing all things. The differences among groups of Americans is also part of what the culture and society are all about. Beyond the orienting ideas, Americans do not agree on what other ideas/values should reflect America. They do not agree on what specific behaviors should be expected of all Americans. They do not agree on how the political, economic, or enculturation systems should work. These kinds of differences create more cultural diversity in America, since those who share similar thoughts and feelings about such things come together to form new cultural groups—political parties and any number of specific purpose or interest groups.

Culturally distinct groups reflect the general fragmentations and complexity that characterize nation-states. This diversity is, in part, a product of how such states come into being. Nation-states originate as already established cultural groups are incorporated in the state by some form of coercion. For example, Native Americans awoke one day to simply find that they were suddenly Americans. Nation-states develop by adding already established cultural groups into their membership ranks or as part of their territorially based political states already in existence or being created. This means that as nation-states are created, the diversity that will characterize them is already part of the process and in place. As their populations grow, fragmented by their backgrounds and circumstances, and as new cultural groups evolve to respond to the core needs of the entire population, that diversity only increases and expands more. Such cultures are not subcultures of the nation-state; rather, they represent constituent cultural groups of the society and culture that are significant to its identity—contributors and sometimes benefactors of the culture as a whole. Americans refer to such groups as subcultures, but this is frequently a grave mistake. For the members of such groupings, the patterns of ideas, behaviors, and products that distinguish them from others provide them with the primary culture to which they will identify. Referring to such groups as simply constituent groups of this multicultural society might be more accurate.

In the context of nation-states, the constituent cultural groups that make them up are special-interest cultural groups. This type of cultural grouping can originate from all kinds of social and cultural distinctions (fragmentation) recognized within the society and culture. For example, there are special interest cultures based on age, sex, and gender; special needs of particular groups; the organizational needs of a complex and diversified society; leisure activities, religious or supernatural activities, and others tied to limited purposes or functions focusing on any number of aspects of trying to live in the United States. Among the most significant special interest cultural groupings that contribute to America's diversity are those that originate with America's organizational structure. Social organization reflects how societies and cultures are organized to meet their core needs of enculturation, social structure and order, and to provide for shelter, food, and the material needs of their members. Thus, there are all manner of cultural groupings that evolve that are tied to education (the primary means of ensuring that each new generation learns the culture) and the political/legal life of Americans (the means of establishing and maintaining social order). Many cultural groups appear out of the economic system or out of the handling of natural resources. This would include the multitude of business and corporate cultures of America and the additional cultures that evolve out of the various activities of such groupings. Age groups reflect the differences between the generations of Americans that arise as culture and times change. Gender and sex groupings evolve in order to pursue their specific interests, as do various religious cultural groupings and leisure activity groupings. Cultural groups evolve that culturally tie people together to pursue other limited interests or goals in religion, politics, conservation, humanitarian and charitable activities, and so forth. The actual number of such groupings is staggering to say the least. It is not generally recognized that the multitude of special interest groups in America represent people with very specific beliefs and behaviors that distinguish them as cultural groups—as constituent cultural groups making up the multicultural or diversity culture and society of America.

The cultural diversity of the United States is found in all the constituent cultural groupings that came together to make up the American culture and society. Each constituent group is made up of people who learn and share beliefs, behaviors, and products. Their shared patterns serve to distinguish them from other groups of people who learn different ideas, behaviors, and products. While it is popular to refer to such cultural groups as subcultures, suggesting their secondary importance to the culture of the nation-state, this has shown itself to be a serious mistake. These constituent cultural groups are not always subcultures, nor are they second in importance to the nation-state culture imposed upon them by virtue of nationality or birthright. Some of these cultures become, very much, the primary cultures for their members, providing them with their most important ideas and standards of behaviors—it is this cultural truth that lies at the heart of the diversity problems. As culture represents truth, when people of different cultures come together, the consequence must always be some conflict, for it is more than people coming into contact. It really means that truths come into contact and that means conflict. Each group tends to believe that its beliefs and practices are the right or more correct ones. They judge others by it and being convinced of its correctness, each group makes every effort to impose their truth on everybody else. As everybody does the same thing, cultural contact will always mean conflict.

SOCIAL CATEGORIES VERSUS CULTURAL GROUPS

The diversity groupings generally thought of by most Americans presents us with the next problem to be confronted. As already suggested, most people have a rather skewed understanding of America's diversity. When asked about cultural diversity, their first thoughts and images are of racial and ethnic groupings. This is not surprising in view of the government's own skewed handling of race, culture, and ethnicity. Unfortunately, neither perceived races nor overgeneralized ethnic groups represent cultural groups. Cultural groups are made up of people who share beliefs and behaviors, but artificially and arbitrarily created "races" are no more than social categories created on the basis of some vague physical characteristic for social purposes—social identification, to provide for generalization, to distinguish "them" from "us," to help in making policy decisions, and so on. Social categories based on race, gender, ethnicity, and/or special interests represent no more than aggregates of people grouped together based on some criteria established for them, not by them, and personal characteristics are assigned based on stereotyping and overgeneralization. The prescribed and composite membership of such groups is based on a faulty perception that people being prescribed into membership based on some physical characteristic(s) also share all the same cultural (learned) beliefs and behaviors.

Cultural diversity does not exist by virtue of racial groups, for such groupings are far too artificial, arbitrary, and generalized to be of any value. All blacks do not think or behave alike, nor do all whites, browns, yellows, or whatever other such "racial" groups one might want to identify. Black people do not share a culture. In fact, there are many different cultural groups represented among so-called black people (even if one could achieve agreement on what "black" means). This same thing can be said for whites, browns, or anyone else. The fact that race continues to play such an important role in diversity questions, issues and problems is amazing considering the fact that it does not really exist except in our social minds. Race is a classic example whereby people are grouped based on observed physical traits (mostly color for Americans). But races are also established on the basis of religion (Jews, Buddhists, Muslims), origins (Latin Americans, Native Americans, Asian Americans), language (Arab Americans, Hispanic Americans), or any number of other cultural criteria or traits. The question of the persistence of race and its relationship to cultural diversity is discussed more fully in chapter 4. There is little doubt that race persists as one of the most pressing problems to be faced in the context of American cultural diversity. Despite all the evidence to the contrary, Americans are convinced of the reality of different races and in the specificity of the differences they learn that accompany them. Race introduces some interesting dilemmas into the diversity topic and into the social and cultural realities of the diverse nation-state. The persistence of race raises serious questions about this nation's ability to ever resolve some of the most perplexing social problems that accompany the cultural diversity that so characterizes American society. While it seems reasonable to assume that what exists by virtue of social learning should be correctable by social learning, in a nation that is so preoccupied with race, the problems engendered by it may be insurmountable.

Much of the same thing applies to the generalized ethnic groups recognized by Americans. But here, too, Americans are more often than not referring to social groupings (categories), not cultural groups. Hispanics or Latinos, Asian Americans, even Native Americans are among the many groupings thought of as "ethnic." But there is no Native American culture, no Hispanic American culture, and no Asian American culture, and so forth. The Hispanic, Chicano or Latino characterization is based on the tendency of a person to speak the Spanish language as their primary language and a somewhat vague geographical affiliation (Central or South America). The social grouping actually consists of people representing many different cultures. Besides speaking the Spanish language or coming from Latin or South America, members prescribed into this group share very little. Within this category may be a Mexican-American, Cuban-American, Colombian-American, Peruvian-American, or any number of other distinct cultural groups that happen to speak Spanish as their primary language. The same can be said for Native Americans and Asian Americans, for these represent social categories as well.

Contrary to popular opinion, there is no Native American culture *per se*. The designation *Native American* reflects nothing more than a social category within which there are many distinct Indian cultures. Also contrary to popular opinion, Asian American is a social category. The inherent suggestion that all members of groups such as these are the same—share the same patterns of beliefs and behaviors—only demonstrates the basic ignorance of most Americans about the rest of the world. These social groups and many more like them immediately come into the minds of most Americans when the term *ethnic* is used. Members of specific groups that identify themselves as ethnic are more prone to use it in association with distinct cultural groups. The same circumstances surround any number of special interests groupings that also should be seen as social categories (e.g., age groupings, sex and gender groups, socioeconomic classes). For example, sex is a biological reality, but gender is a cultural construct. Thus, women might represent a sexual category, but it does not mean they will all share the same set of cultural beliefs and behaviors. Obviously, the first thing that needs to be done is for Americans to recognize that social categories and cultural groupings are not the same thing.

The use of such terms as Hispanic, Native, African, Middle Easterner, Asian and so on, merely obfuscates the actual cultural differences, ideas, and behaviors that distinguish the cultural groupings overgeneralized into such categories. The tendency to focus on such categories simply wipes out the differences among the people being categorized into such a group—differences that are quite significant to the people who may share nothing more than the criteria used by others to group them. To address cultural diversity necessitates that people deal with actual cultural groupings, not social categories. Even in that, there are risks of overgeneralizing, for in all cultural groups, there are variations that can become cultural groupings in their own right. While *ethnic* is simply another word for *culture*, its use in the American context is usually faulty and based on serious overgeneralization and stereotyping. It is assumed that the prescribed membership share the same beliefs, behaviors and products. None of the usually generated groupings represent cultural groups.

Serious debate continues among scholars over the definition of ethnic or ethnicity. With the rise of the complex nation-states, with their territorially-based state political structures and urban environments, ethnicity (ethnic) became a reality as a socially differentiating tool—one of the first ways that people could be grouped together and distinguished in such societies. In the final analysis, *ethnic* is simply another word for culture—it identifies a kind of cultural grouping found in all nation-states. While it initially identified people within territorially based states that moved from one part of the environment to another—primarily rural to urban—it now is applied to immigrant groups within modern nation-states who have moved from one nation-state to another. Contrary to popular belief, ethnic groups are not simply people who continue to practice the cultural patterns of where they may have originated. While they may continue some or many of their former beliefs and/or practices, they have to adjust much of their thinking and behavior in order to exist in the new country. Ethnic cultural groups are identifiable as a group in that they maintain some of their original culture, while adopting new beliefs and behaviors in order to survive in the new context. Ethnic groups, in essence, create new cultural patterns that are unique to them. The cultures they create for themselves are unlike any other in the world. Part of that uniqueness comes with whatever limitations (social stratification) imposed upon them within the new nation-state by virtue of racial, cultural, or social considerations. The cultures they create are unique to the specific nation-state context in which they appear.

Ethnicity has lost much of its original meaning over time, but there is no doubt that it continues to play a significant role in the lives of individuals and groups of Americans, and in the many discussions of diversity. Some scholars argue that the term is no longer appropriate in the modern world of nation-states. Others suggest that its importance has increased because of the steady movement of people from nation to nation. Still others argue that ethnicity serves in the self-identification of specific groups of Americans and their cultures. It becomes an issue in the debates about affirmative action in America and the continuation of bilingual programs originally designed to help people integrate into the American cultural context. In chapter 5, the author considers the many definitions, issues, and debates associated with the terms *ethnic* and *ethnicity* and relates them to various issues and problems of diversity in general.

Special-interest cultural groups are not unlike racial or ethnic groups in that they appear and reflect the complexity and fragmentation of the nation-state. In some cases, they originate from the nation-state's response to organizational needs. Basically, groups of people find themselves in particular circumstances and create their own cultures in order to respond (and survive) within those circumstances. Special-interest groups can be tied to age, sex, or gender; related to any one of the organizational cultures that are a product of the civilized and modern nation-states; or they can be tied to the many differences of opinion as to how the society should respond to or handle its various activities. Additional special-interest cultures are tied to more limited purposes or interests. The actual number of special-interest cultural groupings in America is staggering. But assuming a level of homogeneity for any of these groups, no matter how limited they might be, would be as serious a mistake as assuming a homogeneity for ethnic groups.

Within the actual membership of all identifiable constituent cultural groups of America, there are significant variations and differences that are obscured by the tendency to assume that all members of any particular group are all the same. As suggested earlier, such variations represent the hidden diversity of America, the diversity that is not recognized nor considered in attempting to respond to diversity problems. Most writers on African-Americans make it very clear that not all blacks are the same, nor are African-Americans. This should make a strong case for not overgeneralizing or stereotyping people together simply because they may share some physical characteristic(s). Most Americans ignore this, preferring to go on stereotyping instead. The fact that there is variation even within such a grouping as African-American points to the hidden cultural diversity of America that goes unrecognized for the most part.

With a recognition that cultural diversity in America goes well beyond the social categories to include ethnic and special-interest groupings, one might be prone to believe they have a good grasp of the cultural diversity of America. Earlier a note of caution was introduced about overgeneralizing for even the generally recognized cultural groups. Even with a good case being made for the existence of a Mexican-American cultural grouping, a woman's culture grouping, an educational culture, a business culture, a conservationist culture, and so on, few if any identifiable cultural groups exist in which all the members believe or do the same things. Variations exist within all ethnic or special interest groups. For some members of the identifiable groups, their own pattern of beliefs and behaviors take precedence over the larger cultural group to which they also subscribe. For example, while most blacks born in America recognize their affiliation with African-Americans as a social group, or with the black American category, some might prefer to be identified as Afro-Americans because the particular beliefs and behaviors of those preferring to identify themselves as Afro-Americans are preferred over the beliefs and practices of other African-Americans. Afro-Americans clearly differentiate themselves from Black Panthers or African-Americans who subscribe to the beliefs and practices of the NAACP. While the ultimate goal of obtaining equality with other Americans might be shared, group strategies to attain that goal or further the interests and causes of African-Americans can be quite different. Blacks can even differ in their own perceptions of their identities. The same kinds of things can be said for Mexican-Americans who differentiate among themselves by generation, points of origin, and the best strategies for attaining their goals, and the same has to be said for every other ethnic cultural group in America. The failure to take such cultural variations into account dooms most responses to diversity problems to outright failure right from the start.

The case of special-interest cultural groups is no different. For example, groups of American women differ substantially. Feminists, militant feminists, and more housewife-oriented women represent significant variation with that cultural group. There are variations within political cultures—not all Republicans share the same beliefs and behaviors. Educational culture incorporates a number of distinct cultural variations based on public versus private; elementary versus secondary; community college versus universities, professorial ranks, and disciplines, to name but a few. Wide variations exist for members and different aspects of Generation X, the Boomers, the American Association for Retired Persons, and the emerging Generation Y of the 1990s. Christendom (the cultural version of Christian culture) is replete with variations (Catholic, Protestant, Greek Orthodox, and so on), and even within these denominations (e.g., Protestant with its many subgroupings). Christians believe in Christ and the Bible, but in actual beliefs and behaviors, each specific group or church has a culture of its own.

Assuming homogeneity among any cultural group's members belies the hidden cultural diversity that goes unnoticed, but probably contributes significantly to Americans' inability to resolve the many issues, aspects, problems and questions of diversity. If the term "subculture" has any legitimacy in the culture discussion, it might be with regard to the variations found within nearly all the constituent cultural groups of America and in the cultural groups that develop in response to the organizational needs of complex societies. The term can be used to represent subvariations of some distinguishable cultural group that bonds together by some other characteristics. African-Americans would all basically agree that they are Americans of African origins and as such have a similar identity and similar claims and obligations to one another. Most teachers, be they public or private school or university, recognize their common identity as educators. All Christians recognize their affinity by virtue of their belief in Christ—they are subcultures of their particular denominations. Women generally recognize their cultural affinity with all women, even as they differentiate into subcultural groups based on positions, strategies, and actions. Regardless of the subcultural group with which they identify specifically, they know all women are their sisters. Subculture might be quite appropriate wherever a unifying theme or idea binds the otherwise differing variations together—a binding recognized by all of the people so bound together. But even in this grouping, great caution must be exercised, for in the subcultures or variations within any constituent group, some people find their primary cultures.

The major objection to the term "subcultural" comes with its connotation of subservience, that is, the cultural group is seen as of secondary importance or under an overriding group culture. For many Americans, this is not always the case. In America, African-American culture is not *sub* or secondary to the American culture at all. Members of this group identify with it as their major or primary orientation. Militant feminists distance themselves from other women with whom they do not necessarily agree. For this group, militant feminism becomes their life, their passion, and the central culture of their lives. The same can be suggested for religious cultures and their members. Some Christians make their Christianity the primary orienting culture of their lives, and when their beliefs and behaviors conflict with the national and more secular culture of the United States, the religious one will determine their positions and decisions or otherwise provide the blueprint for their day-to-day living. While many other similar examples can be noted, the point is merely that assuming such groupings are secondary to some other (higher) grouping would many times be a serious mistake. It would lead to major misunderstandings, faulty assumptions, miscommunications, and all the other usual consequences of stereotyping and overgeneralization. Much of the difficulty in responding to the social problems and conflicts created from diversity can be directly related to these kinds of variations within all cultural groupings that in essence prohibit groups from accomplishing their goals, prohibit political leaders from finding solutions upon which everyone can agree, and just makes a complex problem more complex.

The use of the term *subculture* may also be appropriate when speaking of cultural groups that develop in response to the organizational needs of complex societies. It has already been pointed out that all cultures must meet certain needs if they are to survive. In heavily populated nation-states that must provide for these things, new cultural groups appear as states develop ways of handling their educational, economic, and political needs. Indeed, such cultural groups can represent subcultures of the national culture, a product of that culture and specific to it. The higher education culture, the public education culture, bureaucracy of government, workers in all manner of federal programs and throughout the economic system of the United States may well represent cases in point. All such groups are products of the society meeting its core concerns—all could be viewed as subcultures of the national American culture.

Cultural scenes represent another aspect of the diversity of America, albeit part of the hidden diversity along with the variations within recognized cultural groups. As with ethnic cultures, scene cultures simply identify where these particular kinds of cultures originate. Cultural scenes are just like any other kind of culture. People share the same ideas, behaviors, and products, and in that, they distinguish themselves from other groups who have learned different things. The difficulty with all cultural scenes is that they are not as structured, in some cases not as clearly distinguishable, as the ethnic or special-interest groups. They are special interest cultural groupings, but they function within severe time and space limitations. They bring members together at particular times and places (sometimes never in face-to-face interactions), and members recognize themselves as part of the cultural group. Membership is rarely permanent or a given and tends to be much more fluid than that of other cultural groups discussed. Generational cultural groups and groups associated with socioeconomic classes represent cultures of this type. Interestingly, while socioeconomic class can be viewed as a social category on one level, on another it is clearly a culture group whose members share ideas, behaviors, and products. Within the variations of a class, as for example with the lower class, there are specific cultural groupings (e.g., poverty, poor, homeless, and within the homeless, still more specific groups). Much the same can be said for something so easily recognized as Generation X or the newer Generation Y. Generation Xers or Yers will very likely never come together, nor do they have a formal structure. The group's members may only come together at particular times and in particular places. Apart from these times and places, they still recognize their membership in the group and much of their identity will come from that association. Middle-class people recognize their affinity with others identified as being of the same socioeconomic class and believe and behave as those in the same group. But outside of some limited political activity, they may never come together for anything at all. The middle class is also unstructured and its membership is equally fluid.

The majority of Americans prefer to see themselves as middle class. Most recognize the distinction between the bulk of the American populace, which they perceive as middle class, the relatively few that make up the upper class, and the less fortunate that make up the lower class. It is the middle class that most reflects the images engendered by the "American mainstream" and the American Dream. People generally recognize their membership in this cultural group, which clearly learns particular beliefs and behaviors specific to it. With the bulk of America's wealth in the hands of a small number of Americans, the distinction between the upper class and the middle class is quite clear. While most Americans in the middle class are striving for membership in the upper class, realistic prospects of attaining it are minuscule, but that does not seem to deter them from constantly striving for it. Membership in the middle class is determined by almost any achievement toward the American Dream. Achieving any elements of this idealized dream is dependent on the availability of money to acquire those things most indicative of some level of achievement. Money makes it possible to acquire the desired material items such as cars, homes, computers and other technological toys that symbolize some level of success in achieving the dream. The market values of car, home, and technology pretty much determine whether one is in the lower, middle, or upper class; the distinctions between these are important to group members as a sign that they are moving more or less closer to the upper class to which they aspire. Income levels are most assuredly important but are not the sole determinant of class membership. The difference between actual income and the ability to acquire the things that bespeak of class membership can be circumvented by credit purchase and the plastic money of America's economic system. Thus, many people only appear to be succeeding in acquiring significant levels of the American Dream, while in reality they are not. It does, however, lead them to identify themselves with the cultural scene.

Members of this cultural scene, real or imaginary, will never come together. It is with their beliefs, behaviors, and especially their shared products that they recognize a cultural affinity with other Americans. Advertisers, politicians, and religious leaders play to the middle class for support, and it is probably only in providing that support that members of the middle class even remotely come together. The middle class is the most pre-occupied with achieving the American Dream. On issues important to them (anything affecting their aspirations), they may collectively vote for particular political candidates or party positions. The middle class uniformly opposes tax increases because this also would take money from the resources that they devote to the pursuit of the dream. Upper-class people oppose taxes because they can reduce their wealth (the measure of one's success) and potentially threaten their status in comparison with others of their own class. Lower-class members uniformly support tax increases, for in doing so, they believe more money will be available to assist them with basic needs and participation in the American Dream.

There is no permanent structure, nor even a permanent identity marker for the middle class. The income levels used by government to suggest membership are illusionary and constantly changing. What constitutes the American Dream is very fluid—one's level of success is dependent on one's particular financial status at the moment, and, of course, the twist to the American Dream is that there is never enough. So, even within the middle class, distinctions are made by members. It functions at particular times and places and then only with minimal membership actively involved. Americans identify their neighborhoods as middle class, but everyone wants to move up. They want to believe that they will make it to the upper class, but only a very few will actually do so. Class affiliation provides members of the middle class with their specific values on individual effort, work, equal opportunity, future orientation, and much more. Class affiliation accounts for their economic behaviors in acquiring the markers of the dream, and membership status is reflected in the products they surround themselves with, which, they believe, show the world that they are succeeding or have succeeded in achieving the American Dream.

SUMMARY

Each individual American is characterized by any number of cultural affiliations and identities in his or her lifetime. It is in the sum total of all such cultures that the diversity of America is evidenced. The constituent cultures of America each play a vital role in the social fabric of the nation and each can be identified by its own distinct set of beliefs and behaviors. Some of these cultural groups come with the development of the nation-state itself, a product of its origins and as a consequence of the territorially-based political state. Other groups come about as people move from one nation-state to another. Still other cultural groups are a product of the fragmentation and complexity of a modern nation-state as it creates organizational systems (organizes itself) to take care of all those things that any society must if it (and its culture) is to survive. That America is a culturally diverse (multicultural) society does not mean that it does not have a national culture that is shared by all Americans as well. Indeed, America has a unique culture in the world of nation-state cultures, one with a distinct pattern of ideas, behaviors, and products. But, when most Americans think of cultural diversity, limited images emerge. They focus upon broad categories of people based on race, ethnicity, or perhaps sex or gender. Such a tendency is a serious problem in the topic of cultural diversity in America, for until Americans focus on actual cultural groups within which members share beliefs and behaviors—which then represents their truth—they are not going to find adequate solutions to the many problems of diversity that seem to defy resolution. The tendency also obscures the actual diversity that is America. The much used ethnic categories of Asian American, Hispanic, Native American, and so on, for identifying cultural groupings obscure more than they clarify. Broad social categories are not cultural groups for the membership in such groupings is by prescription and constituted members may actually share little more than the one or two characteristics used to create them. It is with actual cultural groups that the problems of cultural diversity come into focus, not social categories, and many of these remain hidden in the tendency to generalize for all groupings.

There is little doubt that the persistence of racism also continues to contribute to the diversity problem. While races are arbitrary and artificial, Americans continue to be pre-occupied with it. The concepts of minorities, prejudice, and discrimination seem to be natural companions of race, but such things are not limited to racial categories alone. They seem to accompany all cultural groupings in one way or another. Along with race, the concept of ethnic (ethnicity) continues to cause problems. There just does not seem to be any agreement on what this means. It was suggested that it might be most appropriately used when discussing people who move from country to country, maintaining former cultural beliefs and practices (in so far that they might be allowed), while they adopt new beliefs and behaviors as might be required in their new national surroundings—in essence, creating new and unique cultures all their own. Some constituent cultural groups such as those established on the basis of all kinds of special-interests, to include socioeconomic classes, or which operate within limited space and time frames (cultural scenes), are difficult to get a handle on for they lack the more formal structure and permanency of ethnic groupings. Still, such groups do represent a significant element of diversity in America and thus should not be overlooked, for they determine the beliefs and behaviors of people just as do the cultural groupings usually considered.

Last, but certainly not least, the conflicts of American values (the orienting ideas of America) that create significant gaps between ideal and real America, pose their own unique problems for cultural diversity. Perhaps no other idea causes as much difficulty in resolving diversity issues and problems than that incorporated in the idealization of individualism in America. Individual Americans are as multicultural as are the nation-states to which they hold membership. But, the existence of the many cultural groups to which the individual affiliates belies the very idea of individualism. Americans hold membership in many cultures at any one time and across their lifetimes. Circumstances determine which of their many cultural affiliations give them direction at any particular time. It is almost as if Americans pigeonhole their lives and call upon the most related cultural grouping for guidance, given the particular set of circumstances they face. This tendency has led many Americans to view their lives in bits and pieces with little awareness or understanding of how the parts all fit together. If the question is a political one, they rarely recognize the economic consequences of political decisions. If the question is social, they do not recognize the political or economic consequences, or that their political or economic decisions may be restricted by the cultures with which they identify. They may not recognize that their religious beliefs and many of their prescribed behaviors go hand-in-hand. They may not recognize that the needs of social living go against the very individualism they value. They may not even know why they react to something the way they do or from which of their group memberships their very ideas might come. They may not understand that different beliefs and behaviors, acquired from different cultural memberships, may even conflict, causing them great difficulties and hardships. Learned culture represents truth and the problems of diversity arise from these truths as they enter into conflict. When truths conflict, members of each culture judge the truth (culture) of the others to be incorrect. To resolve the difficulty or problems of the competing truths, they then proceed to impose their truth (or attempt to impose it) on the other groups and the problems and issues of diversity arise.

REFERENCES

Naylor, L. L. 1998. *American Culture: Myth and Reality of a Culture of Diversity*. Westport, CT: Bergin & Garvey.
———. (ed.) 1997. *Cultural Diversity in the United States*. Westport, CT: Bergin & Garvey.

2

American Core Values and Questions of Diversity

Danny M. Wilcox

Freedom is the driving ideal of American hopes and dreams until someone suggests that people should be allowed the freedom to medicate themselves with drugs of their own choosing as they see fit. Diversity represents the wonderful character of the mythological melting pot and is widely hailed as the strength of this great country, until it causes extreme bitterness when affirmative action programs are designed to foster greater diversity in universities and the work place. Conformity is considered a necessary and positive quality in order to get along with others, to adapt and contribute to life in the community, until it stifles individual initiative and innovation, which is cherished beyond compare. Individualism is the most fundamental concept and crucial to the belief system that constitutes the basic world view that Americans share, at least, until some individual expresses an unpopular approach to some critical aspect of life. Then the value on conformity kicks back in and puts such rampant and dangerous individualism back in its place. It is easy to see that the American cultural ideology is something that is not readily revealed, but is, in fact, buried in a half-conscious cocoon of contradiction and conflict.

Identifying and defining the shared values, ideas, assumptions, and beliefs of mainstream American culture is a difficult and messy task. Some might suggest that there really is no set of values that all Americans share, but if that were true, then the standby phrase referring to a "shared" way of life in so many anthropologists' definitions of culture would be worthless. As a matter of fact, if there is no shared system of beliefs, behaviors, and products in America, we would have to conclude that there is no American culture, and nobody is buying that. Granted, there is a great deal of variability in the way that individuals and groups interpret the values and ideas most basic to the American world view. They vary not only between groups, but within groups as well. There are also enormous differences in the way that groups respond to these interpretations through their actions because beliefs not only influence behavior, but actually determine behavior in some respects (Kearney 1984). Different interpretations based on differences in class, religion, race, and ethnicity, as well as special interest groups, do not preclude the sharing of idealized standards.

Idealized standards are usually derived from a mainstream culture that is usually identified as the dominant, white middle class. Although such sharing would seem problematic to any understanding of the different ways that different groups and individuals view the world, it will become clear that although the interpretations may differ and the behavioral strategies may diverge among many cultural groups, the most fundamental values have still been accepted, integrated, and are shared despite cultural differences. Larry L. Naylor (1997, 1998) identifies individualism, freedom, diversity, and conformity as the four core values (orienting ideas) shared by most Americans and has suggested that these core values generate most of the other orienting ideas and behaviors that are crucial to the American world view.

In order to establish a concept of an American world view, this chapter begins by identifying some major problems presented by a culturally and linguistically diverse population. Then our core values and orienting ideas will be identified to show how they generate beliefs and assumptions about life in America that may or may not have much connection to reality. In this way, the interaction of American values and American diversity in the modern, urban, complex nation-state can be shown to significantly impact people's behavior in their pursuit of the American Dream. Finally, I will take a look at specific examples in real life, as opposed to ideal life, to highlight the contradictions and conflicts inherently generated by the gaps between beliefs and behaviors. These contradictions and conflicts between the idealized standards that are generally accepted by most Americans and the real experience of most individuals and groups are responsible for a great deal of agony in our society. By examining the impact of our values and diversity on economic, social, religious, political, linguistic, medical, legal, and educational systems, it will be obvious that we need to replace assumptions essentially based on illusion and get a better grip on reality if we want to relieve some of that agony.

BASIC PROBLEMS GENERATED BY DIVERSITY

Social Stratification and Class

Despite the generous lip service given to the value of equality in the United States, the inescapable fact is that America is a class-based society. Not only are we a class-based culture, but it seems that we thoroughly embrace the idea that people are not equal and for good reason. We cherish our class differences; we highlight them whenever possible; and we exaggerate them to our own benefit. The interesting thing about class in this culture is how everyone claims to be middle class. It is no surprise that middle-class people claim middle-class status, and it is not that earthshaking that aspiring members of the working and lower classes claim middle-class status, since that obviously works to enhance their self-esteem and probably encourages greater participation in the pursuit of the American Dream. But the really disturbing and revealing development in modern American society is the way that rich and upper-class people claim to be middle class. They object when someone suggests they are rich and privileged, "We're not rich, we're just middle class." They live in a house that costs between a quarter and a half a million dollars; their family members drive cars that cost over a hundred thousand dollars; they live in exclusive, gated communities where the local public school is extremely well supported and more closely resembles a private school; they have an income in the top five to ten percentile of the population of the United States, yet they claim, "We're not rich, we're *just* middle class." The most blatant example of this tendency to claim membership in the middle class by those who actually are among the elite in this country was evident in the Republican primaries during the presidential elections of 1996. Steve Forbes, the beneficiary of an enormous family fortune, and an extremely rich man, stood in front of a group of people and TV cameras and said, "This is a great country, where ordinary people like us can do extraordinary things." Like *us*? Forbes, then, was in the process of spending millions of dollars of his own money to run for president on an essentially one-issue campaign platform that was geared to reducing taxes—the contribution the rich and affluent should give to redistribute wealth—in what, by the admission of many, is the greatest country on the earth and ostensibly the only place the rich and affluent could have realized such personal riches from such humble beginnings.

It is amazing the extent to which the power brokers in this country have convinced the average working class American that he or she has more in common with upper-class members of his or her own racial or ethnic group than he or she has with other working people regardless of ethnicity. This shows how far the idealized value of equality actually applies in reality. The rich and power elites in this country misappropriate middle-class status for themselves as a tool of identity politics in order to maintain the illusion of equality and the "anybody can get rich" fantasy of the average working person. Class differences? Yes, we love them even as we try to ignore them.

The Institutional Machinery of Social Segmentation

Many aspects of the cultural system in the United States contribute in specific ways to the stratification and social segmentation of the society into distinct classes. The very diversity that Americans applaud in theory leads to significant differences and problems within and between cultural groups in actual practice. Economic, social, religious, political, medical, legal, and educational systems are all severely impacted by such diversity. Accommodating all the different individual and group interests on an equitable and fair basis is a massive undertaking with which we, as a society, continually struggle.

Economically, the wide disparity in wealth and income lays the foundation for a society that cannot come close to living up to the sacred value of equality, nor even achieve a modicum of fairness in the daily life of millions. Over the past few decades, the rich have continued to get richer, the poor have continued to get poorer, and the middle class has seen their relative wealth and upward mobility stagnate and begin to degrade. This foundational inequity is the fundamental basis of social segmentation in this country, and most of the other factors that contribute to class stratification depend on the disparity in wealth to begin to work their contribution to the maintenance of maximum diversity in the population. Why is it called *socioeconomic status* rather than just economic *class*?

Socially, some communities are necessarily segregated first by income. In the seemingly natural course of the capital development of living arrangements, entrepreneurs have found it more profitable to build large tracts of homes to be sold to people having comparable financial resources. Upwardly mobile individuals are more likely to pay the premium price for the nicest home available in a whole neighborhood of other people with comparable wealth rather than take a chance on a nice place surrounded by lower-income people. This not only satisfies the need to outwardly demonstrate one's class status, but is also supposed to protect against the fear that someone, usually poor, is going to want your goods and may even resort to violence to get them. Working- and lower-class people simply have no choice. They have to acquire what they can afford. Generally, this means living in older housing or buying in a very modest development. But socially, an interesting dynamic occurs when working- or lower-class people are actually paying just as much or more for substandard housing in a poor neighborhood when they could have something in a better neighborhood for the same amount of money. Are people really willing to stay in the same substandard neighborhood because they would rather be close to other people of the same race or ethnicity?

Religiously, we cannot really suggest that income and wealth have a determining relationship to the major religion that is practiced by any given group of people or even whether they practice a religion at all. After all, there are rich and poor Catholics, Protestants, Evangelicals, Jews, Muslims, Buddhists, and Hindus, to name a few. But, within any religious group, there does seem to be a basic segmentation based on wealth, primarily because these religious organizations tend to be community- or neighborhood-based. When people wander into a religious observance of their choice and find that most of the people there are of a different economic class, their level of comfort generally suffers, and they search for a different community, one they can relate to better. The economic differences in the class structure definitely affect religious communities internally even though accommodations are sought and actualized. Charitable giving is probably higher within religious groups than with any other cultural group. Externally, the tolerance observed or the lack of acceptance, as the case may be, contributes extensively to the continued maintenance of maximum diversity. As long as religious groups see themselves as essentially different from others instead of looking for areas of concordance, then the possibility of accommodation is diminished. Additionally, the large proportion of the American population that claims no religious affiliation and who are intolerant of religious practice add to the conflict.

Politically, the problem revolves around participation in this great, so-called participatory democracy. The history of political participation in this country is a joke. Historically, the right to vote was first linked to the ownership of property. The principle of one man, one vote was legally established and that supposedly ended the domination of landowners, but a man was not black and a man was not a female. It has only been about seventy-five years since women were allowed the right to participate and only about thirty years since people have stopped murdering African-Americans for trying to participate. Let's face it, maximum participation has never been the goal of the power elite. Limited participation is what greases their gears and the tool kit of our modern political system continues to include a huge monkey wrench for the express purpose of suppressing interest and action in the political system by ordinary people. And it works. The people most involved are the rich, the affluent, the ones with the money and property. Most people who are eligible to register to vote do not. Only about half the people who are registered actually vote. India and many other Third World countries have participatory rates for eligible voters that put us to shame. The political professionals know that by keeping the average person either satisfied, disenchanted, or both that, as the Borg say, "resistence is futile."

Medically, the disparity in wealth also enhances the failure of the health care system to adequately respond to the needs of a diverse population. In 1982, 49 percent of the bottom 10 percent of wage earners in the country were covered by health insurance provided by employers, 90 percent of the middle 50 percent were so covered, and some 98 percent of those in the top 10 percent were covered by employer-provided insurance (Pierce 1998). By 1996, the lowest wage earners had dropped to 26 percent, the middle had dropped to 84 percent, and even the top had dropped to 90 percent. Even though all income levels experienced a drop in rates of coverage, the disparity based on wealth is obvious. In addition to the issue of health insurance coverage, the costs of technologically driven medical care have increased dramatically. Lower-income people increasingly use hospital emergency rooms for basic medical services, a trend that is much more costly to the health care system and ultimately to the taxpayer than going to the general family doctor. But for the unemployed, the underemployed, the working poor, and lower-middle class families, the first thing to get left behind in the family budget is health care, particularly regular, preventive medicine. Most people in this situation only present themselves to a doctor when they are experiencing acute conditions. This leads to later diagnosis of serious conditions, a greater financial burden on the system as it tries to belatedly deal with worsening health problems, and higher rates of death for those unable to afford first-rate care.

Legally, well, there are very few rich people in prisons. If one subtracts all the high-dollar criminals from the federal prison system, there are just about no rich people in prison, and very few one could even characterize as affluent. Since the rich have money, they find it less necessary to commit crimes, but even when they do, they spend very little time incarcerated. Lawyers cost a lot of money, and good ones cost even more. The more money one has, the less likely one will do time regardless of the type of offense. Economics has a big influence on whether or not one breaks the law and it affects the quality of legal representation in such a way as to enhance or diminish the chances of incarceration—whether or not one is guilty of an offense. The income disparity of most racial and ethnic minorities ensures higher representations of blacks, Hispanics, and other minorities in prisons.

Educationally, public school systems in urban areas are on the verge of total failure. Again, differences in wealth drive most of the inequity. Schools in poor neighborhoods have the least resources when they probably have the need for the most. As a result, lower-income children are less prepared to attend colleges or universities, or be successful at it. This is so pronounced that many community college districts have given up on many inner-city students, counseling and persuading them to enter vocational training programs instead of pursuing a more traditional university education. Some four-year colleges and universities have begun to curtail remedial course work for unprepared students. Although no one seems to want to face it, the pitiful compensation offered to teachers in the public schools, combined with mind-numbing administrative and bureaucratic exigencies, and very real threats to personal safety mean less effective instruction. If we want quality education, we can have it, but we are going to have to pay for it, and thus far, that is a big problem because people only want to pay for their own kids' education.

Linguistic Diversity: Dialects and Communication

Despite the claims to the contrary by many languacentric and ethnocentric members of American culture, this country has historically been a multilingual nation. At the time the United States was established, it was determined that all government documents would be printed in English, German, and French, depending on where the publications were distributed. This decision was not the result of some philosophical theory, but a practical necessity. Throughout the immigrant history of the country, people have brought their native languages; lived in enclaves; contributed their food and customs; and slowly, but inexorably, assimilated themselves into the fabric of American culture. Some groups took longer to integrate, and some, African-American, Hispanic, and Asian in particular, were legally and/or factually denied integration into the larger society for many decades, but the use of languages other than English has been the rule rather than the exception for over two hundred years.

Our linguistic heritage is truly diverse. We can look at major immigrant groups and see the persistence of many other languages in contemporary society. At the very least, we can see the effects of those languages on the dominant, native, English-speaking population today in the words and phrases that have been borrowed into modern English and in the distinct dialect differences caused by the dynamic interaction of languages originally spoken in an area, geographic barriers, and cultural factors that impact communication. Distinct dialect differences are quite often the result of other speech patterns, phonology, morphology, and syntax. The Pennsylvania Dutch; Scandinavian communities of Wisconsin, Minnesota and the Dakotas; and originally French-speaking communities of Louisiana are just a few examples of the way other languages have resulted in dialect difference. Creole languages, such as Hawaiian Creole, French Creole, and Gullah in South Carolina are distinctive languages in their own right that have developed due to conditions of languacultural contact. The extremely diverse dialect differences in various parts of the country attest to the importance of geography on communication (Bonvillian 1993).

The other critical factor in dialectical differences is communication itself. Differences are minimized in tightly knit speech communities. Here, we can again see the effects of economic class on dialect differences. People tend to speak like the people with whom they speak most of the time. So, people in neighborhoods and communities segmented by wealth will tend to develop their own distinctive speech patterns and variations in the form and sentence structure. Less face-to-face communication means greater linguistic divergence and more specific identity conflict with others that *do not sound right* when they talk. In contemporary American society, we have many dialect differences that are being leveled due to the preferred use of a standard (actually a midwestern) dialect by advertisers, actors, and others engaged in TV and radio broadcast communications. This dialect has been accepted as more prestigious than most of the other regional dialects and has, therefore, been designated "Standard American English." Other variations— some southern, some northern, and, especially, African-American dialects—have been stigmatized as inferior. The linguistic diversity of the country is undeniable and leads to constant problems with communication in schools, businesses, governments, and workplaces. The consequences of such miscommunication are often quite serious.

Race, Ethnicity, and Minority Status

For most Americans, race is real; it matters; and it is here to stay. Just look on the application form for a federal, state, local, or even private sector job. Racial differences exist, but the important question is, why do we pay so much attention to them to the relative exclusion of many other important considerations? The legacy of racism is the massive contribution such thinking has made to the continuation, enhancement, and maintenance of maximum diversity in this country for the foreseeable future. The slavery of Africans and the continued economic, social, and linguistic segregation of their descendants until a mere thirty years ago has effectively spawned a substantial, although diverse, generally poor and angry minority population that presents many challenges to the values Americans say they have always held dear. Asians, particularly the Chinese, were also regarded by the dominant European culture as inferior and no better than animals. After allowing the immigration of the Chinese to work on the transcontinental railroad, further Chinese immigration was actually prohibited by law for a period of time. Other nonwhite immigrant groups have consistently been denied the type of preferential treatment some other (mostly European) groups have received, and the general mood of the country these days is that everything can be neatly blamed on a bunch of foreigners trying to come here and live off the fat of the land. Native Hispanics, whose ancestors were here first, before the U.S. militarily coerced the Mexican government into giving us Texas, California, and most everything in between, have also been excluded from participation in mainstream culture to a great extent.

It has always been easier for the dominant culture to identify racial groups because of the concomitant differences in their appearance, but that is the difficult and shallow aspect about our concept of race. Many Americans perceive African-Americans, Asians, American Indians, and Hispanics as monolithic groups based on race when, in fact, these are all diverse populations with regard to origin, economics, religion, language, and culture. In short, there are many different ethnic groups that constitute most of these groups that we segment perceptually largely based on skin color alone. Over the past thirty years or so, people have begun to recognize the difference between race and ethnicity. They have done such a good job of latching onto the concept of ethnicity that the drive to preserve ethnic, social, and languacultural characteristics has superceded the essential need to integrate different groups into the shared American identity. While this is a much better situation than that one of only three or four decades ago, when Americans were coerced into giving up and throwing away any ethnic vestiges if they wanted to participate and succeed in the pursuit of the American Dream, the cacophony of special interests based on race and ethnicity is out of line when local school boards cannot get anything done due to African-American vs. Hispanic vs. Asian vs. Native American enmity. These kinds of problems, based on the core value of diversity; nurtured by mistrust, misunderstanding, and miscommunication; fueled by economic, social, and political disparity; and encouraged and sanctioned by the power elites, are not so inevitable. But they are counterproductive, tragic, and do absolutely nothing to address prejudice and discrimination in this country.

Prejudice and Discrimination

The very diversity that Americans value in theory leads ironically and directly to prejudice and discrimination based precisely on that diversity. The inherent economic, social, political, religious, and educational differences presented by a culturally and linguistically diverse population generate enormous fear and loathing in a society that is sure there is not enough to go around, that there is only limited good, that others want to take what is not theirs, but yours, and will stop at nothing to get it. Such anxiety is also exacerbated by the fact that there are so many individuals and groups that do not *believe* like we think they should. People discriminate on the basis of physical appearance, not just skin tone, but body weight, hair style, clothes, dental hygiene, physical beauty, and age. Americans also discriminate on the basis of material wealth, the neighborhood or the house a person lives in, the car she drives, the restaurants he frequents. It seems that we are always making visual judgments before people even open their mouths. Once they do speak, we discriminate on the basis of verbal performance, not just the words used, but the speech pattern (accent); the sentence structure; the idiomatic content of speech; vocal volume and speed; and even the silences, the pauses, and etiquette in turn-taking utilized. Americans instantaneously analyze this complex stream of information in an effort to answer the first basic question: Are they *like us* or are they *different* (Agar 1994)?

It is inescapably human to engage in this exercise. It probably had some very important adaptive advantages to our early hominid ancestors. It certainly had adaptive advantages for traditional peoples we know from the ethnographic record. Whether someone is kin, a friend, or an enemy can be very important. Our place among others and our relationship to them is critical to life, liberty, and the pursuit of happiness. As we have noted previously, many economic, social, religious, political, and personal considerations enter into the judgments we make. Human beings are more than adequately equipped to make such judgments in the interests of themselves and the interests of others with whom they have special relationships. The problem is that this facility is not an omniscient one. Human frailty ensures that the exercise must be carried out carefully and prudently, but that is rarely the case. We engage in such activity unconsciously for the most part. Unfortunately, this lack of attention to detail and any thoroughness makes it extremely easy to manipulate people's perceptions of others. The suggestibility of human individuals and groups means that people can be easily blinded to reality, especially when they are afraid. Power elites have effectively manipulated people's fear for thousands of years in an effort to control populations and achieve their goals. This ability is not limited to just the rich and the powerful. Community leaders on all levels can attempt to help their people transcend such base action or they can pander to their own egos and exploit their people's weakness, and encourage the self-centered and destructive animus that leads to prejudice and discrimination.

BASIC CORE VALUES IN AMERICAN CULTURE

Now that we have briefly examined some of the major problems presented by our cultural and linguistic diversity, we need to identify and define the basic core values and associated orienting ideas in American culture. No listing can ever be definitive or exhaustive, since the broad diversity of American culture mitigates against any such determination, but we can identify the core values that most Americans share by virtue of their participation in this culture. Although some groups may interpret them and respond to them differently, there is still enough that we do share that such a discussion will be productive in trying to discover how our values and our diversity work together or result in contradiction and conflict.

Freedom

Freedom is the most central value to American culture. It is also the idea that is most consciously recognized as the fundamental basis for human and American life. We believe in freedom: the freedom of the individual to pursue his or her own course in life; the freedom of groups to preserve their own customs, religions and traditions; the freedoms of expression and assembly; the freedom from injustice; academic freedom; the freedoms of opportunity and participation; the free market; the freedom to tame nature; to develop new technology, to compete; and we believe in the *spirit* of freedom (which also includes all the other unspoken or forgotten freedoms that we will probably think of later). Freedom is what brought our forefathers to this country, and it is what continues to attract immigrants from all over the world. It is the primary reason that most Americans consider this the greatest country in the world because it was conceived and born in the human need to live free from tyranny and injustice. Without freedom, there would be no United States and no American culture, and without the individual, there would be no freedom.

Individualism

We put a great deal of trust and hope in the sacred concept of the individual. Without daring and innovative individuals, there would be no progress, no justice, no freedom. Individualism is the icon of American culture. Click on it and you get a menu of most of the other values and ideas that Americans revere. The role of the individual is critical to what this country is all about. Brave, hardy, intelligent, inspired, and driven individuals are responsible for new and better ways of doing things, scientific discoveries, manufacturing improvements, great art and literature, new world orders, protection of the weak and needy, prosecution of the greedy, truth, justice, and the American way. The character of Superman is the ideal individual and the quintessential American citizen. For most Americans, to stifle the individual in this culture is to dangerously challenge a fundamental law of nature and is an affront to their common sense. The individual is the antithesis of robot, sheep, and communist and is absolutely vital to our way life. The group construct of the value on the individual can be found in the value of diversity.

Diversity

Diversity is the great inner source of the wisdom and strength tapped by the founding fathers to write the Bill of Rights and the Constitution. Different people with different languages, ideas, and ways of life were drawing on their knowledge and that of people with very different backgrounds. This interaction contributed to the individual and group innovations that brought the entire process of establishing the society and culture to life. In the beginning of our country, respect for other peoples' language, culture, social organization, religion, and subsistence strategy was a fundamental necessity. Freedom from oppression by other foreign, dominant groups was the reason these people came, banded together, and codified the rights of individual groups. Protection from prejudice and discrimination was also legally formulated. After the founding of the country, almost continuous waves of immigration from various parts of the world, mostly Europe, contributed to the rich variety of individuals, businesses, languages, customs, food, clothing, and ideas. The melting pot heated up and cranked out more and more Americans because that was the goal of all the poor immigrants: to have a better life, a life of freedom and opportunity, and to leave behind the old ways and the old ideas—to become American, to conform.

Conformity

Even though the individual is considered a hallowed being, the exigency of diversity demands that respect for *other* individuals, not just the individual *self*, be granted. As human beings, we are social creatures. Despite our emphasis on the individual, we cannot escape the fact that we do not live in individual isolation. Social science has thoroughly demonstrated that we live in relationships with others, that depending on the specific culture each person has certain rights with regard to the larger community, and that each also has certain duties and responsibility to others. Within the context of the development of American culture, conformity should provide the natural balance to the individual. Previous immigrants were encouraged to let go of the old ways. Some first-generation Americans went so far as to discontinue the use of their native language with their children in order to more completely assimilate. Some first-generation immigrants did just the opposite. These became the traditionalists who tried to preserve the language and customs of their native lands, but were generally thwarted by their second-generation children. These children, under enormous pressure to melt in the pot and become American, rebuffed the old ways and conformed in an effort to achieve equality.

Equality

Equality is a tricky but necessary assumption to the American world view. Deep down, everyone realizes that there is no absolute equality, that people have variable intelligence, talent, and ability. The practical value we give to the idea of equality is based most firmly in an equal *opportunity* to participate in the American Dream. Although individuals and some specific groups may have variable strengths and weaknesses, the American promise of freedom for the individual and the group to celebrate their diversity as long as they conform and respect the right of others depends on equal opportunity. The American philosophy hinges on the premise that no matter who you are or where you come from you will have the opportunity to "be all that you can be." Given this opportunity, the only way to realize the dream is through hard work.

Work

Hard work is the suggested road to material well-being, happiness, and equal participation in the American Dream. This puritanical, but practical, suggestion is the basis for upward class mobility in American culture. The individual is free to pursue any type of work to which he or she is best suited in order to realize the promise of American life. We are taught that we can have anything we want, but we will have to work for it; nothing comes on a silver platter; there is no free lunch if we want to succeed. If we have a setback or at first we do not succeed, we are counseled to "try, try again" and never admit or cave in to failure or defeat. In fact, in today's sportcentric culture, hard work and never giving up has become synonymous with winning, and winning is what it is all about if you want to *achieve* the American dream.

Achievement Orientation

Achievement is another widely shared idea or accepted assumption generated by the ideas of individualism and freedom. The orientation toward achievement is a consequence of the ideas of individualism and freedom. While there may be many people who inherit wealth or position or opportunity from their families, whether or not the individual is successful is largely a matter of personal achievement. Even in families of great wealth, we can see children who are obsessed with their own personal achievement, of making a name for themselves instead of simply riding on mommy and daddy's coattails. For the rest of us, we are assured that the culture provides the freedom of opportunity and the respect for individual effort necessary to provide the basis for success, but it is up to the individual person to actualize such potential. One must (should) work hard, respect the rights of others, and take advantage of every opportunity in order to achieve the American birthright. One is conditioned to expect setbacks, but progress can only be made if one remains focused on the positive.

Optimism

The "can do" spirit of American optimism is absolutely necessary to progress. This idea is embedded within all the dominant values and a great many other assumptions contained within the American cultural ideology. Without a belief that there is freedom and an equal opportunity for the individual and specific groups to overcome adversities, trials, and tribulations through hard work and personal achievement within the system of American culture, there would be no American Dream. The colonists fighting the Revolutionary War had to believe they would triumph—it was life or death. Abraham Lincoln had to believe that even the carnage of the Civil War was preferable to doing nothing if it would preserve the Union and the dream. The robber barons of the late nineteenth century had to believe they had the right and could succeed in generating and hoarding enormous wealth by whatever means necessary. The labor unions had to believe that they could only overcome the robber barons through unified, persistent sacrifice. The Wright Brothers had to believe that they could design and build a flying machine.

The examples are virtually inexhaustible. We have to believe that there is an American Dream and a cultural mechanism to achieve that promise. But that promise is not going to be fulfilled simply through optimistic persistence and hard work. Achievement can only be realized if positive thinking and effort result in an essential, personal competence.

Competence

This idea is the result of a compromise among the four core values and the assumption of equality. As previously stated, equality *per se* is not recognized as a reality, but rather is manifested in equal opportunity for the most part. Freedom of the individual working within the diverse system of American culture requires that some people will be more competent than others. Through persistent and hard work, the individual is expected to achieve the highest level of competence possible. Success is determined to a great extent by the degree of competence that a person can achieve. By becoming better at the things that we do compared to others engaged in similar pursuits, we are able to effectively compete in the free marketplace of goods and ideas. Such competition is personified in the American obsession with sports and the language used to describe the competitive endeavor and the ultimate achievement of winning. However, the exemplary competitor is not a kicker, biter, and scratcher, but someone who trains effectively to get the most out of one's ability without having to resort to cheating. One is, above all, a clean and honest adversary.

Honesty

Honesty is the best policy. Although there is a great deal of fudging on this idea, most Americans adhere to this basic premise. The values of freedom and equality demand a certain fairness in our dealings with others, and this in turn necessitates the use of honesty. Cheating and lying may benefit the individual, but it seems to grind against the grain of diversity and the respect for others. As we have seen repeatedly, none of the core values or the other derived ideas and assumptions can exist in a vacuum. In order for the American cultural system described and outlined in the American world view to work effectively and equitably, there is a complex and balanced interaction that is expected to take place. This is, of course, an ideal, but there is little or no doubt that the vast majority of Americans consider honesty necessary and appropriate whenever possible. People who have no consideration for others are commonly identified and labeled antisocial.

Sociability

Social responsibility is a fact of human life. This is why we place such a high value on conformity. While Americans do not abide by the ultimate submergence of the individual person into the social fabric, there is a necessary realization that we are responsible to others. For many Americans, this is focused on the family and religious community. For many others, this focus is on the workplace. For some, the neighborhood and well-being of the community is of great importance. No matter where this loyalty to the group is directed, it is important to recognize the need that human beings have to belong. We simply cannot make it in isolation, despite our value on the individual. Even those who claim no group loyalty can be observed worrying about their relationship to other individuals and groups. In the end, like it or not, accept it or not, we always find ourselves subjected to some authority other than ourselves.

Authority

Authority is a wild card. It goes against the stream of individual freedom but is critical to conformity, diversity, responsibility, law, and order. It is often said by politicians, lawyers, and law enforcement professionals that this is a country of laws and that without laws to protect the innocent there would be no order, only chaos and anarchy. Generally speaking, American culture provides a system for law and order. Americans are easily persuaded to form neat lines at concession stands and wait their turn, for Americans are for law and order. A drug may be harmless, but if it is against the law then one should not use it. A war may be unjust, but if the law says that the eighteen-year-old kids who cannot afford to go to college must serve, fight, and die then that is the way it is. You may be perfectly safe speeding on a particular stretch of highway, but if one is exceeding the speed limit, one deserves the ticket. Authority is the strangest of our accepted values because while some authority is generally recognized as absolutely necessary, the overwhelming majority of Americans place a qualitatively negative value on the idea of authority. This is a clear and unsettling indication of the abyss that separates the world view of the idealized American Dream and the reality of human experience in this culture.

THE AMERICAN DREAM, WORLD VIEW, AND REALITY

Anyone paying attention to the description of the pivotal values, ideas, and assumptions that Americans share has already developed a catalogue of objections, exceptions, comments, and outright rejections. It is clear that in trying to explain the historically important core values of American culture and the beliefs and behaviors they generate that America is not Camelot. While these values were gleaned from a number of informed sources and distilled to demonstrate the interdependent and interactive nature of the belief system, so many assumptions scream for exception (Althan 1988; Arensberg & Niehoff 1971; Hall & Hall 1990; Hsu 1972; Spradley & Rynkiewich 1975; Spindler & Spindler 1990; Tiersky & Tiersky 1975). This is to be expected in any discussion of any culture's world view, especially such an extremely diverse, complex, modern, urban culture represented by American society. Still, the previous discussion serves to show how our values generate the ideas and assumptions that we integrate into a specific belief system.

The previous discussion also shows the enormous potential for contradiction and conflict generated in the disparity between our beliefs and our behavior, between what we say and what we do. Individuals and specific groups develop divergent strategies to interpret and operationalize the same accepted values and assumptions. This is where we see the bulk of the objections, exceptions, and rejections of the idealized description of our values and beliefs. Many groups that were previously bound by similar cultural beliefs have fragmented and are no longer a viable or influential unit in the everyday reality of American cultural relations. Other groups have consolidated and grown in such a way as to present a new force with which to be reckoned and a source of changing beliefs and behaviors. Many individuals and groups have had to substantially lower their expectations of the American Dream. Others have given it up completely. In order to more fully explain the massive contradictions and conflicts involved in actualizing the values of American culture in contemporary society, we need to more fully examine the interaction of the problems generated by our diversity and our beliefs in everyday life. Only in this way can we discover the reality of our behavior as opposed to the theory of behavior suggested by our belief system. We need to take a look at real life in late, twentieth-century American culture in the context of the most beloved value of all. We need to critically examine the idea and the reality of our freedom.

ECONOMIC FREEDOM

The American Dream is founded on attaining greater material wealth and higher social status in society. The emphasis on achieving affluence and upward social mobility is based on the concept that any individual, through hard work and persistence, is equally free to pursue a bigger slice of the American pie. This vision of possibilities has historical and contemporary salience for many individuals and groups, but for others, it has absolutely no connection to the reality that they, their families, and their communities have experienced. As such, the American Dream has no real meaning for them. For millions of people in this situation, it is viewed as the unkept promise of the American cultural mythology. The greatest barriers to the achievement of greater wealth and position in this country is, ironically, the lack of wealth to start with and the attending lack of equal opportunity. The rich do keep getting richer. The poor do keep getting poorer. While the rich may be self-serving in denying this, or claim that they achieved it fairly through their own hard work and persistence and that absolutely anyone has the same chance in this country, people without adequate resources are much more aware of reality. Poor people and lower, working middle-class families and communities have no such illusions. By examining some specific economic issues, it will become clear that the values, assumptions, and ideas inherent in an American world view that accepts the reality of the American Dream is, for the most part, even to many individuals and groups that tacitly accept it, the broken promise of an American cultural mythology.

The Free Market

The promise of the free market is supposed to be the foundation of our country and the hope of the average person. This concept is highly touted by most as one of the primary reasons the United States was founded. The historical vision of many is that the colonists in America rebelled in order to free themselves from "taxation without representation." If that had been the case, the Revolutionary War need not have been fought, for the English could have simply extended the privilege of sending government representatives to England. The differences were much more complex. Still, the Boston Tea Party is considered a glorious and watershed event in our history and continues to symbolize the necessity and the productivity of free trade. This value on the freedom to engage in commerce without the tyranny of outside influence is a sacred cog in our ideological wheel.

The theory of free trade (capitalism) is consistent with the core values of freedom, individualism, and diversity. It has meaning when all people have the equal opportunity to participate, but there is no real equality of participation, and there is no reality of a totally free market. From the beginning of this country, there has been constitutional provision for the regulation of interstate commerce and practical restrictions for aspiring business people at home and abroad. Consistent with the orienting idea of conformity and the idea of social responsibility, certain business activities are not allowed by law and the trade of certain commodities are banned while others are closely monitored. Laws against fraud and deceptive trade practices are consistent with the assumption of equality and the orienting ideas of competence, honesty, optimism, and authority. Laws that exclude trade in slaves, child pornography, child labor, murder, robbery, kidnapping, and burglary are also consistent with social responsibility and conformity. Harmful drugs are banned for the same reasons. But even though there is a consensus today about the necessity of such restrictions on free trade, the history of this country has hardly been consistent with regard to what are now viewed as obviously needed controls.

Historically in America, economic freedom and the promise of free trade and entrepreneurial opportunity have been very narrowly restricted. Africans brought to this country and sold as slaves were accorded no freedom or dignity and were treated like animals, with no rights whatsoever, not even the right to life. Although technically freed at the time of the Civil War, their descendants continued to be denied the basic freedoms we all claim to revere. After the Civil War, they were forced to continue to live within their own communities and were excluded from all practical means of participating in the American Dream. They were separated from the opportunity to achieve the kind of success that goes with getting a good education, starting a business, and upward social mobility. These limitations, sometimes legally codified, were only addressed in this country a mere thirty-five years ago with the passage of the Civil Rights Act. Currently, it is very common to hear people express the opinion that slavery and its legacy is a thing of the past and that African-Americans now have just as equal an opportunity as anyone else. But the persistence of prejudice and discrimination is the first indication that this is not the case. Passing the civil rights law and actually making sure that federal, state, and local governments abided by that law was a miniscule beginning to removing real impediments to African-American participation. Many people cite the fact that some African-Americans have improved themselves and their families through hard work, persistence, and seizing the opportunities that were given to them over the past 130 years as examples of their contention that there is something wrong with individual African-Americans and their communities rather than something wrong with the American ideology. While there have been millions of decent African-American people who accepted the limitations of a segregated society and worked hard to afford their children better educations and opportunities, most of these success stories occurred within their own communities, but such success was still limited. Participation with the larger society and opportunities fostered by a truly integrated society has only just begun in recent times, and the limitations imposed by slavery, segregation, prejudice, and discrimination continue for the majority of the African-American population. These continued problems are structural, and they cannot be solved with a flair of the pen. They can only be solved by changing the social and economic structure of the culture.

Although the plight of Africans and their descendants in this country is the most dramatic and disturbing example of the failure of American culture to live up to its creed, the economic disparity they experience and the failure of the values of American ideology in real life is not unique. The historical conflict between the biggest of the capitalist robber barons, entrepreneurs, and workers also leaves us with a glaring example of distance between the ideal of the free market and the reality. It took a long and continued struggle for labor to gain the right to organize and strike, free from the threat of actually being killed or losing their livelihood, as well as generating legislation that would outlaw the use of child labor, unsafe working conditions, and unreasonably low wages. Organized labor helped many individuals and groups to achieve the American Dream, even though the power elites in business and government strongly fought the idea. From time to time, the U.S. government has taken action to assist the individual, but only as a result of intense political pressure. Generally, the government has been most cozy with large capitalist entities. It has passed and still enforces some antitrust legislation, but sometimes one wonders if this is because the government wants to preserve our economic freedom so that the value of genuine, honest competition will result in progress, or if it is just worried that if corporations get too big, they will be calling the shots, which is a very real threat. In fact, it already happens. Big business has always tried to eat up the small competitors and limit workers' compensation, but recent trends are dangerous for the American Dream and scary for most Americans. Fewer and bigger corporations are gobbling up everything, independent business is failing, family farms have all but disappeared, and efforts to pit workers against one another has resulted in a disorganized labor force as fewer and fewer workers have any collective clout to ensure the equality of their opportunity to engage the American Dream. People are forced to go out of business and get a job working for one of these corporations; people are forced to work for less even when there is a shortage of potential workers; and the ability of people to achieve the American

Dream embodied through our core values and assumptions is destroyed.

Actual government restrictions on free trade, practical competitive prohibitions for owners of small or family businesses, and the general absence of an organized labor force clearly demonstrate that the value we put on the free market and our economic freedom is well placed. Big corporations are killing the small-scale entrepreneur and the ability of people to bargain collectively. Small businesses simply cannot compete with them, and workers, while not being legally prohibited from organizing, are falling victim to the value of individualism and the image of limited good. They are pitted against one another by being convinced that everyone is not equal, and it is everybody for themselves—"you gotta look out for number one." So the rich are getting richer, the poor are getting poorer, the middle class is getting squeezed, and the entire process is supposed to be color blind. While some minorities may suffer disproportionately, the process does not discriminate on the basis of race or creed. It is the money that matters. Suffering is over-represented among groups with low incomes, regardless of race or ethnicity. Millions of white people are also excluded from the process based on economic class. The disparity in wealth, resources, and equal opportunity sets the stage for massive contradiction and conflict between our ideals and reality and, if recent trends continue, for a brave, new world.

Welfare: Individuals and Corporations

The fact of poverty in this country is a part of the diversity that we celebrate. "Poor immigrants" is a phrase that we hear repeatedly in any discussion of the history of this country. But the poor immigrants of the American cultural ideology did not remain poor. Given the freedom of the individual and an equal opportunity, they overcame poverty and conformed as Americans. Thus, they have the respect and goodwill of most Americans. At first glance, it would seem that the existence of programs that assist the needy is in direct opposition to the "pull yourself up by your bootstrap" mentality that is so central to the value of individual hard work and effort, but it is in accord with the value of diversity and the social responsibility embedded in the value placed on conformity. Public assistance, as well as private, charitable giving, are good examples of the real interaction of the ideals in the belief system. No value is absolute and all are subject to compromise. Given this, it is no surprise that Americans and the American government have supported programs to help people that cannot help themselves. But currently there are some very serious disagreements between advocates and critics of such efforts.

A vocal and significant number of people in this country have become quite convinced that public assistance, welfare in particular, has been grossly exploited by able-bodied males, welfare mothers, and immigrants who refuse to live up to the American value of individualism and the ideas of competence, achievement, hard work, and optimism. As a group, people on welfare are considered by these hard-core adherents to the American cultural ideology to be bums and societal failures—deadweight at the least, if not outright criminals and cheats. As a group, they are condemned socially, politically, and economically. Government at all levels has focused on these people as wasting the taxpayers' money and has vowed to get them to work and off the public payroll. The implication is that if one does not work and make one's own way, then one is not worth helping or saving. In all fairness, we seem to be just as hard on rich people's children as we are on the poor—the value of equality kicking in again. People are vilified for spending food stamps on beer, as they should be, and people with disabilities are accused of giving up, as they probably should not be. Americans so thoroughly believe in these values encouraged by their ideology that they ignore the way their society and its mythologically generated ideals have failed the very people they criticize.

Of course, the equity mythology has a longer history and is more thoroughly entrenched than public assistance programs in this country. Prior to the passage of social security legislation proposed by president Franklin Delano Roosevelt during the Great Depression, charitable programs were largely the result of individual and religious contributions. Social security is hailed as a breakthrough achievement of humanity within this country. It ensured that the aged would not die of neglect but, here again, only if they had worked and put into the system. But government did not just have an attack of compassion. At that time, there was a depression, labor unions were rapidly gaining support, and the Socialist and Communist parties were growing and starting to be viewed by many people suffering from the disparity in wealth inherent in the capitalist economic system as their best hope. Social security stole that thunder, appeased the worried masses, and preserved our freedom, our individualism, our way of life. It was possible only because the withholding tax had already been instituted and had been widely viewed as taking away the average American worker's just due. Forcing employers to withhold wages to pay taxes was the only way the government could be assured that the average person would be able to pay any taxes. Social security withholding meant that the government (Uncle Sam) was saving it for you. This was widely appreciated and took the sting out of the withholding concept. The first real legislation to address the problems of poverty in the United States was not passed until the mid-1960s during the Johnson administration's bold attempt to build a "Great Society." What we are witnessing today is the backlash to this, made possible by politicians' manipulation of the ideas of freedom and individualism, the ideas of hard work, achievement, competence, and honesty within the context of the false assumption of equal opportunity.

The interplay between the individual, the government, and corporations with regard to assistance is revealing. As we can readily see, welfare sometimes appears almost universally condemned, but unemployment compensation is accepted. That is because a person has to have earned wages in the past year and be out of work through no fault of their own. This type of assistance is considered humane, fair, and necessary. Since people had been working and did not quit or get fired for cause, they were still living up to the American cultural ideals, but again, the assumption that politicians had a spasm of mercy and decided to help the average displaced working person is unfounded. Although there is no doubt that the individual who qualifies for unemployment benefits is helped significantly through this assistance, the biggest beneficiaries are businesses that are seasonal and that experience regular slowdowns and periods of no work for their employees. The major construction industry, oil and gas exploration industry, big car companies, and all types of manufacturing are good examples. When bad weather hits and construction has to stop; when the price of gas and oil plummets, rigs have to be shut down, roughnecks and oilfield service company workers have to be laid off; when the economy goes through a brief recession and General Motors, Ford, and Chrysler have to temporarily shut down their plants; when sales for manufactured goods are down and workers have to be sent to the house for a couple of months, unemployment compensation kicks in to ensure that workers do not have to take just any kind of work to survive but can look only for the kind of work they have been doing. Since slowdowns are usually industry-wide, the requirement to only have to look for the type of work one has been doing means the competition probably would not be able to snag a valuable and already trained worker. It also means the worker has enough income to just wait it out. This means that these industries will not experience a worker shortage or have to retrain new people at the cost of productivity. It allows individual workers to wait for their jobs to start again and benefits the company's bottom line enormously. All these industries experience consistent fluctuations in their businesses and regularly go through this process. Because few politicians have problems with this program, the issue is a politician's match made in heaven. They can tout their compassion and social responsibility for making the burden of brief periods of unemployment less painful for workers and their families, relieving the threat to their freedom in the individual pursuit of happiness, and they can collect campaign contributions from the big boys for helping them to maintain their work force during seasonal fluctuations, saving billions in profits for such companies. In this sense, what is applauded as an effort to save the individual from unnecessary harm is, in fact, also a form of corporate welfare.

Big business demands concessions from government and justifies such demands on the basis of being good for business. The usual argument is that such corporate assistance from the public treasury helps them to compete, creates jobs, and helps individuals in their pursuit of the American Dream. But, it is difficult to see how awarding McDonald's hundreds of millions of dollars in free money to serve Happy Meals all over Europe and Russia creates many jobs or helps individual Americans. Billions of public dollars every year definitely help large corporations to compete, often at the expense of the smaller businesses that are supposed to be the backbone of our ideology and the life blood of the free market principle. Many industries and corporations receive incredible concessions from all levels of government. Local governments are tirelessly put in the position of granting tax abatements, usually in the form of property taxes that fund education in many states, or risk losing a new manufacturing plant or a corporate headquarters being located in their towns. Corporations are constantly holding up governments in this way and fail to live up to what should be their social responsibilities. They justify this by operationalizing the core value of economic freedom. It is true that such activity does generate jobs and economic improvement, but it is individual property taxpayers and small businesses that wind up paying for the so-called developments. In the process, things such as education become even more economically unfair.

Education: Public and Private

The value that we put on education is immense and is the result of the core values of freedom, individualism, diversity, and conformity. A good education is seen as the most fundamental tool of the aspiring individuals and groups in this culture. It is almost universally accepted that anyone who wants to be successful in the pursuit of the American Dream must begin by achieving competence in school. It is assumed that without an education, individuals and groups will not be able to reach the potential necessary for maximum upward mobility. An educated person can expect to enhance equality of opportunity not only within his or her own class, but may be able to raise class status because he or she will be able to more equally compete in the marketplace. His or her skills will have greater value and, thus, chances of greater material wealth will be enhanced.

The idealized value of the public school system reflects the assumption of equality. Theoretically and mythologically, a public system of education means that class differences are leveled and everyone receives the same preparation for a shot at the American Dream. It means that very few (only those so affluent they can afford to send their children to private schools) are privileged. The rest of us participate in the culture as equals. After this equal education, then it is up to the hard working individual to make the most of the equal opportunity he or she has been given. Many people thoroughly accept this scenario despite the fact that they can readily see that it is not true. Most of those who do believe this are affluent. They see the belief system working precisely this way in the public schools their children attend. What they do not consider are the vast differences between well-funded schools in the suburbs and the miserably underfunded schools of urban America.

Until recently, public schools have been funded locally. For example, in Texas, this meant that every district funded only their own schools with property taxes of their own community. As a result, impoverished communities with a poor tax base have produced impoverished school districts that produce poorly educated and impoverished people for the most part. Rich school districts on the other hand, produced educated children, with more valuable after-school experiences. Sports teams were better funded and other clubs and voluntary programs were better supported. Participation in these after-school programs is a big determining factor in whether or not a kid becomes a doctor, juvenile delinquent, or a drug addict. Fewer delinquents and addicts means more achievement in school and fewer threats to the security of students, teachers, and administrators. Combined with the fact that well-funded districts pay the average teacher more money and can afford better benefit packages, they attract and retain the cream of the teaching crop. Poor districts cannot pay as much, offer the same quality or quantity of extracurricular activities, successfully deal with the significant problems of students from poor families growing up in poor neighborhoods, or provide a secure and supportive learning environment for their students or their teachers.

When Texas legislators were forced to address this unfair and unequal treatment under the law, the legislators came up with a revenue sharing program. Opponents, politicians, and journalists dubbed this plan a "Robin Hood" system of funding education. The legendary Robin Hood was famous for "stealing from the rich and giving to the poor." These opponents obviously hit on using the characterization because of the words *stealing, rich, giving,* and *poor.* They objected to what they believed was an unjust redistribution of wealth based on their belief that one has to work for everything one gets in order to give one's children a more equal opportunity and a chance for a better life. They objected to contributing to the education of other, less advantaged children, a definite contradiction to the basic proposition that everyone has some social responsibility if they want to conform to the American ideal. Ironically, they focused on the fact that the poor were "stealing" from them and disregarded the reasons why Robin Hood was engaged in such an enterprise. They forgot that the Sheriff of Nottingham was a rotten, violent tool of the completely unjust ruling classes who bled average peasants dry, demanded more, and then left them for dead in abject poverty and misery. The point here is that if we do not find a way to make public education more equitable, the poor will not limit themselves to stealing from the rich through school funding. They will become even more angry, more belligerent, and commit more robberies, burglaries, drug sales, murders, and form more gangs. For many people who have been shoved aside and forgotten through the malignant neglect of an inadequate educational system, this seems to be the only way to compete. When they turn to criminal activity, such as drug sales, to compete in the marketplace, they justify themselves as simply using their God-given right to freely pursue their individual dreams the way they choose when faced with an unjust social and economic system that is in obvious, violent conflict with the core values, assumptions, and ideals behind the American cultural ideology.

In 1998, a collection of private individuals and businesses pledged to raise fifty million dollars to provide vouchers for students in a San Antonio, Texas, school district to give them the option to go to any school of their choosing. Parents of area children were excited and expectant, but public school officials and others adamantly tied to the ideal of a public school system have thrown up the red flag and warned that if we allow this sort of thing it will mark the demise of public education, opportunity, upward mobility, and all the other advantages suggested by the ideal, but rarely realized. Public education, however, is failing miserably to achieve the promised reality. The voucher program could succeed in providing children with a better education. Private schools are simply superior as a general rule. But if the motivation for rich people to do this is to make private school tuition tax deductible or to make parochial schools into state supported school, then they do not need to even bother agitating for publicly funded voucher systems that politicians have been promoting the past few years. Most of those proposed programs would only benefit the affluent anyway. At some point, unless you directly fund a large number of private schools, fiscally prohibitive, most people get left out. Those are the same people that are left out now, and those are people that need to be included the most.

Some students manage to get an education and maintain a focus on the American value of achieving competence and on the desire to pursue higher education, but given the social and economic problems that are the result of structural aspects of the culture, they are often poorly prepared to successfully pursue college programs, or pursue legal or medical careers. In addition, they are also poorly prepared to deal with the mainstream American workplace. Dialect and cultural variations that reflect guidelines for behavior differ significantly. Trying to show initiative can be mistaken for not following instructions; trying to communicate through a native verbal strategy can be mistaken for rudeness; a friendly touch can be mistaken for harassment; or wearing something to impress might do just the opposite (Bourgois 1995). These kind of languacultural mistakes impede success on the job. Even interested and committed students in the inner city can end up largely unprepared due to the low levels of instruction and the high levels of distraction. These situations are the result of structural problems in this society. Without some massive changes in the structural foundation of the culture, there is no hope for the lower classes, and maximum disruptive diversity will remain. Affirmative action is one program that attempts to change the structural basis of the inequality of opportunity and the economic basis of oppression in this culture.

Affirmative Action

The realization that the structural results of institutionalized racism, sexism, prejudice, and discrimination were not going to simply and quietly evaporate due to good intentions came right on the heels of the passage of the Civil Rights Act. The economic oppression of racial and ethnic minorities was embedded too firmly in the fabric of society. The beliefs generated by the legacy of racism and sexism were entrenched solidly in the minds of many people, despite the fact that such ideas run counter to the values and ideals that produce the American Dream. Minorities and women were faced with people who were not going to change just because a new law had been passed. These people held their views to be unassailable and considered any attempts to change them as meddling by others because they wanted to destroy their way of life. As a result, people were still denied the opportunity to improve themselves through higher education and were still denied employment solely on the basis of their race, ethnicity, or sex. Racial, ethnic, and sexual animosity in schools and in the workplace would be a reality until something forced it to change, and until it did change, there would be no restructuring of the social and economic basis for life in this culture. It would take a bold step and affirmative action was that bold step.

Government agencies at all levels and those educational institutions accepting government funds of any sort, which meant virtually all of higher education, began to institute policies of affirmative action and changes began to occur. Formerly poorly represented minorities and women received preferential consideration for acceptance into institutions of higher learning and employment. The preference was considered absolutely necessary to change society's institutionalized refusal to allow minorities and women to participate in the American Dream. The program has worked dramatically. The growth of the black and Hispanic middle class and the inclusion of women in professions and careers from which they were previously excluded, has been phenomenal over the past twenty-five years or so. In only one generation, the structural, social, and economic transformation of American culture is readily apparent. There are numerous integrated suburbs where people's children are no longer indoctrinated into a culture of hate based on skin tone, but instead are growing up with one another in a climate of mutual respect and affection. There are more integrated workplaces where people communicate and become real human beings to one another rather than some caricature created and promoted by the ignorant and the powerful. There are more black, Hispanic, and female doctors, lawyers, and other professionals. The lead taken by government was followed by corporate America, and they also began to recruit more minorities and women, presenting them with opportunities to achieve the American Dream that they had never encountered before. Even though it needs to be kept in mind that we have a lot further to go, without a generation of preference in education and employment, we as a society could have never come so far. Affirmative action was absolutely essential to restructuring our social and economic reality, and it continues to be necessary if we ever want to build an American culture that is not in such blatant conflict with its ideals.

Presently, there is a good deal of criticism of affirmative action. Critics claim that it is un-American because it does not value hard work, individual effort, freedom, competence, and fairness in the equality of opportunity. People should be judged on their talent. This argument denies the value of social responsibility that is also a part of the ideal, but as we have seen repeatedly, people integrate these values, assumptions, and ideas in various ways in an effort to justify their own version of the American mythology and in ways that enhance their own chances to realize the dream. But we do need to examine the reasons why critics may have a point.

Over the past thirty years, many blacks and Hispanics have justifiably benefitted from affirmative action in an attempt to structurally change society and provide equal opportunity for all. Many of these people received first-rate educations and landed good jobs in working environments that allowed them to achieve upward mobility. They raised their children in affluence and provided them with the quality educational and community environments they never had when they were growing up. When these middle-class children, having been adequately prepared or having had the opportunity to do so, apply to universities and professional schools, is justice served if they receive preference over an equally prepared white, lower class student who had to overcome enormous obstacles to just get there? When an affluent Mexican-American female, whose parents were able to provide her with ample opportunity to prepare, receives the double preference of minority female over an equally qualified white male that did not have such advantages while growing up poor, people correctly perceive that the system is not fully addressing the task of structurally eliminating economic oppression in this country even though it may still be functioning to foster minority and female inclusiveness.

The time has come for affirmative action and concomitant preferences to refocus on the real problems caused by economic disparity. Two years ago, the attorney general of Texas interpreted a fifth circuit court of appeals decision as outlawing the consideration of race in university admissions and hiring decisions around the state. The initial reaction from critics was jubilation, and the reaction of many in public education and those committed to the ideal of affirmative action was the prediction of doomsday for aspiring minorities. The first year, this policy was in effect, dramatic reductions in enrollments in the top public universities and in professional schools around the state were observed and the doomsday people began to talk legal appeal. By the second year passed, some innovative politicians and many educational administrators had made some keen policy changes. State universities and professional schools changed their admissions policies to include a more holistic appraisal of the applicant that included significant consideration of social and economic class, and life experience rather than relying so heavily on previous grades or standardized test scores. The legislature even passed a law that required automatic admittance to state universities of students that graduated in the top ten percent of their own school's graduating class. These changes directly addressed structural, economic disparity regardless of race.

Affirmative action is necessary, but the emphasis may need to change to make economic class the primary consideration. This will include minorities and others who still suffer as a direct result of structural inequality of opportunity but will not include affluent minorities who have been given the chance to adequately prepare themselves. It will also include millions of white Americans that have suffered poor educational and community life and who have not been graced with an equal opportunity to achieve the American Dream. The implementation of successful affirmative action programs in business will surely continue. Many corporations have learned that they must be more inclusive if they want to continue to earn the business of minorities and women and are committed to inclusiveness in hiring and promotion. For those companies such as Texaco that are not committed and shirk their responsibility to participate in the needed structural transformation of society, we still have legal recourse should they attempt to engage in discriminatory hiring and promotion practices. It is time to reassess our needs and direction. If we really want to build a society that produces less conflict as a result of the contradictions between our idealized beliefs and behaviors, it is time to get on with the real work. It is time to move on.

SOCIAL AND RELIGIOUS FREEDOM

The core values of the American cultural ideology demand that we accept others as they are and respect their right to organize, subsist, and believe as they see fit. As we have seen, it is the foundation of the American Dream. But the reality of life in the United States demonstrates the abject failure that we, as a society, have had in effectively operationalizing such acceptance of others. Instead we have perfected the ancient art of inciting intolerance of those we do not understand based on fear and languacentric and ethnocentric attitudes. Through these activities, we have become accomplished chauvinists in thorough contradiction of beliefs central to the American cultural mythology. Debates about abortion, sex, sin, and the American family, and the faith we put in science and technology reveal the depths of the chasm between our idealized beliefs and our behavior.

Abortion

Abortion is one of the most intense, emotional issues of our time. The value we place on the individual supports a woman's free choice about whether to have an abortion or not, but it also supports the position that the fetus has an individual's right to life and freedom from destruction. Of course, the pivotal question here is whether or not a human fetus constitutes an individual, whether or not it is a person. There is no biological doubt that a fertilized and dividing human ovum has begun the process of creating another human life, but cross-culturally there has always been a great deal of difference of opinion as to what point a developing fetus becomes viable, takes on the characteristics of personhood, and acquires inclusion into the society.

The whole debate is more a matter of when personhood begins rather than a question about when life begins. Religious people with strong beliefs in God and the sacred nature of procreation and human life line up squarely behind the idea that life begins at the moment of conception. Many of them are so devoted to the evil of taking a human life that they bomb abortion clinics and murder abortionists just to show the world how sincere they are about their beliefs. These people who claim a sincere compassion for the unborn child apparently have none for their fully developed brothers and sisters engaged in a practice they condemn. They have no mercy when blocking access to clinics, cursing and harassing women trying to enter. Such action can only add to the confusion and sorrow of women seeking an abortion. People who are so adamantly "pro-choice" that they simply deny the objective, biological reality of ending a developing life form and just reformulate the issue in terms of whose rights take precedence—the mother or the fetus—do not show much respect for people who oppose abortion on the grounds of valuing life.

Finally, the most absurd idea in the entire debate is that one must be either pro-choice or pro-life. This is an extension of the mistaken modern American belief that there are always two sides to the story when, in fact there may be three, four, or ninety sides to the story. A position more consistent with American values and the facts is that many people in this culture believe abortion ends a human life and they deplore it, but at the same time, they realize that criminalizing abortion is a great evil with disastrous consequences to individual women, that a person's answer to the whole question depends heavily on religious or philosophical beliefs, and this is hardly an area that government needs to regulate.

Sex, Sin, and the American Family

The massive influence of the individual is readily apparent in the use of sexual images in advertising and entertainment. We are constantly bombarded with the message that human sexuality is there to be utilized and enjoyed for our own personal benefit and that we deserve to get some sex whenever possible and with whomever we so choose. These images and this attitude predominantly conveys the importance of healthy sexiness to our achievement in pursuit of the American Dream, even our competence in the workplace, and unrealistically glorifies youth and beauty in the process. The constant message we get from our parents, families, churches, and schools is a total contradiction that emphasizes personal morality, social and medical responsibility while abstaining from sex until monogamously and heterosexually paired for life. Any other approach is considered sinful by the vast majority of religious people in the country and just plain bad by the majority of the remaining unbelievers. Anyone's sexual orientation other than exclusively heterosexual is quite likely to be condemned despite our stated value concerning diversity and respect for others. The entire situation is one of the saddest examples of the contradiction and conflict between ideal beliefs and real beliefs and actual behaviors.

Faith in Science and Technology

Another significant gap between the ideal and the real is represented in our unwavering faith in the power of technology to overcome obstacles, particularly manmade obstacles such as destroying the environment. Even many who claim to be devoutly religious people believe that Americans have become so efficient and knowledgeable that they will be able to recover from whatever mess they make for themselves, that we need not worry about thinking ahead too much as long as we maximize freedom for individuals and groups in the pursuit of the material dream. Although many religiously inclined people ignore what they purport to be the essence of their beliefs in this regard, the truly disturbing development concerns the large number of people, possibly a majority, that reject any religious affiliation and those who only give lip service to a belief in some vague sense of God, but who put their faith in science and technology to the exclusion of any other consideration of the mystery of the universe and life on this planet. These are the most dangerous fundamentalists in this country. They are only interested in a literal translation of science and the answers it can provide us, and their god of rationality excludes the humility of admitting that we cannot be sure of the purpose of it all or what might happen next. Their faith is unshakable, however, and their minds are closed to any other possibilities, a violation of the implicit conditions demanded by the value of diversity. If it cannot be demonstrated scientifically, it does not matter, and this means turning a cynical and blind eye to many important considerations. Science, technology, and the belief that rational human thought is the only way to believe is an intolerant, self-centered, and dangerous religion. It does not accept nor consider any other alternative. This religion is the faith of those who claim to be faithless but instead believe just as mysteriously that their way of thinking is the only way it makes sense to think, even though such an attitude does extreme violence to many of the ideas necessary to a diverse and democratic society.

DEMOCRATIC AND POLITICAL FREEDOM

The abysmal record of participation in the democratic process by the average citizen undermines the political freedom promised by the laws of this nation. Politicians have successfully developed a clever strategy that ensures they will be held only minimally accountable for their actions. This strategy is also supported by power elites outside government and is the result of the incomplete and unsubstantiated information, propaganda, and outright lies to which the American public is subjected and in which they put their faith, despite denials to the contrary. Americans have so thoroughly accepted the emphasis on individual freedom and pursuit of happiness that if something does not affect them directly they generally do not care. As a result, the political system is funded through a process that should be a criminal offense. Instead, lobbyists for big business, foreign governments, and domestic special interests control the political agenda. The injustice to individuals and groups in this society is just as tyrannical as "taxation without representation." It also destroys people's faith in the efficacy of the political system. Power elites encourage such belief and the accompanying hopelessness because a population that is sufficiently comfortable on the material level and only narrowly concerned about the interests of their own groups are easily satisfied and remain apathetic. Political control is thus achieved by power elites who manufacture the consent of average people. The elite give us contentment and happiness, and we give them authority and control.

Americans continuously refer to politicians and government in the third person plural: "*They* are the problem. If *they* were not so corrupt, we would have a better country. If *they* would just quit stealing from the public; if *they* were not only interested in feathering their own nest; if *they* could relate to other people's problems; if *they* would rise above their petty bickering; if *they* were honest; if *they* had any compassion, we would not have so many problems." The implication is that our elected representatives are somehow not representative of the American people, their core values, and their assumptions and ideas about what is right and proper. We have already seen that all people variably contradict these values and ideals in the process of interpreting and acting on them for their own benefit. That is why politicians can get away with almost anything. President Bill Clinton is vilified as an amoral sex maniac, but his approval ratings go up because we actually would like to have as much sex as possible, no matter what our claims are to the contrary. Politicians lie and evade the real issues just as we lie and evade the real issues in our own lives. Politicians do underhanded things to make more money and power because they are looking out for themselves and so are we. It is not personal; it is just business. Rather than continuing the comfortable belief that politicians are an aberration and unrepresentative of the American people, it would be much more productive to recognize that they are a perfect representation of the reality of American life and the perfect example of the questionable way that we interpret our ideals to guide our real behavior. Collectively, we are guilty of everything that we love to hate about politicians.

LINGUISTIC FREEDOM

The multilingual nature of our society has been a fact of life since the beginning, but most people have discovered through trial and error that to fully participate in the pursuit of the American Dream one should be fluent in English, the *lingua franca* of American culture. Our specific language policies have historically provided for the use and maintenance of other languages, but in order to really acquire the identity of an American, English is helpful. The modern requirement to print voting ballots in other languages that are used by a large proportion of the population helps to ensure that our value of diversity is recognized and respected. Although a ballot in Spanish is of no use to speakers of other languages, it does enhance individual participation in the political process by millions of Spanish-speaking citizens.

Current attempts to legally codify an English-only nation are misguided and misinformed. They are based on languacentric and ethnocentric motivations that contradict the value of diversity and disregard the reality of the United States as a multilingual nation. All efforts to make America an English-only nation should be abandoned as divisive, discriminatory, and devoid of any redeeming social value. Furthermore, what the proponents of these efforts propose is unrealistic and un-achievable. Such efforts disrespect the freedom of the individual and the group. We would do well to closely examine the inherent problems for the modern nation-state that does not incorporate all of its citizens into the culture through proficiency in a single *lingua franca*. The disintegration of the Soviet Union was partially facilitated by the linguistic and cultural diversity that had never been overcome after the forced coalition of many divergent national cultures. If this country should become even more languaculturally diverse and segregate itself, the same thing could occur, and society could be fragmented to the detriment of all. This is not going to occur. There are too many reasons for people to learn English, conform to the American cultural ideology, and participate, but the lesson to be learned is that the well-being of individuals and groups and their needed participation in the business of this country is well served when they are able to communicate. In the mid-1960s, the recognition of this fact led directly to the development of bilingual education.

Bilingual Education

Originally, programs of bilingual education were developed because of the poor performance of students who were native speakers of languages other than English. Policy officials realized that high dropout rates due to the failure of these students to learn English, much less the reading, writing, history, and government studies with which they were presented, contributed to the institutionalized and structural problems of the society and the economy. Theoretically, students would be taught subject matter in the native language while receiving intensive instruction in English as a second language. When this is done properly, it is very successful. The data are mixed and seem to demonstrate either a total failure, total success, or ambiguous and insignificant results depending on which side of the issue with which one aligns.

The passage of the proposition #227 in 1998 to eliminate bilingual education in the California public schools is an instructive example of the motivations driving people on both sides of the issue. People who oppose bilingual education include some Hispanics with children and who have direct experience with the failure of some programs, but for the most part, those in opposition to it are people who have participated in the anti-immigrant bashing of the past few years. Contradicting our reverence for the poor and downtrodden who came to this country in search of a better life, these people simply want it stopped and are not open to discussion. People who work in bilingual education or are otherwise wedded to the principle are almost unconditionally and uncritically opposed to the discontinuation of bilingual education programs. What is needed is an analysis of the problems, failures, and successes of such policies in order to better determine how we might continue to make progress in the effort to structurally transform the social and economic systems of the culture so more people can be included in the American Dream. California's solution, advocated by reactionaries and naively supported by many others, reflects linguistic ethnocentrism and ignores the real needs of many students.

A few years ago, Republican governor George W. Bush of Texas was asked by reporters about California's passage of a (unconstitutional) proposition to curtail services, including education, to illegal immigrants. His immediate reply was that he thought Texas should educate and take care of all the children in the state. This is an answer in accordance with the core values of American ideology. The same answer is the correct one with regard to bilingual education. Some programs failed. The employment of many non-native speakers of the English language who were more comfortable in their native languages than in English may have contributed to this failure. The segregation of these students into different classrooms certainly contributed. The fact is that what we have been calling bilingual education are not truly bilingual programs—they are ESL (English as Second Language) programs. The first bilingual education programs were truly bilingual with Spanish-speaking and English-speaking kids in the same classroom learning each others' languages. Such an approach is valuable to both groups. Speaking a second language is a personal, social, and economic asset. In addition, the integration of kids from different languacultures in one class diminishes the fear and loathing of the other and directly addresses the structural basis for social misunderstanding and the economic oppression. Bilingual education needs to be retooled, not rejected, if we want to minimize the contradiction between what we say and what we do.

MEDICAL FREEDOM

As the number of people who have no insurance and very little access to medical care increases, the structural inequities of the American health care system become more pronounced, contributing significantly to the further separation of a diverse population. Those that have money and resources are getting healthier due to technology and education. The have nots, understandably preoccupied with the basics of economic survival, do not benefit from such scientific and social advances. Instead, they go untreated when sick and die earlier. Their exclusion from the health care system is justified on the basis of the value we place on freedom, individual effort, hard work, and achievement. We do not want to fund any giveaway programs for people that cannot take care of themselves. It is interesting to note that Medicaid, specifically condemned as a giveaway program, is directed to assist low-income people, particularly those with children, in gaining access to health care. Welfare mothers and "other deadbeats" are accused of eating up the taxpayers' money when they do not really deserve it, since they have not lived up to the American cultural mythology. On the other hand, Medicare is accepted as a part of social security, and people believe they deserve it because they paid into the system through their individual effort and hard work. It is always ironic and somewhat perplexing to see some affluent, retired person complaining about government hand-outs, or what a terrible president Lyndon B. Johnson was, while Medicare pays thousands of dollars in health care costs for him every year. The real task is to find a way to make health care accessible to everyone in this society. The value we place on social responsibility demands such a program.

Rejection of National Health Care and the Rise of
Health Maintenance Organizations (HMOs)

National health care was first proposed shortly after World War II. George McGovern made it one of the primary platforms in his presidential campaign of 1972. In 1990, Bill Clinton took office and immediately went to work developing a policy and program of national health care. For almost two years, planning continued and a program was finally proposed by his administration. He was promptly crucified for the money it would cost, and proposing managed care in an effort to contain the spiraling cost of medical care. The American Medical Association promptly denounced the plan as the death knell of modern medicine and the demise of the best medical care in the world. The insurance and drug industries got squarely behind the effort to defeat the legislation as well. The

American public was overwhelmed with millions of dollars in advertising designed to discredit the plan and the Clintons personally. Among the most effective charges were that individuals in need of medical attention would no longer be able to choose their own physicians, doctors would no longer be free to treat patients as effectively because they would not be able to aggressively treat them without clearing the expense with a third party, doctors would lose control of their own fees (an affront to free enterprise), fewer people would become doctors, shortages of qualified doctors would become common, and the greatest medical system in the world would become mediocre. The general American public bought it, and their representatives in Congress defeated it so soundly that Republicans rode the coattails of public opinion to gain control of the House of Representatives. The public may have been fooled and convinced that the whole scheme was an idiotic idea, but the insurance industry was paying close attention, recognized a good idea, and rapidly began the change from their traditional methods to health maintenance organizations—in other words, managed care. Senator Jay Billingworth Bulworth (Warren Beatty in the movie *Bulworth*) was right when he stated that insurance companies take 25 percent of total revenues to pay administrative costs, while the government manages to handle Medicare and Medicaid for about 3 percent. Obviously, the profits necessitated by having insurance companies arrange medical care are excessive and a drain on the accessibility and quality of care. Yes, there needs to be a law—that law should be national health care.

LEGAL FREEDOM

Our system of government insists that the individual and groups have recourse to the rule of law in their pursuit of the American Dream, but people have variable access to the legal system, and legal representation is based almost entirely on social status and economic class. This is another prime example of the way that structural problems within American society sabotage the intention of the American cultural ideology to provide equal opportunity for all individuals. This situation undermines the concept of justice. The death penalty is a good case in point. Aside from the fact that the United States is the only so-called civilized society to still put criminals to death and aside from the absurd notion that mercilessly killing people is the most effective way to demonstrate that killing is morally reprehensible and unacceptable to society, it has been repeatedly demonstrated that the death penalty is not a deterrent to more murder; it has been applied to innocent people; it is inequitably applied more to minorities than whites; and it is unequally applied to poor whites as opposed to the middle class and the affluent, minority or not. The disparity in legal representation caused by the almost exclusive use of public defenders by people convicted and sentenced to death ensure substandard legal representation and, hence, the greater probability that an innocent person will be put to death.

Legal remedies to the drug problems in the country are also another good example of the way that the structural disparities in social status and economic class drives injustice. Poor people simply do not have any choice but to have public defenders represent them. In the Dallas County Criminal Court District, public defenders are hired and assigned to one court and one judge. They effectively work for that specific person and generally provide the court with a valuable docket clearing service. It is a pitiful situation that goes completely against the idea that every individual is a valuable and worthwhile human being. It certainly violates the assumption of equality under the law. As a result, drug offenders make up nearly half of the almost 150,000 prisoners incarcerated in institutions operated by the Texas Department of Criminal Justice (a larger prison population than almost any country in the world). Furthermore, drugs are endemic in our culture, and the middle class and the affluent have as a high a rate of drug use and drug sales as poor people do, but the poor are the only ones in jail. People with insurance or money can send their kids to rehabilitation centers at five thousand dollars a week, but people without money who have to deal with the problems caused by a resident drug addict in the family have to just let them sit in jail. Nowhere among these situations can the reality of American cultural values be seen to be anything other than contradictory.

One other highly visible contradiction between the ideals we cherish and the reality within which we live is reflected in the system of civil law. Nobody wants to take responsibility for their own actions. This is a heresy concerning the importance and value placed on the individual and freedom. When a woman slips on a patch of ice on the front porch of her apartment building, she sues. When a man falls out of the upper deck at a sporting event because he got drunk and made a mistake in judgment trying too hard to catch a foul ball, his family sues the ballpark for wrongful death because the railings were not high enough. When a woman burns her mouth on a hot cup of coffee at McDonald's, she successfully sues. When a man willingly smokes cigarettes for decades, knowing full well it is dangerous, and gets cancer, he sues. This cult of "victimology" is absolutely ridiculous and is in direct conflict with not only individualism and freedom, but conformity, social responsibility, and competence as a thinking human being.

INTELLECTUAL AND ACADEMIC FREEDOM

The freedom to express one's opinions and to challenge accepted interpretations of events and situations is a closely guarded right in both the American legal and ideological sense. It is grounded in the core values of freedom, individualism, diversity, and conformity. The American system of higher education adopted the tenure system in order to protect scholars and scientists from attacks based on such differences of opinion. The idea is that the free expression of ideas and the freedom to conduct rigorous, scholarly investigations into matters of extreme importance to the society will result in progress, enlightenment, and a better world. This principle is central to the American world view, but it is increasingly coming under attack.

Politically correct world views that seek to direct the flow of information and to narrowly restrict inquiry in an effort to transform the perception of reality for everyone are misguided attempts to force everyone to think and believe in the same way. Such a strategy also contradicts all the core values of American cultural ideology and in reality encourages conflict and strife and generates anger and belligerence. Teachers all over this country are currently hypersensitive to such politically correct criticism, and whether they will admit it or not, many stifle themselves and avoid potentially messy topics and research. This is tragic and sad. While it is true that educational leaders are sometimes wrong or insensitive in their evaluation of the reality they perceive, and that they have a responsibility not to add to misunderstanding, resentment, anger, and the structural problems of society. Unfortunate remarks or actions that were not intended to be defamatory or demeaning need not be the basis of demands for the immediate dismissal of even tenured professors. Such remarks should be productively viewed as a beginning point for fresh discussion and re-evaluation of reality. They can be utilized to come to a better understanding of ourselves and those around us.

Unfortunately, higher education has been transformed into a market-driven business. Colleges and universities were overbuilt during the demographic bulge of the late 1960s and early 1970s created by the coming of age of the baby boom generation and the war in Vietnam. Now institutions are in a competitive drive to attract and retain students. Curriculums have suffered, as have relative qualitative standards, as more and more teachers receive pressure from their institutions to pander to student demands because it is good for business and enhances the prospects for institutional survival and prosperity. In order to ever increase the number of choices students have through additional course offerings, the use of part-time faculty has become ubiquitous and exploitive. Over 60 percent of college and university courses are taught by part-time faculty. In Texas, the community colleges appear to be the biggest offenders, but universities make ample use of such bargains. Most part-time faculty are dedicated to their disciplines and their work, but they are poorly compensated. They are a bargain and a money maker, but they encounter little institutional recognition or reciprocity for their efforts. They are used up, discarded, and their chances of realizing the American Dream are not very good. They become convinced that American cultural mythology is just that—a myth.

GETTING A GRIP ON REALITY

It is very clear that the American value system that generates the American world view is not a monolithic set of principles to which everyone adheres, but rather a variable set of interpretations by different individuals and groups that form the basis for their commitment to various sorts of behavioral action (Goodenough 1990). It is clear that variations are often based on self-interest, self-satisfaction, and self-justification regardless of the actual facts. It is clear that most people hold these beliefs on an almost unconscious level and fail to recognize the conflict and contradictions, even though they can articulate exceptions to the rule and are constantly bombarded with the consequences of such conflict. It is also clear that the principles encoded in the values, assumptions, and ideas of the American world view are worthwhile and important. But finally, it is clear that the exaggerated value placed on the individual has generated a culture in which people are expected to be independent, not needing anyone, and not having any responsibilities, obligations, or duties to others (Nash 1993; Wilcox 1998). Social anthropology has long recognized that people in any culture who claim total independence with no obligation to others are deluded and asocial. We need to change the way that we accept the supreme importance, even the deification of the individual, because right now we are raising an entire culture of asocial human beings (Kuper 1977).

REFERENCES

Agar, M. 1994. *Language Shock: Understanding the Culture of Conversation*. New York: William Morrow.

Althan, G. 1988. *American Ways: A Guide for Foreigners in the United States*. Yarmouth, MA: Intercultural Press.

Arensberg, C. M., and Niehoff, A. H. 1971. *Introducing Culture Change*. Chicago: Aldine.

Bonvillian, N. 1993. *Language, Culture and Communication: The Meaning of Messages*. Englewood Cliffs, NJ: Prentice-Hall.

Bourgois, P. 1995. *In Search of Respect: Selling Crack in El Barrio*. Cambridge, MA: Cambridge University Press.

Goodenough, W. 1990. Evolution of the human capacity for beliefs. *American Anthropologist* 92(3):597–612.

Hall, E. T., and Hall, M. R. 1990. *Understanding Cultural Differences*. Yarmouth, MA: Intercultural Press.

Hsu, F. 1972. *Psychological Anthropology*. Cambridge, MA: Schenkman, pp. 241–262.

Kearney, M. 1984. *World View*. Novato, CA: Chandler and Sharp.

Kuper, A. (ed.). 1977. *The Social Anthropology of Radcliffe-Brown*. Boston: Routledge and Kegan Paul.

Nash, D. 1993. *A Little Anthropology*. 2nd ed. Englewood Cliffs, NJ: Prentice-Hall.

Naylor, L. L. (ed.). 1997. *Cultural Diversity in the United States*. Westport, CT: Bergin & Garvey.

———. 1998. *American Culture: Myth and Reality of a Culture of Diversity*. Westport, CT: Bergin & Garvey.

Pierce, B. 1998. Benefits in unskilled jobs erode along with pay. *Dallas Morning News*, June 14, 11A.

Spindler, G. et al. 1990. *The American Cultural Dialogue and Its Transmission*. New York: Falmer Press.

Spradley, J. P., and Rynkiewich, M. A. (eds.). 1975. *The Nacirema: Readings on American Culture*. Boston: Little, Brown.

Tiersky, E., and Tiersky, M. 1975. *The U.S.A.—Customs and Institutions: A Survey of American Culture and Traditions*. New York: Regents Publishing Company.

Wilcox, D. M. 1998. *Alcoholic Thinking: Language, Culture, and Belief in Alcoholics Anonymous*. Westport, CT: Praeger.

3

Official and Unofficial Culture: The U.S. Navy

Clementine K. Fujimura

The United States (U.S.) Navy, like the other military services, distinguishes itself from the civilian United States in its specific beliefs and behavior. This chapter examines some of these military/civilian distinctions by discussing the navy's underlying values. Upon investigating these differences, it becomes clear how and why the U.S. Navy must be considered, not only as a variation of the military, but also as a subculture of American society. While naval officers are in many ways "American," they also hold values and abide by rules that are unlike values and rules held by other U.S. citizens and, moreover, maintain principles and lifestyles that may even conflict with those of the general American public.

The following description of the U.S. Navy as a subculture of American culture is based on a number of interviews conducted in 1995 and extensive participant observation over a period of two years. Naval officers attached to the U. S. Naval Academy (USNA) were interviewed about their daily lives as a part of the U.S. Navy. The USNA may be considered to be the fountainhead of navy culture in as much as it exists to take the most promising of American youth and subject them to a four-year process in which they are transformed into midshipmen engaged in a business of preparing for service as officers. Throughout the interviews, the officers expressed a sense of their daily lives as different from that of mainstream U.S. citizens, and at times, they found their world view conflicting with certain of the American values that they are trained to defend. It must be pointed out that the opinions expressed are specific to the officers at the USNA and that many other opinions regarding the navy have, therefore, not been represented. Like any other institution, the U.S. Navy includes people representing a variety of jobs as well as ethnic socioeconomic and educational backgrounds. All officers at the USNA are unique in that they hold graduate degrees and are tasked with training midshipmen to become not only officers, but thinkers as well.

GENERAL DESCRIPTION OF THE NAVY

The history of the U.S. Navy goes back more than 200 years, during which it has created social organizations that tend to mirror those of the larger American culture (American Forces Information Service 1995; Zimmerman 1995), including medical, government, education, and even consumer institutions. The government of the navy is established by a separate code of law, the Uniform Code of Military Justice (UCMJ), and is maintained by a separate legal system. The educational system includes rigorous training programs for all its members, some of which is specific to officers. All of these programs educate and socialize (or "indoctrinate" as the navy prefers to call it) new members to become part of the military society. The navy also offers markets for grocery and other shopping for its members throughout the world, including in the United States. These facilities are for military personnel and are off-limits to civilian U.S. citizens. Creating institutions and traditions exclusively for its members is just one way in which the navy indexes its separations from civilian America and from the rest of the world. In effect, the navy has made itself into an independent society as has the entire military establishment.

The military establishment represents a unique and clearly distinguishable category of diversity in the United States. It also qualifies as a subculture within the society and thus helps justify the idea that the United States is a pluralistic society. Generally, American subcultures buy into the beliefs shared by American society at large and act within the same organized systems. The same, however, cannot be said for the military. All branches of the U.S. military operate under their own set of principles and practices, which can sometimes be in direct conflict with those of the broader American culture. Perhaps most telling in this regard is the reliance of the UCMJ. In essence, the UCMJ represents a system of social order that is in many ways unlike that of the society at large and to which citizens of the United States are not subjected.

The main subdivisions of the U.S. military are the Army, Navy, Marine Corps, Air Force, and Coast Guard. Each of these services represents a cultural grouping within the military category, and within each of these, a variety of subgroups exist as well, which are usually, but not always, mutually exclusive. The main divisions separate the military into those who are officers and those who are enlisted. Of the military services, the navy is the second largest, totaling 509,950 members as of September 30, 1993 (American Forces Information Service 1995). Each of the categories is further subdivided according to pay grade. For example, following initial officer training, the ranking of officers is as follows: ensign, lieutenant jr. grade, lieutenant, lt. commander, commander, captain, rear admiral (lower half), rear admiral (upper half), vice admiral, admiral. These titles are different for other services. The majority of the officers are lieutenants (23,618 out of 66,348 total) (American Forces Information Service 1995). Minorities counted include black Americans (4.9 percent officers, 17.8 percent enlisted), Hispanic Americans (2.8 percent officers, 7.2 percent enlisted), and "other," meaning Native Americans, Alaskan Natives and Pacific Islanders (3.3 percent officers, 6.0 percent enlisted)

(American Forces Information Service 1995). While these statistics point to a great range in backgrounds, they do not mirror the minority representation in the United States at large.

REPRESENTATION OF MAINSTREAM AMERICA IN THE NAVY

It is generally believed by most of the male officers interviewed, that the navy is composed of a solid cross section of American society. According to one male Marine Corps captain, the navy-marine team serves as the ultimate melting pot that blends all economic and racial backgrounds (John Schneider [pseud.], interview by author, tape recording, May 16, 1995). The Marine Corps, while in uniform and culture a separate service, is administered by the Department of the Navy and has as its civilian head the secretary of the navy. The Marine Corps originated as naval infantry and evolved into a separate service, operating in tandem with the navy.

While the navy in recent years has attempted to improve quantitatively the representation of minorities (see previously mentioned statistics), it has not yet been able to attract enough minorities at the officer level to mirror the racial mix of American society. The same is true for gender. For example, only 12.5 percent of the officers and 10.6 percent of the enlisted personnel in the navy are women, whereas in the United States the population is composed mostly of women (95.3 men for every 100 women) (American Forces Information Service 1995; U.S. Dept. of Commerce 1994).

Female officers interviewed did not stress the proportional numbers when speaking on the topic of representation. Rather, there was more of an emphasis on common values maintained between the two societies. In terms of ideals, one female lieutenant described the navy as a microcosm of American society. She explained that while differences exist, certain likes and tendencies in American culture are represented in the navy. Examples include a love of law and order. According to her, it is not that Americans inherently love the extreme structure emphasized in the navy, but that both Americans and naval officers have faith that a legal system can serve justice. Justice, in turn, is based on a common ethical standard held by both mainstream America and the navy.

Officers also see a parallel between American and naval social development. One example cited includes the move toward political correctness (PC) in both cultures. However, the definitions of PC vary from American culture to navy culture. Politically correct for civilian America refers to respecting and being sensitive to the values and lifestyles of others, even when these do not coincide with one's own values and lifestyle. For the navy, PC has two applications. As one officer described: "For the authorities in the navy, it is acting so as not to attract undue attention. For the rest of the navy, PC is acting as told by authorities (Kevin Ridgely [pseud.], interview by author, tape recording, May 20, 1995).

A both politically correct and conservative attitude toward the use of alcohol is one example of overlapping values. Americans would agree with Europeans, for example, that American views on drinking are conservative (the drinking age in

America being twenty-one, whereas in most of Europe it is sixteen), and it is also considered "politically correct" by Americans to drink little. Given the recent public focus on navy drinking policies, the navy is also attempting to limit the consumption of alcohol in response to ensuing criticisms.

Interestingly enough, none of the officers interviewed described American social development as influencing the direction naval culture takes. According to the officers interviewed, the navy at first glance appears to be more a part of American culture than a separate one, in that it represents an American tradition in itself. Furthermore, as one officer put it in a personal communication: "We are very American in what we're defending, the ideals we have are American. But there is a difference between our ideals and our behavior." While officers strive to realize and maintain democratic society, the ideal for U.S. citizens, their own day-to-day lives are often compromised.

DIFFERENCES BETWEEN MAINSTREAM AMERICA AND ITS NAVY

The officers interviewed all acknowledged differences between American and navy culture. Stated most plainly: "The naval person has much more of a group ethic than the individual American has. It is quite clear that the military is in many ways on the one hand quite socialistic. On the other hand, we're much more authoritarian than the average American would like. We're closer to a Chinese-Communist model (Kevin Ridgely [pseud.], interview by author, tape recording, May 20, 1995). This comment reflects the observer's understanding of the Chinese Communist political system as a top-down hierarchy wherein party members exist not to aggregate the political will of the people, but instead to carry out the political will of the masters. In similar fashion, the naval officer corps functions to carry out the decisions of the navy leadership and not to elicit the opinions of individual members. In this sense, it is a complete antithesis of Western political ideals of self-determination and democracy.

Military cultural behavior is expressed not merely in day-to-day lifestyle, but also in its social structure. The social structure of the navy simply does not lend itself to democracy; it is extremely hierarchal, and communication between the levels is more often than not unidirectional. One example is the clothing policy. In civilian society, fashion can symbolize individuality and, at times, is an expression of world view. In the military, "proper" attire even while off duty (on liberty/leave) is mandated by military authorities. Individual expression is subordinated to the image the leadership wishes to project. There is no choice or debate in the matter—when crew members depart a navy ship for liberty ashore, representatives of the commanding officer (watchstanders) inspect all departing personnel and deny permission to leave for those who do not comply. Idiosyncrasies such as requiring shirts with collars, prescribed sleeve length, or tucking in of shirts are a few of the standards imposed. Because of this imposition, military personnel find subversive ways to express themselves. In recent years, the navy has received criticism for the inability for all to know what is going on at all levels and the stifling of potential beneficial creativity. As a result, naval scholars are focusing their attention on how to restructure interaction in the military to achieve more efficient command.

Because of the major differences in lifestyle (regulated behavior and daily schedule, regimentation, and a rigid hierarchy) between the navy and American society, many American ideals are more difficult to realize in naval culture. The first ideal that comes to mind are the basic methods of communication and the values that underlie these methods. Ideally, in the United States, problems are discussed and agreements reached by consensus. Our elaborate communication options and capabilities help to realize this ideal. We can call meetings, hold conference calls, and log onto the Internet. In the military, however, this is not an option. While telephones and computers do exist, discussing and factoring opinions and emotions are not always practical, especially in times of crisis, such as war.

There is at least one unofficial organization for self-regulation at the junior officer level, which is called the Junior Officer Protection Association (JOPA). This organization, while unofficial, has become a tradition throughout the navy. It is headed by the most senior junior officer and serves a variety of functions, one of which is to ensure that junior officers are treated fairly. It is often organized quite informally, usually on the occasion that a group of junior officers feel that they are not being treated justly. The most senior junior officer will represent this group to his or her superior to bring attention to the problem. JOPA also serves other functions, which may be viewed skeptically by outsiders. More about this group will be discussed toward the end of this chapter.

While JOPA acts as an official venue for officers to voice their concerns, over the past few years, the navy has been trying to incorporate more official cross-communication, thus making the system less hierarchical. High-ranking officers are learning to listen to those of lower rank during meetings. The American ideal, however, is hardly the rational choice for the military system. There are times when a senior officer needs to make decisions and act quickly without waiting for individual opinions and feelings. Only in less dire circumstances is a democratic decision-making model effective.

Navy officials have begun work on W. E. Deming's Total Quality Management (TQM) business model and renamed it Total Quality Leadership (TQL) (Bodnar & Dengler n.d.). In an attempt to become more like American business, TQL is based on the notion that there is communication between all levels and that a superior will have occasions during which it would behoove him or her to listen to subordinates' opinions. Many officers, however, find it hard to implement this new theory without losing some of the discipline and control they are used to having. Since TQL's appearance, scholars have tried to make similar models work for the military. Currently, a retired naval officer, Dr. J. Bodnar, CAPT, USNR (Ret.), suggests leadership with more of a network orientation, one that, as he puts it, is flexible "not only in adapting to changing missions but also adapting to changing size of the organization" (Bodnar & Dengler n.d.).

OFFICIAL VERSUS UNOFFICIAL CULTURE

Official culture may be described as containing those values openly maintained by members of the community. In the navy, there is an internal document called the *Navy Core Values* that, theoretically at least, unites all of the members as part of the navy. Within this cultural haven, there are also a number of other official cultures by which members of the U.S. navy distinguish themselves from other members. This level of official culture is a subdivision, dependent on the warfare specialization and hierarchy. Some of these occupational subdivisions include flight, submarine, SEAL (Sea Air Land—or the navy's special warfare), to mention but a few. Ranks (more commonly referred to as "paygrade") also clearly mark a member as belonging to a certain subgroup and are even more pronounced when distinguishing enlisted men from officers.

The member's ethnicity and gender-identity (female, male, or homosexual) unofficially mark a person as part of a subgroup. It has been expressed, for example, that female African-Americans feel a close bond mainly because they are marked as minorities; they are women, and they are African-Americans. Other factors figuring into their identity become less pronounced, and these women tend to bond with one another, regardless of their personal histories, family background, or personal values. At the USNA, for example, one midshipman described: "It's funny, but any woman of color immediately becomes part of the black female community, even if outside of this place, we would not usually relate to one another. And it doesn't matter if you are more white than black. If you are of color, you are considered black. To evoke the presence of our black culture, to feel at home, most of us are part of the church choir. We feel close there, not alienated, not different" (Carol Smith [pseud.] interview with author, 1995). With little support given to the maintenance of (ethnic) minorities, culture, and traditions, boundaries between specific minority or ethnic groups are often blurred, uniting them as simply different and yet equal.

Ethnic minority groups, while openly acknowledged by the members themselves, are not officially recognized as subgroups and may therefore be classified as unofficial culture groups within the navy. This is due to the commonly upheld myth that the navy is colorless and classless, and distinction and privilege are based on ability and experience. In reality, a person's color, family background, and gender are important to a military member's identity and how the person is viewed by others.

In the navy, as in most cultures, many people hold beliefs that would be considered subversive by the mainstream establishment and may therefore not be openly discussed because they contradict or conflict with the official value system. Ironically, in the navy, one conflicting belief is the freedom of speech. While naval officers pride themselves in defending a country that stands for, among other things, freedom of speech, in the naval community the exercise of the freedom to speak one's mind is not feasible. A member is only allowed to voice her or his opinion when asked to do so by an authority. One example is when one is asked to act as a character witness to give a personal opinion about the officer in question.

Officially, one can only speak when specifically addressed or called upon.

Keeping in mind the premise that a naval officer is representing the navy at all times, that is, she or he is always considered to be "on duty" to some extent, an officer cannot openly disagree with official policies of the navy. It is also illegal to become involved in any political activity while in uniform. Such behavior not only would undermine the navy authority, but it could also lead to serious problems during a crisis, the most extreme example being in time of war. In a battle, it may be critical that the officer respect and follow orders in order to successfully complete a mission, thereby not only hitting a target but securing the safety of fellow officers and possibly the United States. In a time of crisis, there is little room for argumentation.

Given the premise that officers are always on duty and the belief that always being on guard is the best preparation for the real crises, naval officers work at containing their individual opinions, even though they defend the right of other Americans to express theirs. For instance, in military aviation pilots and aircrew have the ability to eject in case of an emergency. This process is potentially crippling, while at the same time potentially life saving. The difference between life and death in such a situation is measured in fractions of seconds of reaction time; there is no margin of error or time to hesitate. When any crewmember so much as uses the word "eject," it is taken as a command of execution and is responded to immediately. In such a situation, one simply cannot question the direction.

This does not mean that individual officers do not disagree with some of the navy's policies or basic values and beliefs. It also does not mean that there is no subversion in the navy. Subversion here refers to a member's conscious decision to act counter to the official line. While there is no official information on subversion in the navy, it is evident from interviews and unofficial rituals to be described later that subversive activity is deeply imbedded in the navy tradition, in a sense functioning as an unofficial venue for dissent.

As in any society, in the navy, there exists acts of rebellion that continually test the system. Some of these acts of rebellion have become extremely widespread and even traditional, although the navy could never officially condone such behavior. The use of alcohol is an example. While the navy does not officially support the use of alcohol to excess—even claims to be "dry at sea"—alcohol abuse is a common aspect of naval culture. Most officers interviewed acknowledge on the one hand the hazards of drinking alcohol, yet on the other hand, most have been privy to, and even part of, traditional ceremonies promoting intoxication.

One such tradition is the unofficial *wetting down ceremony*, which is part of any officer's promotion. Traditionally, the one being promoted buys all the liquor for colleagues who ostensibly help the officer pass from one rank to the next by drinking heavily. While fellow colleagues partake in this rite of passage by joining the drinking activity, the focus is on the officer undergoing the change. It is a tradition that continues to this day in various forms. One extreme might be compared to a bachelor-type of party; the other extreme is a less rowdy cocktail hour.

Other similar functions include *drinking your wings* for naval flight officers and *drinking your dolphins* for the submarine officers (wings and dolphins are emblems of qualification). The latter celebrates qualifying in submarines. Drinking your wings follows the more official ceremony, the winging ceremony, and begins with a congratulatory champagne toast. Traditionally, after the toast, glasses are thrown into the fountain at Pensacola (the training base or "Cradle of Naval Aviation"). The newly qualified officer then has wings dropped into a pitcher of beer. In order to get the wings back, he must drain the entire pitcher, catching the wings in his teeth. It is only recently that women have been included in such ceremonies. Moreover, it should be noted that the combination of alcohol and tradition is not unlike events that take place in the rest of American culture. Examples of alcohol traditions include those of college fraternity parties, family ceremonies such as weddings and many more. Subversive activities such as heavy drinking is therefore one way in which the naval culture mirrors American culture.

In addressing the issue of alcohol, related traditions must be addressed that, because of changing times, are becoming obsolete. These involve attitudes toward women, a theme that will be discussed in greater detail later on. Many in and outside the navy who remember the days of Tailhook (the name "Tailhook" refers to the hook at the end of the planes designed to land on carriers which catches on a cord as it lands) admit that it was common for a convention to be held yearly for those who had completed at least one arrested landing aboard an aircraft carrier. Until recently, this was an all-male event, a fraternity of male aviators. As women began working on aircraft carriers, the culture aboard the ships began to change, as did the social events. Traditionally, it was at this convention that women were regularly harassed. Most members in the navy knew about it, yet no one openly admitted to it or to agreeing with its traditions. Nothing was done about it because it was seen as part of the culture—a once-a-year outlet for the officers engaged in this hazardous occupation (Zimmerman 1995). What is interesting about this affair is that it included women from within its own culture as well as outsiders. Far more frequently, "sex" traditions, while ingrained as part of unofficial naval tradition, involved civilian women and even more frequently, non-American women,

As mentioned previously, JOPA has a reputation for ensuring that all officers stick together. This function sometimes extends to the social sphere. As was described by officers interviewed, JOPA does not look kindly upon those unmarried male officers who do not partake in popular pastimes. A new junior officer will be escorted around the local hangouts, which in the Phillippines, for example, included bars with striptease dancing and prostitution. The question inevitably arises: Why this peer pressure to partake in behavior that is shunned by some? Answers include: "To make sure he doesn't tell on us;" or " To make sure he's one of us, part of the team;" or, "To make sure he's not a fag." With women now on board, this situation might ease up (Zimmerman 1995).

GENDER AND ETHNIC CULTURES IN THE NAVY

It is often assumed that women in the navy compose a subculture, a group with similar values, but one that also stands in opposition to the larger naval culture. While women do see themselves as women—a distinct gender—they also do not wish their gender to be a handicap in their profession. Many believe they can make it to the top, like any man, if given a chance. In order to avoid victimization, they feel it is necessary for women to fight the battle on an individual basis and not succumb to the notion that they need help (Joanne Moore [pseud.], interview by author, May 18, 1995). They do not want to be labeled as part of a less able group, much less as a subculture distinct from that of men. Most women interviewed admitted that, although networks through which women can find and give support to one another exist, these do not establish enough continuity to warrant labeling women as part of a subculture. In fact, many women choose not to participate in these networks, since to them, such groups only help marginalize women by setting them apart from men.

While women today have a choice of joining women's circles, many choose not to do so. The first women to enter the USNA commonly complained that there were not enough support groups for women and that they felt extremely isolated among the larger number of men. At the time, women tended to feel competitive rather than sympathetic to each other's needs. While women today at both the academy and in the navy have more support, some still feel the isolation and, more specifically, feel that they are not listened to or respected by the men. As one woman informant put it: "No one ever asks us how we, as women, feel about women in combat. Sure there are problems, but somehow our often more supportive comments and opinions aren't taken as seriously and there is no forum for us to express our opinions." Decisions such as who is to serve in combat are still largely made by men, since they represent the majority and because they are the ranking officers. Career paths to command have not been open long enough to turn out many women in leading positions.

African-American women feel more of a bond within the Caucasian-dominated naval culture, simply because of their shared identity. As mentioned above, it does not matter if one woman is blacker than another. As one informant remarked, "Whereas we might have completely different social backgrounds, we still identify with one another, simply because we are black." Again, there are few institutions that support this cultural grouping, and it is hard to even see them as an independent group. The only organizations that do support the African-Americans include clubs such as the USNA's Black Midshipman Club, which meets once a semester to listen to guest speakers and to watch films. Other meetings may occur in church, choir practice, and during sports events.

It is apparent that much less support exists for other ethnic minorities groups. At the USNA, there are a variety of clubs such as the Japanese-American Club, the Spanish Club, the French Club, the German Club, and the Russian Club. But, these groups only exist as an adjunct to the academic programs and, more specifically, language studies. Beyond such groupings, there are no groups comparable to those for African-Americans.

NOTIONS OF HOMOSEXUALITY AND GENDER IN THE NAVY

A third gender, that of homosexuals, is put into an even more tenuous situation as homosexuality is not recognized officially in the navy, has zero support and few opportunities to communicate. Given that language, communication, and tradition are all part of a culture, one cannot identify homosexuals as a culture grouping in the navy, at least on an official level. Like in any society where a certain group is oppressed, the only means for survival of that group is for members to remain hidden, since their lifestyle poses a huge risk to their careers. In this case, the risks are one's career, loss of friends, and much more.

One example of such loss is the story of Edmond Bonnot, who, after allegedly coming on to a male colleague and friend, was reported to Bonnot's superiors. Bonnot was threatened with a court-martial but, in the end, got off lightly with a sentence of alcohol counseling and a warning (Zimmerman 1995:107). In this event, not only was the reputation of a man put into question because of sexuality, but a friendship came to an end. Usually, the penalty is even more severe. Along with a loss of reputation and friends comes the loss of a career. Homosexuality is officially documented upon dismissal and read by future employers.

While homosexual women and men in the navy may perceive their situation as offensive and highly problematic—an issue that counters the politically correct ideology—heterosexual officers interviewed do not see it as a problem. As one officer stated:

Gays in the military is an issue that came from without, not from within. It is perceived as a problem because it conflicts with a certain American civilian ideology. But in the Navy, we do not have that same ideology. Sure we represent the American way of life, we fight for it, but in order to live that life, some of us have to forego that lifestyle. Our lifestyle does not allow for all the freedoms of American society (Personal communication by officer in the USNA 1995).

From this officer's perspective, disapproval of homosexuality ensures that the navy function most effectively. Just before 1995 (and still today, unofficially), the same opinion was voiced about women on ships. The issue of accepting homosexuals on ships, like the issue of accepting women on ships, is often disguised as a question of warding off potential problems due to sexual acts on ships. It is widely believed that such acts could potentially interfere with the work environment. Dating among officers (fraternization) is not allowed simply because it would be too much of a distraction during work. Moreover, many heterosexual men feel uneasy around homosexual men and do not like the idea of being eyed. Many of the individuals interviewed mentioned the close living conditions and complete lack of privacy in one's sleeping quarters and bathrooms as adding to the unease experienced by heterosexuals.

But, the issue lies on a deeper level. It boils down to an issue of homosexual and heterosexual cultures in conflict. There is a deep-rooted homophobia built into the traditions and structure of the navy. Suspicions of homosexuality are traditionally tested (as in examples of peer pressure to join in heterosexual acts), and anti-gay jokes and comments are commonly heard and accepted. Homosexuality has been openly compared to bestiality (Zimmerman 1995:233) and has developed into a taboo of naval culture. Overriding this deep-rooted taboo would take as much time as would changing a taboo of any other culture. It implies not merely a change in rules, that is, the acceptance of homosexuals in the navy, but also a change in the entire naval culture's attitudes, values, and world view.

Yet, the change is not completely out of sight. The navy is, as already suggested, questioning its hierarchical decision-making pattern, and it has accepted women into the fleet. However, the rate of change will not in all likelihood appease the tension between the civilian and military America, since such a change asks for a change in cultural values. These values do not simply develop in the navy, but in the homes of individual members. After all, the navy is made up of individuals from American society at large—individuals who come with certain ideas already well established in their minds. Their values also represent values held by some of civilian America. Thus, the tensions exist not only between the military and civilian societies, but among civilian Americans as well.

CONCLUSION

The idea that military life conflicts with the values of civilian America is an accepted truth among naval officers. This notion, however, extends beyond the level of understanding these differences to the level of dislike for extreme nonmilitary behavior. The conflict between civilian and military America goes both ways. This general sentiment is a public one and has even been described in the media. According to one marine: "I think America could use a lot more military discipline" (Ricks 1995). Some midshipmen at the USNA have expressed their belief that they are models for the civilian world of how to act. Just as civilians might not feel comfortable with the military lifestyle and complain that it is too regimented and limited, so members of the military do not always agree with the civilian lifestyle and claim that civilians lack discipline, direction, camaraderie, and honor. This lack of understanding between military and civilian America has led to much emotional and political hostility as evidenced by Oliver North's testimony before Congress regarding lying and deception within the legislative branch of the government. While Oliver North is not a representative of the mind set of all the U.S. military, he does speak for a significant segment.

Indeed, naval culture is different, if not separate, from mainstream American culture. Yet, it must be kept in mind that, at the same time, it is an American tradition. In terms of social stratification, structure, and ideology, the American navy could be seen as "un-American." The people who serve, however, consider themselves to be "all-American." They see themselves as people willing to die for their country, a country containing values and ideals they only experience in passing. This question remains: What exactly prompts a young person to join a culture that forces her or him to exit a life of freedoms that he or she values for a life that so bluntly seems to contradict these values. There is a paradox in becoming a member of a repressive society, while claiming to defend an open society. The resolution of this paradox lies deep in the psyche of the individual. Answers such as "there are some ideals worth sacrificing for" may be labeled martyrdom by some and heroism by others.

REFERENCES

American Forces Information Service. 1995. *Defense 94*. Vol. 5. Alexandria, VA: U.S. Department of Defense.

Bodnar, John W., and Dengler, R. n.d. The emergence of a command network at the national level. Unpublished manuscript.

Ricks, Thomas. 1995. New marines illustrate growing gap between military and society. *Wall Street Journal*, July 27.

U.S. Department of Commerce. 1994. *Statistical Abstract of the U.S., 1994*. Washington, DC: United States Government Printing Office.

Zimmerman, Jean. 1995. *Tail Spin: Women at War in the Wake of Tailhook*. New York: Doubleday.

4

The Persistence of Racism in America's Cultural Diversity

Erma Jean Lawson and Vijayan Pillai

INTRODUCTION

Racism continues to plague American society and remains a major dilemma at the end of the twentieth century (Bell 1992; Cose 1993, 1997; Gibbs 1985; Hacker 1992; Morris 1984; West 1993). For example, a national survey found that blacks continue to experience discrimination in acquiring a job and confront workplace social discrediting (National Opinion Research Center [NORC] 1994). Blacks with postgraduate education report more incidents of racial discrimination compared to those with less than a high school diploma (Feagin & Sikes 1994; Schuman, et al. 1985).

In the United States, blatant acts of racism have been replaced by a subtle ideology of cultural inferiority (Cose 1993; Essed 1991; Hacker 1992; Sigelman & Welch 1991). Thus, the complaints of highly educated blacks involve feeling irrelevant in most white organizations, coping with white stereotypes of blacks, observing subjective criteria used to dismiss qualified blacks from managerial positions, being surrounded by mediocre whites in authoritative positions, and noticing the promotions of whites that are based on personal influence and cronyism, rather than merit (Bell 1992; Collins 1983; Sigelman & Welch 1991; Crosby, Bromley & Saxe 1987; Wilkinson 1977).

The persistence of hate crimes and white supremacy groups and the attempts to eliminate affirmative action programs are also signs of the continual racial tension (Farley & Allen 1987; Feagin & Sikes 1994). Consequently, a large number of blacks believe that the subtle racism in the 1990s is more treacherous than the overt racism in the 1960s (Blackwell 1988; Bobo 1988; Cose 1993; Dalton 1995; Hacker 1992; Pinkney 1993).

Simultaneously, a large number of whites continue to claim that they have never discriminated against blacks; therefore, they should not be responsible for social inequality. In fact, McConahay and Hough reported that 60 percent of whites believe that discrimination is not the main reason blacks experience low income, since most of them "do not have the motivation to pull themselves out of poverty" (1976:33). In fact, American white youths often believe that most qualified whites are more harmed by affirmative action policies than are qualified blacks harmed by racial discrimination (Blackwell 1988; NORC 1994).

Stereotypes and prejudices prevent the destruction of racism. For example, a national survey reported that most whites subscribe to one or more antiblack stereotypes. Evaluating a list of eight antiblack stereotypes, including "prefer to accept welfare," and "having less native intelligence, over half of the white respondents agreed with two or more racial stereotypes (Feagan & Sikes 1994). In another poll, whites were asked to evaluate the work orientation of blacks. Only 16 percent ranked blacks as hard working; half selected "lazy" to identify the approach of blacks toward work. In contrast, the majority of white respondents ranked whites as hard working; only 7 percent placed whites in the lazy category (Schuman et al. 1985). Finally, Jones (1986) documented the fact that during job performances, white managers evaluate the best characteristics about their own color and the worst about blacks, which resulted in job promotion discrimination.

Although whites often view blacks as achieving equality of opportunity in education, employment, and housing, blacks perceive social inequality and race-based discrimination as increasing over the past years (Blackwell 1988; Farley & Allen 1987; Hacker 1992; Jackson 1988; Pinkney 1993; Yates & Pillai 1992; West 1993). Many of the factors that contribute to the polarization of racial attitudes and subsequent racist behaviors of Americans are addressed in this paper. First, we discuss the historical facets of racism. Second, we address the various theoretical frameworks used to explain the persistence of racial subordination. Finally, we present manifestations of the continuance of racism and suggest that even whites who do not profit directly from the consequences of racism behave as if they do, thus enacting an adherence to a racial ideology shaped by the interests of earlier generations of whites.

RACISM IN THE UNITED STATES

The ratification of the Thirteenth, Fourteenth, and Fifteenth Amendments to the Constitution established the constitutional basis for racial equality in the 1860s. However, the rights guaranteed by these amendments did not materialize until the mid-twentieth century. A major legal breakthrough was the 1954 historic *Brown vs. Board of Education* of Topeka, Kansas. This Supreme Court decision judged "separate educational facilities as unequal," which later applied to a number of public facilities (Benokraitis & Feagin 1978).

Black protest against discrimination escalated with the Montgomery, Alabama, bus boycott when Rosa Parks refused to give up her seat to a white person on a segregated bus. This event triggered a successful boycott of public transportation by Montgomery's black residents. Additionally, black resistance to segregation propelled the creation of the Southern Christian Leadership Conference (SCLC) led by Dr. Martin Luther King. In the spring of 1963, SCLC launched a series of demonstrations in Birmingham, Alabama, that gained national and international publicity because fire hoses and police dogs were used against the demonstrators. In 1963, the civil rights era resulted in the massive March on Washington with King's famous "I have a dream" speech, which dramatized black aspirations for freedom and revealed the depth of racial inequality to national and international audiences (Feagin & Feagin 1996; Morris 1984).

The Civil Rights Acts of 1964 and 1968, and the Voting Act of 1965 were important events in the black struggle for racial equality. These acts provided a mechanism for fighting discrimination in employment, housing, voting, and public accommodations. They also denied federal funds to local and state governments that permitted any form of discrimination. In addition to these things, President Lyndon B. Johnson's administration established Head Start and initiated the Food Stamps Act to counter the effects of discrimination (Feagin & Sikes 1994; Pinkney 1993). A series of federal assistance programs, such as the Higher Education Act of 1965, the Economic Opportunity Act of 1964, and Job Corps, also were established to upgrade the skills of blacks (Feagin & Feagin 1996).

The actual discrepancy between legal equalities and social inequalities, however, remained. Consequently, Watts, a black section of Los Angeles, erupted in riots during the summer of 1964, which lasted for five days. Thirty-four persons were killed, more than 1,000 persons were injured, and property damage was estimated at forty million dollars (Pinkney 1993; Pinkney 1968). In fact, between June 1963 and May 1968, more than two million Americans demonstrated and rioted to express their political demands (Feagin & Feagin 1996). Riots resulted in 191 deaths, and 23 deaths were racially motivated (Morris 1984; Pinkney 1968).

Northern blacks also participated in direct actions against segregation that consisted of boycotts in Harlem, sit-ins in Chicago, and mass demonstrations in Cairo, Illinois. As a result, the number of organizations oriented toward black nationalism and self-help gained prominence. The Congress of Racial Equality (CORE) accelerated their protests against housing and employment discrimination. The Black Panthers started breakfast programs for children and engaged in surveillance of local police officers to prevent police brutality in the cities. The Nation of Islam (Black Muslims) initiated black-controlled businesses in such places as restaurants, bookstores, and publishing companies. Cultural nationalism was emphasized in the Nation of Islam by the establishment of schools that taught self-respect and pride in an African cultural heritage (Morris 1984; Pinkney 1993; Staples 1985).

In the mid-1960s, the United States experienced more civil strife than most nations in the world. In fact, the struggle for racial equality moved from the streets to the walls of the academy. College students demanded black student unions and black cultural centers. First, the black student movement insisted on a pedagogical approach that included group discussions and informal lecturing, as well as emphasizing the importance of black community studies. Second, proponents of black studies declared that the interdisciplinary approaches toward learning were superior to narrow, selective teaching methods that concentrated on one single subject. Additionally, black students were urged to devote their research activities toward the transformation and liberation of black communities. Thus, the black studies movement emphasized a relationship between theory and practice, since it was viewed irrelevant in most institutions of higher education (Carmichael & Hamilton 1967).

The Student Nonviolent Coordination Committee (SNCC) created the "Black Power Movement." which accelerated the civil rights movement. Progressive black professionals were hired in the African-American studies departments on white campuses. Additionally, black social scientists such as Vincent Harding, Lerone Bennett, Robert Allen, Manning Marable, and Robert Staples argued that blacks have fought to secure the economic and political tools for self-determination, even though the impact or discrimination remained painful, stifling, and cumulative. As a result, the 1960s have been viewed as the golden period for civil rights (Feagin & Sikes 1994; Marable 1983; Morris 1984; Sowell 1981; Staples 1985).

Social Retreat

By the 1980s, many blacks feared that the gains made in the 1960s were eroding. For example, President Ronald Reagan expanded military spending and cut back many social programs aimed at minorities, such as job training, and funding for civil rights enforcement. Reagan and his associates strongly opposed strengthening the 1965 Voting Act and reversed the federal government's commitment to address education, housing, and employment segregation (Pinkney 1993). The Reagan administration also de-emphasized the significance of race and argued that black leaders exaggerated the magnitude of racism (Yates & Pillai 1992). As a result, the Justice Department was no longer a major proponent of civil rights.

The situation of blacks also deteriorated because of the Bush administration's high defense spending. Bush declared that the Civil Rights Act of 1964 was unconstitutional (Morris 1984; Pinkney 1993). The Bush administration's increased military budget had a negative effect on blacks as well. According to Yates and Pillai (1992), military spending was least concentrated in disadvantaged economic areas, such as the Mid-Atlantic and East North Central States. This created a loss of employment opportunities for blacks living in northern urban cities. Cutbacks in housing assistance programs, food stamps, the school supplemental breakfast program, programs such as Aid to Dependent Children, and supplemental programs for low-income aged provided evidence of a social policy aimed at solidifying white dominance (Bluestone & Harrison 1982; Pinkney 1993; Yates & Pillai 1992).

From 1989 through 1993, the administration of George Bush continued the negative approach to civil rights. Bush appointed conservative Supreme Court justices, whose decisions limited discrimination victims' right to sue. Bush vetoed the Civil Rights Act of 1990 and signed the 1991 Civil Rights Acts only after a long political struggle. These events demonstrated that the government had failed to consider civil rights as a national priority. According to Pinkney (1993), the Reagan-Bush administration position on civil rights was as follows: (1) racial and sexual discrimination no longer exist in the United States; (2) affirmative action discriminates against white males, and thereby violates the Constitution; and (3) affirmative action is a form of reverse racism.

As a conservative political base solidified, the Ku Klux Klan, a leading white supremacy group, gained strength. Other racist groups, such as the White-Aryan Resistance (WAR) emerged in recent years. More than 300 Klan, neo-Nazi, skinhead, and other white supremacist hate groups that involve an estimated 200,000 white Americans, exist in the United States. Additionally, approximately 25,000 whites are thought to be passive supporters of the white supremacist ideology (Langer 1990). Thus, it is not surprising that in 1980 Jesse Jackson declared that a large number of blacks believed in a white conspiracy of racial genocide. Indeed, newspapers have reported the existence of paramilitary training camps where white supremacist groups are preparing for a "race war"(Langer 1990; Nichol & Lee 1998).

In recent years, political leaders have pleaded for increased penalties for hate crimes. For instance, Michael Donald was lynched by Klan members, who testified that they had selected their victim at random. Donald's family sued the United Klans of America and in 1987 won a seven million dollar reward (Feagin & Feagin 1996). In 1993, an appeals court upheld a 12.5 million dollar judgement against WAR for its role in a skinhead gang murder of a black man. Additionally, citing the murder of a black man in Jasper, Texas, Senator Royce West introduced legislation to allow the death penalty if a murder is racially motivated in Texas. Mr. James Byrd, Jr., a forty-nine-year-old disabled black man, was chained behind a truck and dragged along a remote road until his head and right arm were severed from his torso (Nichol & Lee 1998). Senator West stated, "I want to make sure the people who participate in this kind of crime will be punished and will be made to pay the ultimate penalty" (Nichol & Lee 1998).

In 1994, more than 3,500 race-related, hate-inspired crimes were committed and 13 hate-motivated murders were reported to the FBI. Most of these crimes were committed by white attackers targeting people of color and Jewish-Americans (Feagin & Feagin 1996). Of interest, reports of hate crimes increased 20 percent in 1995 (Sigelman & Welch 1991). In fact, in 1997, there were 360 hate crimes in Texas, and the greatest number were at residences and directed toward blacks (Nichol & Lee 1998). In one incident, the home of a black family was pelted with eggs, and their car was set on fire in the street outside their home. More than half of all known hate crime offenders were less than twenty-one years of age, although this group composes only one-third of the total population (Feagin & Feagin 1996).

Political Protest

The persistence of widespread racism propelled organized movements to expand civil and economic rights. For example, in 1984 and 1988, the Rainbow Coalition registered two million new voters to support Jesse Jackson's presidential campaign. Jackson won nearly four million votes in the Democratic party primaries and went to the Democratic national convention. Although Jackson lost the nomination, he created a multiracial political organization in a number of states. Additionally, he was the first presidential candidate in U.S. history to develop a strong public position on issues of concern to blacks and other people of color (Dalton 1995; Pinkney 1993).

The Rainbow Coalition supported the Equal Rights Amendment, choice on the abortion issues, and the selection of a woman as a vice-presidential candidate. According to West (1993), however, Jackson's television style resists grass-roots organizing and, most important, democratic accountability. Although Jackson's brilliance and charisma sustain his public visibility, his lack of a moral vision, prudential judgment, courageous defiance, and organizational patience undermine its progressive potential. Nonetheless, a problem for any black candidate is that a significant proportion of white voters will not vote for a black president under any circumstance (Bell 1992; Dalton 1995; Hacker 1992; NORC 1994).

Bill Clinton's presidency brought renewed hope among blacks for aggressive enforcement of civil rights laws. Clinton's civil rights record was much better than that of presidents Reagan and Bush. He appointed more black men and women to important government positions, including judgeships, and his administration placed emphasis on the enforcement of civil rights laws by the U.S. Department of Justice. However, in 1994, for the first time in several decades, the Republican Party won control of both houses of the U.S. Congress. The new leadership showed hostility toward affirmative action, and some even advocated the abolition of all public welfare while championing "the minimal state." The views it espouses have had a continued impact on public policy. The dramatic resurgence of white political power at the national level generated political cynicism among blacks that also discouraged the development of a black infrastructure to address social inequality. As a result, many blacks became frustrated by the indestructible, ingrained, and immutable acts of racism that permeate every facet of American society (Cose 1993; Crosby et al. 1987; Feagin & Sikes 1994; Lawson & Thompson 1995).

In summary, the social, economic, and political progress of blacks have been restricted by legal segregation and systematic white privilege supported by a ideology of white supremacy (Sowell 1981; West 1993). Although the civil rights acts have made formal acts of discrimination illegal, they have not brought an end to blatant, subtle, and covert discrimination in business, jobs, housing, education, and public accommodations. Reflecting on the costs of racism, a black educator commented on what it is like to be a black man in a predominantly white society: "As a black man, most whites view me as a threat. My job has never gone smoothly and my chances for advancement have not been great. I have worked hard for years to earn as much money as a white man with my same qualifications. Throughout my entire life, I have been treated as a second class citizen. This in a country my forebearers helped to build and where I pay taxes to support the very organizations that discriminate against me" (Lawson & Thompson 1995:213).

Explanations of the persistence of racism are extensions of theories that reason why racism occurs. Modifications of these theories occur when attempts are made to accommodate significant sociopolitical events such as the civil rights movement. The following discussion addresses theories that explain the persistence of racism in a post-civil rights era.

EXPLANATIONS FOR THE PERSISTENCE OF RACISM

The term *majority*, as used here, refers to ethnic (cultural) groups who belong to the social category of Anglo-American. The most common definition of *ethnicity* is one offered by Max Weber (1929). According to Weber, members of ethnic groups hold to their common descent based on physical similarities, customs, shared colonial experiences or migration. The concept of a cultural minority refers to such ethnic groups as African-Americans, Mexican-Americans and American Indians. More broadly, in this paper, *ethnic* is used to represent ethnic groups who claim identities different from those of Anglo-Americans.

The word *racism* represents the belief that abilities such as intelligence are predetermined by one's racial group membership and *racism* refers to the belief that minority group members are inferior to the majority. One explanation of the persistence of racism focuses on the lasting influences of decades of slavery on the world view—the historical explanation. During the early part of the twentieth century, job opportunities for minorities were limited to low-paying menial, manual jobs on the farms and in the households of the wealthy majority. Socioeconomic mobility among minorities was limited by a series of unjust laws. The civil rights movement was a fight against these unjust laws. The success of the movement led to the enactment of civil rights laws and establishment of human rights agencies. This to an extent marked the end of explicit legal racism.

The expectations with respect to the pace and consequences of change during the post-civil rights movement were not the same among the majority and minority. Legal changes do not dramatically alter the political and economic inequalities between the majority and minority that have prevailed over decades. Those among the majority sympathetic to the claims for social and economic equality view the emergence of new social and political institutions founded on new civil rights as an evolutionary process. Blacks, however, often view the lack of rapid transformations required for fair and equitable sharing of power with suspicion. The value systems among the oppressors and the oppressed change slowly over time. The memories of oppression, in combination with an economic and political system that has moved very slowly in favor of minorities today, mold the perception of opportunities among the minorities. Thus, the historical explanation focuses on the persistence of old values and societal arrangements, on opinions and world views, that shape the current perception of racism. The perception of persistence of racism is likely to differ between majority and minority groups. The bid for power and equitable wealth sharing by minority groups is seen as a challenge to the power base that the majority has historically enjoyed. By the same token, the fear of losing the gains that blacks have made in recent years is a real one.

As already pointed out, the historical explanation of the persistence of racism emphasizes the role that old values and institutional arrangements play on the current social and economic conditions of the minority groups. As blacks demand swift movement toward achieving economic and social equality, various factions among whites question policies and programs that pave the way to power sharing. The threat to the power that the majority has historically enjoyed results in open acts of violence and prejudices against the minority. As previously discussed, there are a growing number of factions, such as the Ku Klux Klan and other militia groups, who voice their concerns against ideologies and policies that protect the interests of only whites. In addition, these extremist groups among the majority view ethnic diversity as a threat to their power. The recent increases in hate crimes and the burgeoning of militia groups may be seen as a reaction to the perceived loss of power that the whites have historically enjoyed. Such groups seek racial unity as opposed to diversity, in order to effectively compete for the control of scarce social, economic, and political resources.

In addition to publicized acts of violence against minorities, there is a nonviolent, but wide-spread, movement spearheaded by the majority groups to reinforce the ideologies of white racial superiority. The violent actions of militias and freemen may arguably be few and far between. The ideologies of these groups, however, are shared by a large number of people in the majority groups, even though the strategies they advocate for the prevention of the erosion of the power base are less dramatic and nonviolent. A case in point is the recent controversy surrounding the book, *The Bell Curve* by Hernstein and Murray (1996).

The Bell Curve reopened the issue of the significance of race for public policy making. This book suggests that the amount of intelligence one possesses (IQ), is highly correlated with several desirable outcomes such as education and wealth. The authors of this book argue that IQ is positively related to education and income as well as with morality. The more intelligent are morally superior. Those who possess a high IQ are more likely to be highly educated and more successful in accumulating wealth. Since these "cognitive elites" are also morally superior, they are less likely to commit crime, abuse alcohol, use illicit drugs, or become a teen mother dependent on welfare.

The authors argue that blacks score lower than whites on IQ tests and that this IQ differential is most certainly genetically determined. The policy implications are clear. Since the source of inferior intelligence and morality among blacks is largely genetic, the opportunities for making any improvements in their life are limited. Thus, welfare programs, which are often the only source of support for a large proportion of single-parent black women, should be eliminated. According to Hernstein and Murray (1996), these women can only perpetuate the welfare problem by having inferior children and federal monies should be channeled to support social programs that will benefit the children of the "cognitive elite." In schools, lowered educational performance expectations for black children is justified. The proponents of this view question why the government would spend scarce resources on special education programs? Instead, they assert that funds should be allocated to the more realistic and quantifiable job skills training for black children. Indeed, the book served an unmet demand for the reaffirmation of racial superiority among many whites and received nationwide publicity. It was debated and discussed by policy makers, academicians, and the interested public. Although the scientific merit of this book was widely questioned by well-renowned scholars, it captured the attention of elite educational policy makers and welfare reformers. The book also gained entry into the reading lists recommended by white extremist groups.

A second explanation for the persistence of racism hinges on demographic determinants, in particular, minority population size. The overall population size of minority groups tend to be small compared with the population size of the majority. This difference in population size does not necessarily result in the oppression of the minority. For example, in South Africa, a small population of Afrikaners wielded power over the majority of South African native population. Members of a group with a relatively small number of members compared with the majority are likely to feel out-numbered. While competing for scarce resources, the concerns of the minority groups are likely to be taken less seriously. This is particularly true in democratic societies where strong political representation is necessary to force majority opinion.

The political strength of the majority is a result of their relatively large population size. Very often political support of the majority is needed if minority groups are to gain access to resources. This lack of independence brings about perceptions of economic and political insecurity. The lack of access to resources in a political system based on majority opinion and vote is viewed as an outcome of institutionalized marginalization of the minority groups. As long as whites are demographically dominant and have gainful access to the scarce resources, they are more likely to be less mindful of the real concerns of the minorities. Thus, the demographic size explanation suggests that marginalization of blacks is likely to occur where political power is shared on the basis of demographic size. It is significant that when a minority group is persistently vocal in their demands for equitable access to scarce resources and political power, the demographic size of that group is likely to be exaggerated by the majority group.

A third explanation for the persistence of racism is supported by the ideology of assimilation. If only minority groups would give up their ethnic identities and adopt the cultural values and aspirations of the majority, racism would disappear. The assimilation perspective suggests that ethnic conflicts can be reduced and cooperation enhanced by dissolving ethnic distinctions. The assimilationists aspired to create one "American" identity at the discordance of the diversity of ethnic identities that early American settlers and immigrants brought to this country. The emergence of one American identity, it is contested, would lessen the ability to discriminate against "they" who are not like "us." The persistence of assimilation ideologies are indicated by resistance against multicultural and bilingual programs in primary and secondary education. As long as minority groups assert their ethnic pride and identity, the majority is likely to see the minority as belonging to "out groups" against whom the majority must compete successfully for scarce resources. This particular explanation suggests that racism will persist for as long as those desiring assimilation are resistant to ethnic diversity.

Finally, the persistence of racism may be attributed to the socialization process. Despite the socioeconomic progress blacks have achieved during the post-civil rights era, minorities remain physically and socially segregated to an extent from the majority. Blacks are more likely to live in inner cities. Blacks and Hispanics are less likely to share residential areas with the majority. Minority children are more likely to attend public schools where the majority of the student population is from the minority. This results in a lack of contact between the majority and minority during early childhood. The lack of opportunity for whites to socialize with black and Hispanic children contributes to the lack of appreciation of cultural diversity by white children. Social class plays a crucial role in determining intergroup relations and this has implications for race relations. That is the most important difference between the black and white categories. It reflects a major difference in the political and economic power that these two categories possess. The following discussion shows that these factors are observed in income, education and housing.

INCOME DISPARITIES

Family Household Disparities

On every economic indicator, blacks fare poorly, and in some cases, they have actually lost ground relative to whites. Blacks have been disadvantaged by the economic recessions of the early 1980s and have not shared in the recovery of the second half of the decade. During economic recessions, black workers tend to lose their jobs twice the rate of white workers and tend to be recalled at a slower rate than whites. Table 4.1 shows that between 1970 and 1990, the median income for white families increased from $34,419 to $36,915, representing an increase of 8.7 percent. During these decades, black family income barely changed from $21,151 to $21,423 (U.S. Bureau of the Census 1996). Since the 1950s, the income of white families income has remained 55 to 60 percent higher than that of blacks. In addition, the black per capita income is 56 percent less than white per capita income in the nation's largest cities such as Washington, DC, and Dallas, Texas (U.S. Bureau of the Census 1996).

Although the proportion of black households with incomes over $50,000 increased by 46 percent between 1978 and 1987, the percentages of black families with annual incomes below $15,000 also increased from 8.9 percent to 13.5 percent (U.S. Bureau of the Census 1995). The increase in black families with the lowest family incomes increased four times the number of black families receiving the highest incomes. In the mid-1990s, blacks were three times as likely to live in poverty. One-third of blacks and 46 percent of black children fell below the poverty line. The number of blacks living in poverty increased from 7.2 million to more than 10.9 million between 1974 and 1993 (U.S. Bureau of the Census 1996).

Table 4.1
Income Distributions by Race and Year

	White Families		Black Families	
	1970	1990	1970	1990
> $50,000	24.1	32.5	9.9	14.5
$49,000-$35,000	24.1	20.8	13.9	15.0
$34,999-$25,000	20.6	16.5	17.6	14.0
$24,999-$15,000	16.9	16.0	24.0	19.5
<$15,000	14.3	14.2	34.6	37.0
Median Income	$34,419	$36,915	$21,151	$21,423

Source: U.S. Bureau of Labor Statistics 1991

Moreover, many whites inherited significant economic wealth from their parents and earlier ancestors. Because of past slavery, legal segregation, and continuing informal discrimination, blacks have had little opportunity to build up multi-generational wealth. Compared to white households, black households possess a much lower net worth. The median net worth for white families is $44,408, compared to $4,604 for blacks, almost ten times that of black households (Swinton 1988). In addition, the types of assets held by white households are different from the types held by black households. Almost three-fourths of the assets of black households are durable goods, such as housing and vehicles, compared with less than half of the assets of white households. White households hold more than three times as much of their wealth in interest-bearing bank accounts or stock shares than do black households (Swinton 1988).

Unemployment

For decades, the unemployment rate for blacks has been about twice that of whites (see Table 4.2). In 1985, the black-white unemployment ratio reached a record high of 2.4 and remained about 2.1 in early 1995 (U.S. Bureau of the Census 1996). In some cities, the unemployment rate for blacks has risen to more than four times the rate of whites. Among the major reasons for this has been the movement of capital and jobs to the suburbs. The majority of new jobs have been created outside the central city areas where most blacks live. Of great significance is the unemployment of college-educated blacks. Table 4.3 shows that 4.5 percent of blacks who completed college are unemployed compared to 2.2 percent of whites. One explanation for this finding is that public and nonprofit organizations account for a large number of the college-educated work force. Unfortunately this results in blacks being vulnerable to public budget cuts (Hacker 1992).

Even greater than the unemployment rate for blacks is the *underemployment*

Table 4.2
Unemployment Percentages of Whites and Blacks

Year	White	Black
1960	4.9	10.2
1965	4.1	8.1
1970	4.4	8.2
1975	7.8	14.8
1980	6.3	14.2
1985	6.2	15.1
1990	4.1	11.3

Source: Adapted from Hacker 1992:103

rate, which includes individuals with no jobs, those working part time, and those making wages below the poverty line. Surveys have found that a large number of blacks are only part-time workers, even though they desire full-time jobs, or are discouraged workers (those who have given up looking for work). It is estimated

Table 4.3
Unemployment and Educational Attainment (Ages 25 to 34)

	White	Black
Completed College	2.2%	4.5%
Completed High School	5.3%	12.9%
Dropped out of High School	11.4%	25.3%

Source: Adapted from U.S. Bureau of the Census 1996b

that one-third of black workers fall into these subemployment categories, while the proportion for whites is much lower (U.S. Department of Labor Statistics 1991).

The unemployment rate of blacks is primarily influenced by recruiting practices. Traditionally, word-of-mouth recruiting served a positive function for employers by providing inexpensive advertising. Indeed, word-of-mouth advertising is the most widely used method of employee recruitment. When the existing work force is mostly white, however, word-of-mouth recruitment practices result in few black workers. The information networks are often shaped by widespread discrimination in housing. Blacks who live in central cities have little opportunity to enter the critical word-of-mouth recruitment networks when many industrial and retail trade operations are located in suburban areas. Moreover, using present white employees for new job referrals perpetuates the existing make-up of the labor force (Farley & Allen 1987; Feagin & Feagin 1996; Feagin & Sikes 1994).

Employed Blacks

The position of blacks in the work force is dismal. For example, in 1987, 5.6 percent of all corporate executives, administrators, and managers are black. The positions where blacks have greatest representations tend to be jobs that whites are reluctant to take (hotel maids and nursing aides) and lower civil service levels, such as correctional officers and postal clerks (U.S. Bureau of the Census 1996). A large percentage of blacks perform repetitive office chores such as data keyers and telephone operators. Occupational fields offering more job openings, such as bus drivers and social workers, are the ones serving clienteles that appear to have already become disproportionately black (Hacker 1992; Pinkney 1993). Table 4.4 shows occupational representation of blacks from 1960 to 1990. The proportion of

Table 4.4
Occupational Representation of Blacks (1960 to 1990)

Occupations	1960	1990
Telephone Operators	2.6%	19.7%
Accountants & Auditors	1.6%	7.4%
Secretaries	2.0%	7.6%
Lawyers	1.3%	3.2%
College Professors	4.4%	4.5%
Domestic Servants	53.3%	24.7%
Hairdressers	12.7%	9.2%
Physicians	4.4%	3.0%

Source: Adapted from U.S. Bureau of Labor Statistics 1991

black physicians has decreased and that of black professors has increased since 1960. Telephone operators, accountants, auditors, and lawyers have expanded.

In recent years, black women have composed a significant part of the black professional work force. Black women account for some 63.8 percent of all black professionals, whereas white women represent 50 percent of the whites holding professional positions (U.S. Bureau of the Census 1996). In the technical and managerial groups, black women are even further ahead, while among military officers, the black figure is double the rate for white women (U.S. Bureau of Labor Statistics 1991). There are two reasons for the dominance of black women in the professional work force. First, organizations generally prefer to hire black women rather than black men. Black women, like all women, are perceived as being less assertive and more accommodating, which increases the comfort level of whites. There is a belief that black women tend to show less resentment or racial hostility than black males. Second, there is a concern among white employers, although not always openly stated, that having black men and white women working together might lead to familiar relationships that could be easily misunderstood or cultivated

(Hacker 1992; Pinkney 1993; Turner et al. 1991).

Further, many companies also worry about hiring too many black employees or promoting black men too liberally (Hacker 1992; Wilkinson 1977). They may fear that promoting too many black males might jeopardize their image of competence and credibility. Firms also become uneasy if their organizations attract a large number of black clients. They report that white customers are reticent to associate with black preferences and tastes (Bell 1992; Hacker 1992). Simultaneously, businesses argue that they are color blind and seek the best talent, irrespective of race or gender. They often insist that the lack of blacks on their payrolls is because of the lack of qualified blacks. What is not explained very well, however, is how the possession of skin of a certain color or a certain look (blue eyes, blonde hair) figures in perceptions of qualifications (Cose 1993, 1997; Crosby et al. 1987).

The Glass Ceiling

Although black applicants experience discrimination at the entry stage, they also confront barriers in job promotions. Blacks are often denied access to higher-level jobs in an organization, whether it is in business, government, or education. Blacks, women, and some people of color refer to promotion barriers as the glass ceiling because opportunities for job progression are denied. A study found that white men, who make up about 39 percent of the adult population, accounted for 95 percent of the top corporate executive positions (Feagin & Feagan 1996). The glass ceiling has a negative effect on the promotion of blacks and it acts as a barrier for job progression because promotions are often based on subjective criteria. Indeed, promotion and hiring procedures often involve the subjective judgments of whites (Cose 1993; West 1993). While most companies have formal, written regulations for promotions, informal, unwritten rules often have a much greater impact. A black person might be passed over for promotion for "lack of initiative or aggressiveness," or because he or she is "not a good team player." Organizations hiring new people frequently ask whether the individual interviewed will "fit in here." Seasoned interviewers indicate that they can determine if a person has the traits and attributes their organization requires. Hence, it is difficult to obtain the real reasons why someone has been passed over for a promotion, or has been failed to be invited for an interview (Feagin & Feagin 1996; Hacker 1992).

EDUCATIONAL ATTAINMENT

High School

The actual completion of high school is often irrelevant for a number of blacks. Approximately 73 percent of blacks complete high school compared to 82 percent of whites (U.S. Bureau of the Census 1996). The secondary school drop-out rate among blacks is especially high among black males. One explanation is that when a black man perceives the opportunity structure as not allowing his upward mobility through education, he is more likely to divert his attention into sports, music, or hustling (Staples 1982). A study by the American Council of Education reported that public secondary educational systems tend to have low expectations of black males. Thus, a number of cities have created special schools or programs within the public schools just for black men. Another explanation for high black dropout rate in high school is the lack of resources available to blacks in many secondary institutions. Black high school students are provided with much less educational resources compared with students in other school districts. In fact, black high school students have fewer access to computers, less extracurricular programs, and fewer experienced teachers than the white students, factors that significantly affect their employment possibilities (Jackson 1988; Kozol 1991; Pinkney 1993). Moreover, black students are more likely to attend high schools with poorer physical facilities compared to their white counterparts (U.S. Department of Education 1994).

The type of high school education offered to black youths may also influence their dropout rate. Black students are more likely to be enrolled in special education programs, less likely to be enrolled in programs for the gifted or talented, and are over-represented in vocational education. In fact, secondary educational institutions tend to have low expectations of blacks, in general, and black males, in particular (Feagin & Hahn 1973; Marable 1983; Hacker 1992). Additionally, the dominance of elementary and secondary education by women diminished the number of male role models in public schools for black men. For example, traditional classrooms are oriented toward feminine values and black women tend to volunteer more in class than black men (Mitchell 1991; Hacker 1992). Consequently, the general success of young black females during their high school years helps to explain their occupational mobility as adults.

College

The same general educational attainment trends also apply to college education. In the 1990s, the proportion of black students entering college immediately following high school was less than three-fourths that of white students. In 1995, only 9.6 percent of blacks compared to 15.8 percent of whites completed four years of college (U.S. Bureau of the Census 1996b). Blacks enrolled at graduate schools also declined by 7 percent compared to a white decrease of 1 percent during 1980 (U.S. Bureau of the Census 1995). The enrollment of black students in mostly white colleges, however, obscures the retention issue. Predominately white colleges enroll considerably more black students than they graduate. While composing 10.2 percent of enrollees, blacks receive only 6.5 percent of the degrees granted (U.S. Department of Education 1994). Race is a significant factor in the retention rate of black college students. Feagin and Feagin (1996) note that often black students find white universities hostile where they are seen as "special admits" and beneficiaries of affirmative action.

Another problem blacks often confront on predominately white campuses is white hostility. Ehrlich (1990) reported an increase of campus ethnic violence, citing 200 events involving ethnic bigotry over a two-year period. At least two colleges had crosses set on fire in front of black residence halls. On another campus, a white fraternity gave a ghetto party with racially demeaning decorations (Ehrlich 1990). A black undergraduate at the University of Texas reported that he was confronted at gun point by two white students who wore Ronald Reagan masks. At another school, a student claimed that a professor called her a "black bitch" after she had charged him with racism for failing her in a class. Ehrlich (1990) concluded that bigotry and racism exist in major U.S. college campuses.

According to Feagin and Feagin (1996), the tragic aspect of the racial barriers at predominately white colleges is that black students perceive their educational experiences as an "agonizing struggle" rather than an experience to be savored. Thus, black students often leave white institutions of higher education rather than tolerate racial insensitivity. Indeed, the United States has more of its black men locked in prison jails than are attending classes on college campuses (Bloom 1997; Farley & Allen 1987; Hacker 1992; Kozol 1991; Massey & Denton 1993; Staples 1982).

HOUSING DISCRIMINATION

Rental Discrimination

Blacks continue to confront large-scale discrimination in housing in most urban environments. A survey involving twenty-five metropolitan areas found that most black renters face discriminatory treatment about one-half of the time, while black home seekers faced discriminatory treatment 59 percent of the time (NORC 1994). The U.S. Department of Housing and Urban Development report that some ten million cases of housing discrimination occur annually (*Chicago Tribune* 1993).

White Movement to the Suburbs

In the past decade, housing segregation has become increasingly prevalent. The major demarcation is between whites in the suburbs and blacks in the cities. For example, in the 1960s, the white population of the central cities in the Northeast declined by 10 percent (U.S. Bureau of the Census 1995). During the same period, the white population of suburban areas increased by 15 percent. Between 1970 and 1980, the central cities lost one percent of the white population annually (U.S. Bureau of the Census 1995). In 1970, the black population of suburbia was at 3.4 percent; ten years later blacks made up 6 percent of that population (Farley & Allen 1987). However, the migration of blacks to the suburbs does not mean that racial segregation in residential housing has decreased to any large extent. In many cases, black suburbanization is the result of central city black neighborhoods expanding across city boundaries into the inner suburbs—often older suburbs vacated by whites that have begun to deteriorate. While whites moved to the suburbs, blacks moved to the cities in large numbers. During the 1960s, the black population of New York City increased 38.2 percent, and Dallas, Los Angeles, Boston, and Detroit populations increased over 20 percent (Feagin & Feagin 1996). Although the white migration to the suburbs and black migration to the cities declined in the 1970s and 1980s, a segregated pattern of housing had been firmly established (Farley & Allen 1987).

One pattern that contributes to high rates of segregation is racial steering, in which real estate brokers refuse to show houses outside of specific area to black buyers. Although restrictive covenants—agreements among home owners not to sell their property to people who are designated as undesirable—is illegal, it still occurs (Farley & Allen 1987). Because it operates below the surface, with no written agreements, racial steering is difficult to detect. Blacks also are denied bank loans for housing purchases in certain neighborhoods. In fact, the total number of blacks who own their homes is less than whites because of mortgage lenders' discriminatory practices against blacks. Blacks are more likely to be rejected for a mortgage than whites with similar incomes. Approximately 71.3 percent of whites are homeowners, compared with 43.6 percent of blacks (Farley & Allen 1987; Swinton 1988). The outcome of such racist practices is to restrict the ability of many blacks to accumulate home equity and thus accrue subsequent financial resources.

CONCLUSION

The previous discussion has shown that racial categories, and hence their importance, have been influenced by the following factors: (1) the historical experiences of blacks in the United States, (2) demographic factors with whites as the majority, (3) power relationships and social hierarchial arrangements, and (4) a dominant ideology of racial superiority, which contributes to income, education, and residential segregation. Although there are many cultural diversity workshops, retreats, and seminars in academic institutions and private industries, every major poll has revealed a wide gap in black and white perceptions of race. A large percentage of whites believe that blacks have advantages over whites in educational opportunities due to reverse racism. This view is called the new racism in which social inequality is denied.

The previous discussion has also shown that the persistence of racism is the result of values and institutional arrangements that supported racism during the pre-civil rights era. The civil rights movement destroyed the legal foundations for racism. Subsequently, many blacks expected swift changes in the institutional arrangements favorable to an equitable distribution of wealth, education, and occupational opportunities. The source of threat to consolidated power among whites is not limited to the economic and political ascendency of ethnic and racial minority groups. The changes in white attitudes occur in the context of increasing competition for jobs and changing social values that have polarized races and classes. Racial polarization is a volatile issue that can result in racial and ethnic conflict. Moreover, we have shown that blacks experience a number of incidents of racism in income, education, and housing. Although legal slavery has ended, segregation and racial subordination have been allowed to persist. America imposes a stigma on every black child at birth. The restriction of educational, income, and housing opportunities, along with the long history of systematically discrediting blacks, have had a profound effect on blacks and whites.

An underlying contention of this discussion has been that racism is deeply ingrained in the collective historical practices and behaviors of American society. Throughout the evolution of the cultural organization of the American social system, racism has supported a social milieu based primarily on meanings assigned to color. It has sustained and legitimized segregation, restriction of opportunities, and the spatial isolation of descendants of slaves. Racism, as with political and psychological processes, has served to reaffirm the designed racial ordering of American society. While politicizing the identities of each racial group in society, racism superiorizes the self-images of whites and undermines an appreciation of cultural diversity. More importantly, racial social subordination prohibits inter-racial collaboration and precludes an ideological orientation of white and black destinies as profoundly interlinked. The continuance of racism also poses a moral question for whites: Is it moral to adopt negative stereotypes and white supremacist ideals about blacks and other minorities, then expect them to be quiescent—a characteristic that has never been demanded from the white majority population?

REFERENCES

Bell, D. A. 1992. *Faces at the Bottom of the Well: The Permanence of Racism.* New York: Basic Books.

Benokraitis, C., and Feagin, J. R. 1978. *Affirmative Action and Equal Opportunity: Action, Inaction, Reaction.* Boulder, CO: Westview.

Blackwell, J. 1988. Dynamics of minority education: An index to the status of race and ethnic relations in the United States. *Trotter Institute Review* 2:5–13.

Bloom, A. 1997. *The Closing of the American Mind.* New York: Simon & Schuster.

Bluestone, B., and Harrison, B. 1982. *The Deindustrialization of America.* New York: Basic Books.

Bobo, L. 1988. Group conflict, prejudice, and the paradox of contemporary racial attitudes. In *Eliminating Racism.* Katz, P., and Taylor, D. (eds.). New York: Plenum, pp. 85–114.

Carmichael, S., and Hamilton, C. V. 1967. *Black Power: The Politics of Liberation in America.* New York: Random House.

Chicago Tribune. 1993. Civil wrongs: As blacks go house hunting, too often the door is closed. November 14, C1.

Collins, S. M. 1983. The making of the black middle class. *Social Problems* 30:369–81.

Cose, E. 1993. *The Rage of a Privileged Class: Why Are Middle-Class Blacks Angry? Why Should America Care?* New York: HarperCollins.

————. 1997. *Color-Blind: Seeing Beyond Race in a Race-Obsessed World.* New York: HarperCollins.

Crosby, F., Bromley, S., and Saxe, L. 1987. Recent unobtrusive studies of black and white discrimination and prejudice. *Psychological Bulletin* 87:546–63.

Dalton, H. L. 1995. *Racial Healing.* New York: Doubleday.

Ehrlich, H. J. 1990. *Campus Ethnoviolence and the Public Options.* Baltimore, MD: National Institute Against Prejudice and Violence.

Essed, P. 1991. *Understanding Racism.* Newbury Park, CA: Sage.

Farley, R., and Allen, W. R. 1987. *The Color Line and Quality of Life in America.* New York: Russell Sage Foundation.

Feagin, J. R., and Feagin, C. B. 1996. *Racial and Ethnic Relations.* 5th ed. Upper Saddle River, NJ: Prentice-Hall.

Feagin, J. R., and Hahn, H. 1973. *Ghetto Revolts.* New York: Macmillan.

Feagin, J. R., and Sikes, M. 1994. *Living with Racism: The Black Middle Class Experience.* Boston: Beacon Press.

Feagin J. R., and Vera, H. 1995. *White Racism: The Basics.* New York: Routledge.

Gibbs, J. T. 1985. Can we continue to be color-blind and class-bound? *Counseling Psychologist* 13:426–435.

Hacker, A. 1992. *Two Nations: Black and White, Separate, Hostile, Unequal.* New York: Charles Scribner's Sons.

Hernstein, R., and Murray, C. 1994. *The Bell Curve: Intelligence and Class Structure in American Life.* New York: Free Press.

Jackson, J. 1988. The program for research on black Americans. In *Advances in Black Psychology.* Jones, R. (ed.). Richmond, CA: Cobb & Henry, pp 38–40.

Jones, E. 1986. What it is like to be a black manager. *Harvard Business Review* 64:39–43.

Kozol, J. 1991. *Savage Inequalities.* New York: Crown Publishing.

Langer, E. 1990. The American neo-Nazi movement today. *Nation*, July, 82.

Lawson, E., and Thompson, A. 1995. Black men make sense of marital distress and divorce: An exploratory study. *Family Relations* 44:213–218.

Marable, M. 1983. *How Capitalism Underdeveloped Black America: Problems in Race, Political Economy and Society.* Boston: South End Press.

Massey, D. S., and Denton, N. A. 1993. *American Apartheid: Segregation and the Making of the Underclass.* Cambridge: Harvard University Press.

McConahay, J. B., and Hough, J. 1976. Symbolic racism. *Journal of Social Issues* 32:38–50.

Mitchell, E. 1991. Do the poor deserve poor schools? *Time,* October 14, 60.

Morris, A. 1984. *The Origins of the Civil Rights Movement.* New York: Free Press.

National Opinion Research Center. 1994. *General Social Survey.* New York: National Opinion Research Center.

Nichol, B., and Lee, C. 1998. Jasper scarred but healing, Jackson tells mourners. *Dallas Morning News*, June 14, 1A, 38A.

Pinkney, A. 1968. *The Committed: White Activists in the Civil Rights Movement.* New Haven, CT: College and University Press.

———. 1993. *Black Americans.* 4th ed. Englewood Cliffs, NJ: Prentice-Hall.

Schuman, H., Steeth, C., and Bobo, L. 1985. *Racial Attitudes in America.* Cambridge, MA: Harvard University Press.

Sigelman, L., and Welch, S. 1991. *Black Americans' Views of Racial Inequality.* New York: Cambridge University Press.

Sowell, T. 1981. *Ethnic America.* New York: Basic Books.

Staples, R. 1982. *Black Masculinity: The Black Male's Role in American Society.* San Francisco, CA: The Black Scholar Press.

———. 1985. Changes in black family structure: The conflict between family ideology and structural conditions. *Journal of Marriage and Family* 53:221–230.

Swinton, D. H. 1988. Economic status of blacks, 1988. In *The State of Black America.* Jacob, J. E. (ed.). New Brunswick, NJ: Transaction Books, pp. 129–152.

Turner, M. A., Fix, M., and Struyk, R. 1991. *Opportunities Denied: Discrimination in Hiring.* Washington, DC: Urban Institute.

U.S. Bureau of the Census. 1996. *Statistical Abstract of the United States.* Washington, DC: U.S. Government Printing Office, pp. 229–231.

U.S. Bureau of Labor Statistics. 1991. *Employment and Earnings.* Washington, DC: U.S. Government Printing Office.

U.S. Department of Education. 1994. *The Condition of Education, 1994.* Washington, DC: U.S. Government Printing Office.

————. 1995. *The Black Population in the United States: March 1994 and 1993.* Current Population Reports, Series P-20. No. 420. Washington, DC: U.S. Government Printing Office.

————. 1996. *School Enrollment: Social and Economic Characteristics of Students.* Current Population Reports, Series P-22. Washington, DC: U.S. Government Printing Office.

Weber, M. 1929. *The Protestant Ethic and the Spirit of Capitalism.* New York: Charles Scribner.

West, C. 1993. *Race Matters.* Boston: Beacon Press.

Wilkinson, D. 1977. The stigmatization process: The politicization of the black male's identity. In *The Black Male in America.* Wilkinson, D., and Taylor, R. (eds.). Chicago: Nelson-Hall, pp. 145–158.

Yates, D. and Pillai, V. 1992. Public policy and black inequality: A critical review of the 1980s. *Indian Journal of American Studies* 22:23–31.

5

Discrimination and Prejudice Run Amuck

Debra A. Harley, Carolyn W. Rollins,
and Renee A. Middleton

DISCRIMINATION AND PREJUDICE

Discrimination is broadly defined as an act of distinguishing between two entities in a prejudicial manner. It presents itself in numerous forms (e.g., stereotyping, denial, sexism, and racism as related to gender, age, disability, sexual orientation, and so on), while in essence, its core function is primarily to exert control over the opportunity structure of America through oppression. According to Susan Fiske, "stereotyping and power are mutually reinforcing because stereotyping itself exerts control, maintaining and justifying the status quo" (1993:621). Implicit in discrimination and prejudice is the syndrome of revictimization—repeated acts as opposed to one-time victimization.

Acts of discrimination involve both overt and covert privileges exercised by those of the majority group over those of the minority group. Minority status refers to a "socially defined group whose values and aspirations are not validated by those persons who wield the balance of power in a given society" (Gaines & Reed 1995:98). For example, males have assumed authority over females, whites have assumed authority over African-Americans, the young over the elderly, and so forth. Thus, discrimination is a reward or positive reinforcement for those in the majority who conform to the social roles and group dynamics of the status quo. On the other hand, any level of discrimination places an unnecessarily heavy burden of revictimization and stigma on those of the minority groups.

Understanding the definition of discrimination requires an examination of equality, environmental conditioning, and the evolution of progress through the means of self-empowerment (e.g., civil rights movements) and legislation. Although discrimination is defined, implicitly and explicitly, with reference to both its political significance and with reference to social control, most of the current issues appear to be influenced by majority status "bonding" and the larger organizational context within which they are embedded (Pettigrew & Martin 1987; Sleeter 1994).

Equality

The concept of equality has been discussed and analyzed for centuries by various individuals, including the Greek philosophers Plato and Aristotle, the educator De Tocqueville, President Abraham Lincoln, the American philosopher and educator John Dewey, scholars such as Carter G. Woodson, and the literalist writer W. E. B. Du Bois. While the exploits of these individuals did not produce a conclusive definition of equality, Louis Fischer (1989) was able to offer a summary of four types of equality that have evolved over the course of time: ontological equality, equality of opportunities, equality of condition, and equality of outcome or result.

Ontological equality stresses the natural equality of all persons (as in all people being created equal). Equality of opportunity enables all types of individuals to achieve desirable ends (as evidenced in equal treatment under the law and freedom from discrimination in social and economic matters). Equality of condition, aspires to make living conditions and opportunities of life, equal for various social groups (as might come with affirmative action programs). Equality outcomes utilize legislation and other governmental actions to achieve equalities for individuals—this despite any inequities they might experience in other areas of social life (as with advantages specified for disadvantaged groups) (Fischer 1989). Equality is a primary focus of social philosophy with substantial consequences for both law and education (Fischer 1989), and for the identification of the "universal" mental antecedents of prejudice (Gaines & Reed 1995).

Environmental Conditioning

Environmental conditioning is also known as "social interaction"—the feelings of belonging or not belonging to a group (Gaines & Reed 1995). A crucial part of socialization (interacting and learning behavior) is categorization. "Nature does not create discrete categories of human traits or identities. People create categories to simplify the complexity of multiple identities and multiple realities" (Reynolds & Pope 1991:175). Discriminatory and prejudicial hostilities are directed by erroneous generalizations predicated on the essential component of categorization: "One must categorize the targeted individual as a member of a certain socially defined group" (Gaines & Reed 1995:97). Instead of environmental conditioning leading to an exploration of human diversity, it gives way to fragmentation and dichotomization.

Socialization factors impacting discrimination and prejudice that are found in the world view of dominant Western culture are centered on segmentation and/or beliefs (Reynolds & Pope 1991). Since stereotypes tend to exert control through prejudice and discrimination (Fiske 1993), and environmental conditioning is based on "subjective culture" (social norms, roles, beliefs and values of particular groups), individuals of the majority status are socialized to seek power (Triandis 1989). "Because power is control, people pay attention to those who have power" (Fiske 1993) and socialize those without power into a world view that is non-advantageous, resulting in a fragmented identity which allows oppression to be the order of the day (Myers et al. 1991).

Evolution of Progress

The difficulties inherent in challenging the subtle and institutionalized aspects of discrimination and prejudice are enormous. Bringing about social and political change in American society and culture—inundated by the majority subordinating the minority by using stereotypes and bigotry—requires multiple strategies. The most progressive change in discriminatory practices has been forged by the self-advocacy of those in the civil rights movements and legislation. Historically, individuals experiencing discrimination often found themselves with few viable options because of "ghettoization" by rigid laws that usurped their access to equal protection and due process within the jurisdiction of the laws.

The social reality for individual minorities based on race, gender, age, sexual orientation, disability, and so on, is that they must assume the role of change agent and the responsibilities attendant on that role. As individuals of the minority status, they are stigmatized and marginalized (Atkinson & Hackett 1998; Healey 1993; Reynolds & Pope 1991). By virtue of belonging to a minority group, individuals share a common agenda item—civil rights.

In America, several civil rights movements have evolved over the last four decades. The American civil rights movement of the 1960s served as the impetus for subsequent movements. Prior to this movement, the landmark decision from *Brown vs. The Board of Education* began the dismantling of discriminatory practices (Alston et al. 1994). The era of emancipation had begun.

In the years to follow, a growing militancy among minority individuals began to develop. Out of the blood and sacrifice of a great many African-Americans during the civil rights movement of the 1960s (among others), a foundation was laid for the anti-discrimination movements for women, persons with disabilities, gays, and lesbians (Middleton et al. nd.). While each of these started after the African-American civil rights movement, being largely based on that movement, the status of women (Cortese 1992), various persons with disabilities (Alston et al, 1994), gays and lesbians has surpassed that of African-Americans. For example, disproportionately higher rates of educational attainment for white women has consistently translated into improved success in the labor force, while sharp decreases occurred for African-American men (Cortese 1992). Gapasin (1996) discusses other inequities of the neo-conservative movement that have emerged since the passage of the Civil Rights Act of 1964. According to Gapasin, this movement is used to justify the concept of "reverse discrimination" and leads to "color blind" race politics and a nonresponsivist state policy (1996).

Gains by other cultural minorities include: the passage of disability legislation such as the Americans with Disabilities Act of 1990; the 1992 Amendments to the Rehabilitation Act; and the Rehabilitation Act of 1973. Persons with disabilities continue to improve their status as a protected class while African-Americans lose ground, as evidenced in the current efforts to repeal affirmative action. Likewise, Proposition 209, prohibiting state or local agencies from using preferences based on race or gender in employment, education, or contracting (Schmidt 1996), will adversely affect people of color who have limited protective avenues. Although the Civil Rights Act of 1991 was mainly designed to discourage discriminatory practices, enforcement is still limited and major companies (e.g., Denny's and Texaco) continue to discriminate against African-Americans. Those companies that continue to discriminate limit the access of African-Americans not only to employment and promotion opportunities, but to social equity as well.

"As equality is most often denied through governmental classification" (Fischer 1989:67), it is ironic that minorities have been able to achieve any victories at all. A plausible explanation for their success, however, comes from the "strong presumption of constitutionality of legislation or government policy" (Fischer 1989:67). Regardless of the reasons for the accomplishments of minorities, minority individuals have set the tone for the evolving standards of civil rights.

PREJUDICE AND DISCRIMINATION IN THE CONTEXT OF RACE

Discrimination in America today is deeply rooted in the stereotyping and prejudice related to race, particularly that of African-Americans, who are the primary recipients or targets of that discrimination. While the focus here is on the attitudes and behaviors of the white majority status toward the minority status, it does not suggest or imply that whites are the only problem. It does suggest, however, that the white majority has produced the greatest amount of aversive racism. Aversive racism is a subtle form of discrimination that is based on the strong egalitarian values of many white Americans, who also happen to believe that they are not prejudiced (Dovidio 1993). Unquestionably, white Americans have been the greatest perpetrators of overt racism throughout history—evident in public lynchings; legally enforced segregation; slavery; activities of ultra-right white supremacy groups as the Ku Klux Klan; discrimination in employment, housing, and in the administration of justice; assimilation; and acculturation (Blassingame 1972; Davis 1981; Du Bois 1962).

Prejudice is also manifested in the practice of categorization based on race. That categorization occurs instantly upon meeting a person and is based on what one sees. Since race is one of the most obvious and first-noticed aspects of another person, "racial categorization can form a foundation for prejudice"(Dovidio 1993: 52). Given that aversive racists actively and consistently express negative feelings, those expressions of prejudice and bias will eventually create a disadvantage for minorities and an advantage for the majority (Dovidio 1993). Aversive racism is difficult to dismantle because, since the majority status expresses their biases in subtle ways, they can rationalize and/or deny their own attitudes and behaviors (Dovidio 1993; Walters 1996).

Many Americans argue that African-Americans and other minorities have made substantial gains in education, employment, and housing (Pettigrew & Martin 1987). When people have been denied access to certain social, political, and/or economic arenas, any subsequent access can be considered an improvement. But racial discrimination, intentional or unintentional, produces the same effect—harm to those of the minority status in their individual or group situations (Walters 1996). In addition, the fact that racial discrimination is inherent and pervasive in the government responsible for the enforcement of social justice is the strongest confirmation of its power (Holzer 1994; Walters 1996). Unfortunately, in the post-1980s, the political climate is one of "race-neutralizing," whereby many people experience discomfort with the permanence of racial inequality and respond to it by denying, avoiding, and minimizing this reality (Bell 1992; Hacker 1992; Thompson & Jenal 1994). Evidence of the majority's unwillingness to address discrimination is offered by Sam Fish (1994) who discusses the use of "speaking in code." Fish asserts that liberals and conservatives use this technique to perpetuate their own discriminatory self-interest while cloaking themselves in the politically correct arenas of tolerance and equality.

Racism continues to survive and thrive because of the way people's values are determined. Once established, the value attached to particular minorities appears unchangeable. People of color have always been devalued by many whites despite their contributions to the economic, educational, and social structure of American society. Over sixty years ago, DuBois offered a perspective on the value of people of color in relation to their white counterparts that remains valid today. DuBois wrote: "In Africa, a black back runs red with the blood of the lash; in India, a brown girl is raped; in China, a coolie starves, in Alabama, seven darkies are more than lynched; while in London, the white limbs of a prostitute are hung with jewels and silk" (Du Bois 1962:728). The current racist value placed on people of color is illustrated by a series of recent events: the 1998 death of James Byrd Jr. who was dragged to his death by three white men in Jasper, Texas simply because he was African-American (*Associated Press*, 1998); the dragging and beating of a seventeen-year-old African-American youth in Belleville, Illinois by three white youth in 1998 (*Knight Ridder News Service* 1998); the abduction of two African-American women who were then beaten and set on fire by two white males in Montgomery County, Maryland in 1992; and the killing of Yusef Hawkins in Brooklyn by white youth (Walters 1996). These types of events are occurring with regular and alarming frequency.

The low value placed on people of color is also evident in the racial disparities in death penalty cases. For defendants whose victims are white, the odds of them receiving a death sentence are significantly higher than for those defendants whose victims are African-American. This is double discrimination—one, against the victim, and two, against the offender. The recent shooting incidents in small-town schools by white youth (ranging in age from eleven to thirteen years) have been portrayed in the media as evidence of a crisis. The offenders are portrayed as victims. Conversely, when similar incidents occur in the inner-city schools (attended by mainly minority students) the event and the offender are both portrayed as criminal. This is a classic example of discrimination and prejudice run amuck in American society.

The malignant devaluing of people of color by whites reflects an absence of what Cox (1974) refers to as "social ethics." That is, those of the majority status fail to employ critical judgment against society, utilize subjective viewpoints, and disregard any alternative perspectives. The devaluation of the African-American cultural heritage (and those of other minority groups) "reflects a conservative assimilationist ideology that blames contemporary racial inequity on the presumed cultural deficits of African-Americans" (King 1991:138). Such ideology, however, fails to consider how the facts of American history have been falsified "to save face" by a nation that simultaneously fought to perpetuate slavery and establish democracy.

Racism, discrimination, and prejudice are manifestations of both descriptive and prescriptive beliefs (Terborg 1977). Descriptively, stereotypes "tell how most people in the group supposedly behave, what they allegedly prefer, and where their competence supposedly lies" (Fiske 1993:623). Prescriptively, a stereotype "tells how certain groups *should* think, feel, and behave" (Fiske 1993:623). Descriptive and prescriptive stereotypes compete for superiority and primariness in the rationalization processes of the majority in their attempts to understand the minority perspective. Ironically, the majority is able to accommodate both positions as equally correct, even in light of contradictory challenges and facts. Clearly, the partnership of discrimination and prejudice is able to maintain a constant course, because when they intersect with subordinating the minority status, white racial privileges are preserved.

SUMMARY

Discrimination and prejudice are age-old problems. They exist because they are beneficial to the majority group. White people have gained economically, socially, and politically as a result of subordinating people of color—the majority has gained at the expense of the minorities (men over women, the non-disabled over those with disabilities, heterosexuals over gays and lesbians, and younger adults over the elderly). Racism, sexism, handicapism, homosexism, and ageism all clearly demonstrate that discrimination and prejudice are reinforcing for the perpetrators of such behaviors.

As America prepares to enter the new millennium, discrimination through dichotomization, segmentation, and societal stratification that favors the majority will continue to gnaw at the ideal of equality. The ideal of equality is elusive simply because the existing social order cannot provide unlimited (or equal) opportunity for minorities while maintaining the privileges for the majority group (Wellman 1997). Discrimination in any form or disguise serves to deactivate any civil rights movement or constructive agenda designed to combat inequality and inequity. Fundamental change in one's society is the ultimate goal of civil rights movements. Challenging both the liberal and conservative ideologies on racism, discrimination, and prejudice would appear to be the most promising approach for bringing about that change.

The free reign of discrimination and prejudice, along with society's attempts to simultaneously control it and benefit from it at the same time, can only be understood (and eventually altered) by systematically deconstructing the antecedents of its dominance. For any real chance of success, efforts toward deconstruction must address: the historical perspectives held on race, class, and gender; the cognitive distortions of dysconscious racism (King 1991); aversive racism (Dovidio 1993); and multiple oppressions (Reynolds & Pope 1991). Because bias can occur on any of the cultural, institutional, and individual levels of society (Dovidio 1993), multidimensional examinations and strategies must be the order of the day.

Discrimination and prejudice have run amuck in American society. They are analogous to a large and powerful machine out of control, destroying everything in its path. Therefore, the machine must be intercepted and control re-established. Knowing what to do, however, does not translate into how to do it. That is the question for the future: How can America rectify a shameful past riddled with injustices, maintain an inclusive social, political, and economic structure for the present, and establish a constructive agenda that embraces the "full complexity of human diversity" (Reynolds & Pope 1991)? A similar question was posed by Walters (1996) in reference to the African-American struggle for civil rights. While this question was prefaced to African-Americans, it has merit for members of all minority groups. According to Walters:

At all ends, America must come to terms with the poison of racism and the fact that there are no good substitutions that black people will accept in exchange for a respectable place in society predicated on an open opportunity structure. That is the primary basis of the struggle for civil rights and social justice in America, and if the blatant signals that are now being sent by every major political institution in America are interpreted to mean that a line is being drawn in the sand, then, the question which faces black America is not whether, but when and how to cross it—again (1996:7).

Can discrimination and prejudice be eradicated? The answer is yes, but only if every bigot, racist, and prejudicial thought can be lobotomized and their seed sterilized. Despite the enormity of the challenge, minorities cannot wait for a spur to action or a change in the social conscience of the majority group. The *when* of the new civil rights movement is right now, and the *how* is through consistent, persistent, intense and collective assaults on the social, economic, and political fronts. The reality is that the minorities are knocking on the door and they *will* come in. In the words of Nelson Mandela (1991), "Our march to freedom is irreversible."

REFERENCES

Alston, R. J., Russo, C. J., and Miles, A. S. 1994. Brown v. Board of Education and the Americans with dis-abilities act: vistas of equal educational opportunities for African Americans. *Journal of Negro Education* 63 (3):349–357.

Associated Press. 1998. Hundreds mourn man dragged to his death in Texas. June 14, 16.

Atkinson, D. R., and Hackett, G. 1998. *Counseling diverse populations.* Boston, MA: McGraw-Hill.

Bell, D. A. 1992. *Faces at The Bottom of the Well: The Permanence of Racism.* New York: Basic Books.

Blassingame, J. W. 1972. *The Slave Community: Plantation Life in the Antebellum South.* New York: Oxford University Press.

Cortese, A. J. 1992. Affirmative action: Are white women gaining at the expense of black men? *Equity & Excellence* 25(2–4):77–89.

Cox, G. O. 1974. *Education for the Black Race.* New York: African Heritage Studies Publishers.

Davis, A. Y. 1981. *Women, Race, & Class.* New York: Vintage Books.

Dovidio, J. 1993. The subtlety of racism. *Training & Development* 47(4):51–57.

Du Bois, W.E.B. 1962. *Black Reconstruction in America 1860–1880.* New York: Atheneum.

Fischer, L. 1989. Equality: An elusive ideal. *Equity & Excellence* 24(2):64–71.

Fish, S. 1994. *There's No Such Thing As Free Speech.* New York: Oxford University Press.

Fiske, S. T. 1993. Controlling other people: The impact of power on stereotyping. *American Psychologist* 48(6): 621–628.

Gaines, S. O., & Reed, E. S. 1995. Prejudice: From Allport to DuBois. *American Psychologist* 50(2):96–103.

Gapasin, F. E. 1996. Race, gender and other problems of unity for the American working class. *Race, Gender, & Class* 4(1):41–62.

Hacker, A. 1992. *Two Nations: Black and White, Separate, Hostile, Unequal.* New York: Charles Scribner's Sons.

Healey, S. 1993. The common agenda between old women, women with disabilities and all women. *Women & Therapy* 14(3/4):65–77.

Holzer, H. J. 1994. Black employment problems: New evidence, old questions. *Journal of Policy Analysis and Management* 13(4):699–722.

King, J. E. 1991. Dysconscious racism: Ideology, identity, and the miseducation of teachers. *Journal of Negro Education* 60(2):133–146.

Knight Ridder News Service. Illinois teen's attack resembles fatal dragging of Texas man. June 14, 12.

Mandela, N. 1991. Poster. Corte Monterrey, CA: Cortal Publishing.

Middleton, R. A., et al. n.d. Affirmative action, cultural diversity, and disability policy reform: Foundations to the civil rights of persons with disability. *Journal of Applied Rehabilitation Counseling.* Forthcoming.

Myers, L. J., et al. 1991. Identity development and worldview: Toward an optimal conceptualization. *Journal of Counseling & Development* 70:54–63.

Pettigrew, T. F., & Martin, J. 1987. Shaping the organizational context for black American inclusion. *Journal of Social Issues* 43(1):41–78.

Reynolds, A. L., & Pope, R. L. 1991. The complexities of diversity: Exploring multiple oppressions. *Journal of Counseling & Development* 70(1):174–180.

Schmidt, P. 1996. An end to affirmative action? Californians prepare to vote. *Chronicle of Higher Education,* October 25, A32–34.

Sleeter, C. E. 1994. A multicultural educator views: White racism. *The Education Digest* 59(9):33–36.

Terborg, J. R. 1977. Women in management: A research review. *Journal of Applied Psychology* 62:647–664.

Thompson, C. E., & Jenal, S. T. 1994. Interracial and intraracial quasi-counseling interactions when counselors avoid discussing race. *Journal of Counseling Psychology* 41(4):484–491.

Triandis, H. 1989. The self and social behavior in differing cultural contexts. *Psychology Review* 96:506–520.

Walters, R. 1996. The criticality of racism. *The Black Scholar* 26(1):2–8.

Wellman, D. 1997. *Portraits of White Racism.* Cambridge, MA: Cambridge University Press.

6

Diversity among Black Americans: Part of America's Hidden Diversity

Tyson Gibbs

THE SECRET

After the 1964 Civil Rights Act was signed into law, and after years of attempts to achieve the promises of that law, a major secret in the black community in America became evident to those outside and those within this community. The secret revealed that not all black people were alike. Prior to the 1960s, black people were forced by the larger society into a segregated way of living, requiring the majority of the black population—regardless of wealth, power, or influence—to remain within particular geographical borders and social groupings in most parts of the United States (Higham 1997). Further, there was a collective ideology, supported by most blacks that suggested that white Americans should allow black Americans full access to all of the rights and privileges that they as Americans should be able to enjoy.

To change the level of survival of black Americans required that for a while there was a need for black Americans to think in unison about the lack of access to the rights that white Americans enjoyed. There was probably little disagreement among most blacks about the need to press for access to their share of America's plenty and for better access to American culture at large—its hotels, restaurants, gas stations, employment agencies, housing offices, legal services, educational institutions, and financial services. Carson Clayborne describes this unity amongst blacks (1986:21). He believes that the activism (unity) among blacks during the civil rights movement resulted from a distinctive mindset that was shared by the activists. Protest participation was more likely among blacks who had become increasingly aware of the discrepancies or dissonance between their conditions of life and the alternatives made possible by a rapidly changing surrounding society. Black protestors were distinguished from other blacks by a higher awareness of the wider society. According to Clayborne, it was this collective understanding among the middle-class blacks initially, and the other economic and social classes of black Americans later, that fueled the success of various marches, sit-ins, picket lines, mass arrests, street demonstrations, and all kinds of boycotts designed to unite black Americans, regardless of their personal ideology.

But, such collective unity in thought about the need for social change in America provided blacks and whites a false picture of unity in all other aspects of black lifestyle. During the civil rights movement, the variation in ideas about what the black community needed to achieve a feeling of parody with the white American manifested themselves for the first time in the public arena. Rhoda Blumberg (1988) describes part of this variation in ideas as a fissure developing in the 1960s whereby the nonviolent direct action approach was overshadowed by an evolving black power philosophy among some activists. Both versions of black protest were aimed at improving conditions of America's largest minority group but differed sharply on the means to that end. Clayborne writes that there was a constant tension between the national black leaders, who saw mass protest as an instrument for reform, and the local leaders and organizers, who were often interested in building enduring local institutions rather than staging marches and rallies for a national audience (1986:27). Local black leadership sought goals that were quite distinct from the national civil rights movement. Richard Davis points out that blacks have always followed the divergent paths defined by color, class, religion, ethnicity, aptitudes and abilities, opportunities, and constraints (1997:134). During the late 1960s, and even today, many blacks and whites are still discovering that not all blacks are the same.

One of the key reasons for developing a critical understanding of the differences within ethnic and racial minority groups is to understand that gaining knowledge about group differences can change the perspective one has of that group. For example, the diversity among black Americans demonstrates clearly that on such major issues as political thought processes, identification issues, and gender questions, not all black Americans think or behave similarly. Outsiders viewing the black community, or for the matter any other ethnic minority group, often find it easier to consider that group a monolith—feeling, acting, and creating a social life in the same manner. It is easier to consider people within these groups as "the same" because of the effort involved in segmenting the population. The average American will not usually take the time to read, go to a lecture on, or otherwise gain knowledge of "the other Americans." Further, and unfortunately, such limited thinking about ethnic (cultural) minority groups provides fertile ground for bigotry, stereotyping, and discrimination.

Within-group differences also illustrate reasons why such groups do not often react as one during a social or political crisis affecting the group. As with the civil rights movement, for example, different populations among black Americans participated at different times, in different ways, and for different reasons. The activities ranged from those who contributed money as a way of participating, to those who were on the front lines of civil disobedience. Attempts at understanding group differences provides Americans with the greatest opportunity to break down the barriers caused by ignorance of a group and provides the chance to overcome stereotyping of a group. For all ethnic and racial minorities, diversity within populations is the rule, not the exception.

LABELING DEBATE IN THE BLACK COMMUNITY

One of the early areas of disagreement among blacks surfaced in the call for changing the names by which blacks called themselves. The names debated are well known. One of the major areas of disagreement centered on those blacks calling themselves *colored people*. This particular label was very popular among older black Americans. It has been argued that this term called attention to the complexion of the skin and, thus, re-enforced the concept of *we*—meaning white people or people whose origins lie mainly in Europe—are different from *them*—the people of African descent (Gibbs 1997). It is important to emphasize here that in the 1960s, many blacks over sixty years of age used the word *colored* to describe themselves.

Considerable disagreement between younger college-educated blacks, members of such groupings as the Student Non-Violent Coordinating Committee or the Congress for Racial Equality, and middle-class, lower-income blacks who grew up in the 1930s and 1940s resulted in the continued use of the term *Negro* to describe black Americans. The term *Negro* became popular during the early 1900s and may have gained in popularity because anthropologists used it to describe one of the four major races of man recognized by many at that time (Negroid, Caucasoid, Australoid, and Mongoloid). Many people of African descent used this term to describe themselves, rejecting the *colored* label as demeaning. The anthropological definition of *Negro* during the early 1900s referred to those dark-skinned people living south of the Sahara Desert in Africa, but this was not acceptable to those who wanted to further distinguish black Americans from their past.

The term *black American* became a popular label as the result of the civil rights movements of the 1960s. Philip Kasinitz believes that the term *black American* was an ascribed racial identity violently imposed (Davis 1997:157). According to Kasinitz, the boundaries of this identity were defined for the convenience of their oppressors and not based on any cultural characteristics of the group. However, once historical circumstances created black Americans (by virtue of their shared experience as slaves and in living together in a segregated society), their shared historical experience and shared cultural commonalities did produce a sense of shared ethnicity. Thus, while the term *black* had become a purely racial term used to describe a person's phenotype, it also was to become an ethnic term used to refer to a self-conscious group of people, their history, and/or their culture. When this group later redefined itself as *African-Americans*, another ethnic dimension was added to the definition of self (Davis 1997:157). During this time, many black Americans decided to adopt the African-American label to symbolize their African association with dark-skinned people who live in other parts of the world. The term *black* was also intended to be a statement of the way people of African descent could unite themselves as a political group (Anderson 1990:2). Not all people readily adopted this label, however. During the 1960s and beyond, many black Americans still preferred to describe themselves as *Negro* or *colored.*

Following the 1960s, an internal political struggle took place between the black intellectuals who were the teachers and promoters of Black studies, militant blacks whose politics included using any means necessary to gain parity with white America, and the general body of people of African descent who formed the masses and whose income ranged from poor to wealthy. The choice of whether or not to use terms such as *colored, Negro, black,* or *African-American* demonstrated the divisions along both political and ideological lines and the differences across generations of blacks. Many older blacks refused to change the conceptualization of themselves as *colored* to the dismay of the younger generations (grandchildren, sons, and daughters). Many middle-class blacks were very comfortable with the *Negro* label, considering it far more palatable than simply being called *black.* Anecdotal data from discussions within the black communities across the United States suggests that there were many heated debates about the need for a new name for referring to the black people in America. These differences in label preferences clearly demonstrated that the black community was not one huge monolith, with a whole people thinking, feeling, and acting in unison.

Caught up in this internal debate was the thorny issue of what to call immigrant Africans (e.g., Nigerians, Ghanians, Ethiopians, Kenyans, Liberians, and so on) and immigrant Jamaicans, black Cubans, black Puerto Ricans, and/or black Panamanians who were beginning to immigrate into the major cities in the United States. Many of these groups preferred to be called by their country or group of origin, not as *blacks, colored, Negro,* or anything else. Davis says that today the black community is constantly being inundated by wayfarers from around the world (1997:vii). While this level of immigration is unprecedented, a significant number of West Indian and Africans have coexisted with native-born blacks for the better part of this century. Most of these West Africans and Africans have elected to become part of mainstream white America; others have chosen to live in separate communities and remain culturally distinct. To the dismay of native-born blacks, most of these dark-skinned foreigners also refused to take part in a struggle with which they did not identify nor view as their own. Although their skin color matched the dark skin of the native-born blacks, their foreign speech patterns and accents, along with their dress, provided these black foreigners access to many of the advantages of American culture unaccessible to native-born blacks prior to the 1960s civil rights movement. Seeing that many of these dark-skinned foreigners had access to a lot of the advantages of American culture, many black Americans viewed them as a negative influence on the civil rights movement. This view of black foreigners was particularly strong among college students and within the communities in which these black foreigners lived. There was little support from these black foreigners for the civil rights activities in which native-born blacks were participating. To be sure, at least in the South, to be called *African* was the height of insult for native-born black adults and children. To be called African in the company of one's friends could easily start a fistfight. In spite of the desire by many black leaders to link all black Americans to black Africa, the word *African* remained a term of insult and not one of pride in many communities. The internal struggle about labeling clearly demonstrates that not all black people living in America were of one mind. The split on this question occurred between different generations, income levels, and political ideologies and, in many ways continues to separate and divide the black population into different ideological groups today.

AFROCENTRICITY

In addition to the issue of label, some more dissension appeared out of differences in political ideology. During the civil rights movement, all native-born black Americans were challenged, encouraged, or pressured by leaders of the civil rights movement to stop calling themselves *nigger*—even in jest—and to seek a better understanding of their heritage or "roots." Many books, films, and college courses were created to reflect what many saw as a new era in the black social movement in the United States. But, it was also during the post-1964 era that many other differences within the black communities were revealed. The hunger for more access to the lifestyle of the majority white population by blacks was placed in full view of those who had designated themselves as the keepers of the new black social movement in America.

The differences among blacks were becoming clear in the post-civil rights era. Politically, blacks wanting to align themselves with more aggressive tactics for change opted for affiliation with such groups as the Black Panthers, Student Non-Violent Coordinating Committee, Congress of Racial Equality, or the Freedom Riders. Moderates within the black community sought out such groups as the Southern Christian Leadership Conference and the National Association for the Advancement of Colored People, and participated in church rallies and a great many local community political activities. Differences in how this new era of black power should be promoted began to surface. There were calls from within the black community, by those civil rights leaders who supported native-born blacks developing a linkage to Africa, for blacks to change the ways they dressed and adopt the so-called African style of clothing. For example, the *kente* cloth and other colorful materials were made into garments as a demonstration of the political and cultural connection between Africa and native-born black Americans.

Edward Reed et al. (1998) provides a discussion of the Afrocentricity issue. They believe that three major ideologies resulted from the discussions about labeling, political linkage, and dress wear. Their discussion focuses upon the ideas of writers such as Gerald Early (1996) who suggests that Afrocentrism is an intellectual movement, a political view, a historical evolution, and/or a religious orthodoxy. It stresses the culture and achievements of Africans. Molefi Kete Asante believes that Afrocentricity reorganizes the black frame of reference so that blacks become the center of analysis and synthesis (1992:33). As such, it becomes the source of regeneration of black values and beliefs. Indeed, this movement recaptures the collective will that was responsible for ancient Egypt and Nubia.

Types of Afrocentrists

It is argued that there are three basic types of Afrocentrists: race-distancing elitists, race-embracing rebels, and race-for-profit (Reed et al. 1998). The first type is dominant at the more exclusive universities and colleges. These Afrocentrists often view themselves as the *talent tenth* who have a near monopoly on the sophisticated and cultural gaze of Afrocentrism. This type of Afrocentrist revels in the severe denigration of many African-Americans who fail to adopt the view of Afrocentrism as a linkage to Africa. For example, these Afrocentrists may denigrate other native-born blacks who do not wear African clothes or wear braids. Interestingly, Afrocentrists distance themselves from other African-Americans by ironically calling attention to their own marginality.

The second type of Afrocentrist is the race-embracing rebel, who often views him or herself in the tradition of Malcolm X, Stockley Carmicahel or Eldredge Clever. The race-embracing Afrocentric rebels express their resentment of whites but reproduce similar hierarchies based on class and gender within the black context. They rebel against the insularity and snobbishness of whites, yet their rebellion replicates them by excluding other black Americans with doubled marginality such as gays, lesbians, and those in the under and lower classes. They tend to advance their own interests and to hunger for higher social status. Hence, their rhetoric on the glorious African past becomes a substitute for analysis; their discussions on the merits of Africa become little more than a replacement for serious analysis and reading of the predicament of black Americans.

The third type of Afrocentrist is the for-profit-Afrocentric who is usually an individual self-taught in Egyptian history and other histories from the African continent. These Afrocentrists mimic the cultural style and even the moral stance of capitalism. They are usually committed to convincing African-Americans to consume primarily African goods, including clothes from the "motherland." This kind of behavior is not only symptomatic of the alienation and desperation of black Americans, it further fragments black Americans by making symbols of African clothing and dress, while making them the essence of what one considers under the label of African-American. For the average black American, indeed for whites and other Americans, these three types of Afrocentrism appear to reflect one mode of thinking. However, these ideologies represent the variability in sociopolitical thinking among black Americans. Afrocentrism often links the psychological redemption of black Americans with their re-acquaintance with Africa. According to Afrocentrism proponents, Afrocentrism is the ideological glue that could bring black Americans together as the expression of a cultural and spiritual level that transcends class and geographical lines. Black American solidarity also is viewed as critical, since there is an extensive internalized sense of oppression among most black Americans, a product of slave holders deliberately dehumanizing African-Americans during slavery. Thus, it is important to recognize that black Americans share a common history, punctuated by slavery and producing a common sense of oppression. The ideology of the for-profit-Afrocentrist has led to an even more frequent appearance of the Afrocentric ideology among younger blacks, and it provides for some middle-class black Americans' idealized sense of oneness.

There are other reasons why Afrocentrism has such an appeal to so diverse a group of black Americans, including that concept offered by Early, in which he discusses why blacks dream of a world without whites (1996:115). What Early proposes is that Afrocentrism is a mood that has largely erupted in the past ten to fifteen years in response to integration, or perhaps because of the failure of integration. Noting that the bourgeois black middle-class element of Afrocentrism is very strong, he sees Afrocentrism as a demonstration of their race loyalty and solidarity with their brothers and sisters throughout the world—whether in American cities or on African farms. Early also argues that the black middle class has given Afrocentrism its force as a consumer ideology by making it possible to buy into Afrocentrism through the clothing one wears, the books one reads about Africa, or the works of art one may collect from Africa.

Afrocentrism is also embraced by black American college professors who use it as a mechanism to call attention to racial differences and as a buffer against actual and perceived racism. Black college students seeking their own identity on predominantly white college campuses are attracted to Afrocentrism because it can be used to solidify their membership in the black middle class to which they aspire or already belong. A number of black students may feel guilty for not being poor. For them, Afrocentrism represents the ideological glue for bonding across class lines. In addition to the college educated blacks seeking some sense of identity, black American prisoners, too, are attracted to the ideology and philosophy of Afrocentrism. Reed et al., found in his work experience in four state prisons that many black American prisoners in search of personal identification adopt the ideology presented in Afrocentrism as a way of finding their identity (1998).

Another reason proposed for the appeal of Afrocentrism comes with its widespread commercial possibilities during the summer months at black American and African festivals held nationwide in America's largest cities (e.g., New York City, Detroit, Chicago, Gary, Indiana, Chicago, Los Angeles, Cleveland, and Seattle). At such gatherings, many "high profile" rap stars, singers, dancers, and professional athletes wear African garb and use the symbolism of the Afrocentrism philosophy. Many seem to be more interested in selling or buying their way into an Afrocentric ideology, rather than necessarily believing a particular ideological viewpoint. Lastly, many blacks find that Afrocentrism satisfies an emotional as well as a psychological need. This is evident in the practice of blacks from across the classes electing African names for their children, and it is also evident by the numerous trips middle-class blacks have taken to Africa.

Early (1996) argues that the greatest psychic burden on the black American is that he or she must not only think constantly about being different, but about what the difference means. He makes the point that affirmative action, which promotes separate group identifications and group differences, tends to intensify black self-consciousness. Early surmises that blacks, through no fault of their own, are afflicted with a debilitation of self-consciousness when around whites.

CLASS AS SYMBOLIC OF BLACK DIFFERENCES

Whitney Young states that there is a grave potential danger in the alienation of the middle-class Negro from those of his or her race who are in the almost dependent category of the lower class (1964:315–316). The alienation works both ways. Both unconsciously and consciously, members of the black middle class often disassociate themselves from the lower-class black. On the other hand, the black in the lower class group sees in the flight of the middle-class black from the lower-class black neighborhood a desire to disassociate from the rest, and this causes some tensions. The withdrawal of the middle-class black also fosters the development of different values and the establishment of different goals by the two groups. Some middle-class blacks now exhibit a tendency to be indifferent, if not hostile, to those black Americans less fortunate or privileged.

During the post-civil rights era, blacks were quick to seize the opportunity to send their children to what were once all-white elementary schools, junior high schools, high schools, and colleges and universities in an effort to obtain an education at a predominantly white college, which had been unavailable to the black community for many years. This rush on the part of many to send their children to newly integrated schools further illustrated some of the differences among black Americans. Sidney Kronos argues that education became almost an obsession for middle-class blacks (1971:9). Going to college or some other post-secondary school for training became a high priority goal for them. The flight to the integrated schools also started a flight from the predominantly mixed middle- and lower-class black communities such that in many cities, poor communities became "middle-class black people poor" with the exit of blacks to predominantly white communities and/or to middle-class black neighborhoods.

In the pre-1960s era, professional blacks in many black communities often found themselves living close to lower-income blacks. They were forced into such living conditions because as blacks, they were excluded from living, en masse, with whites. Although the majority of the black population resides in metropolitan areas of the major cities, Thomas Clark indicates that significant enclaves of middle- and upper-class black areas now exist in the major cities (1979:1). Such a change in the character of inner city and black middle-class neighbors has caused significant resentment and anger from those blacks left behind. Terms such as *oreo, uncle tom, handkerchief head,* or *whitey's boy* or *girl* were hurled at those who only thought they were doing the best for themselves and their children.

Fragmentation of the black community continued as black colleges, which formerly were the mainstay of black higher education for many years, began to experience a decline in student enrollment, forcing many of them to operate close to bankruptcy as parents sent their children to predominantly white colleges and universities. Debates among blacks over the need for black children to attend black schools because of what black schools could offer were fueled by stories indicating that as many as 50 percent of those blacks entering predominantly white colleges and universities were failing to graduate within the four- or five-year period. Even within the white colleges and universities, there was little agreement among black students as to how the new era of black social change should be promoted. Black students were often criticized for dating anyone of another ethnic group, and many of them were ostracized and prohibited from participating in the functions of Black Student Unions and other Afro-American organizations, and some were even branded as traitors to the black community and causes. In this post-civil rights era, middle-class blacks could be identified by their strong belief in the power of education, their heavy emphasis on individuality and personality, isolation from lower-class blacks, class consciousness, and conservatism (Kronos 1971).

POPULAR CULTURE AND SOME FURTHER DIVISIONS

The popular culture of films, TV shows, music, and sports served to highlight the increased recognition within the black community that all was not one. Movies such as *Shaft, Superfly* or *Uptown Saturday Night* were criticized as depicting blacks as pimps, drug dealers, prostitutes and/or stupid. Older movies in which blacks appeared as lazy, watermelon eaters, or scared of ghosts were scrutinized, and the actors of such movies portrayed as "uncle-toms." Television shows became the focus of discussions about the image of blacks in America. The popular show *Sanford and Son* was contrasted with such shows as *Julia* and *I Spy*, which appeared to present a much more positive image of blacks. Other television shows such as the *Jeffersons* were criticized for presenting blacks as stupid, even when blacks got enough money to live as upper-class whites. Any music that appeared to reflect the burgeoning black influence was given a "thumbs up" by the black community watchers, while any music that was considered inappropriate for "The Movement" was considered a negative influence on the black community. For example, the Jimi Hendrix Band received mixed reviews because of Hendrix's use of drugs. Many thought that even though he was a black musician, the image he projected was not a good one for the black community. Major black sports figures, movie actors, actresses, prominent political figures, or just about anyone else in the public eye were evaluated in terms of their roles or personal activities. For example, while a great many blacks were happy to see the late Senator Edward Brooke of Massachusetts become a senator, he was condemned for marrying a white woman. Such scrutiny was also directed at such people as Sammy Davis, Jr., Lena Horne, Quincy Jones, and Sidney Poitier; they were soundly criticized for marrying or dating people of other racial or ethnic groups, in spite of their notable contributions in their respective fields.

As debates became more intense within the black communities around the United States, they were not lost on the white population or anybody else. Many whites became confused about what to say or how to react to people of the new black movement taking shape within American culture. How to address a black person became an important question in the minds of many whites who wanted to respect the rapid changes taking place in the black community. While some whites remained entrenched in their beliefs about the inferiority of blacks, others saw the changes as opportunities for social growth in American society and culture, as opportunities for new business opportunities, new educational opportunities, or simply as new ventures. For these whites and other non-black Americans, it became important to keep up with the latest preferred forms of address, the handshakes that became a way of determining who was in and who was outside of the black movement, or the terminology that was rapidly becoming part of the lexicon of the black community's dialogue. Whites, who may have had little contact with blacks prior to the 1960s, were suddenly realizing that the black community was not one cohesive group, with the same beliefs and feelings. Many whites were caught off guard by the behavioral differences between Southern blacks, Northern blacks, Midwestern blacks, or blacks from the Far West. Many were discovering that black men and women did not all think alike on education, economics, dating, marrying, or what clothing to wear. Each of these cultural traits and behaviors became ways for blacks to signal each other as to which blacks were inside and which were outside the burgeoning black social movement.

While the literature on black Americans is replete with instances of variability within the black community, and as the economic charts are showing signs of black Americans in all levels of wealth in American culture, for many within and outside of the black community, there is still debate about the unity of thought and social behavior of black Americans. These debates are especially important, since blacks in leadership positions purport to speak on behalf of the entire black community in the United States, as such activities as the Million Man March on Washington, DC continue to give the impression of a black monolith in America.

GENDER DIFFERENCES IN THE BLACK COMMUNITY

There are clear differences in males and females in the United States. Black and white males earn more money than black and white females. Males commit more crimes than females, regardless of ethnicity. The issue for black Americans in the post-civil rights era focuses on whether gender issues or black American social issues are more important. Prior to the 1960s, the pervasiveness of segregation supplanted the issues of gender within the black community. Black Americans, both male and female, were subjected to the problems caused by the issues of race and ethnicity. After the civil rights movement, issues of gender in America took center stage, alongside the debates over issues of ethnicity, and provided further evidence of the nonexistent black American monolith. Arthur Eckardt reports that while the Black Power movement spawned the assimilationist goals of the politically conservative black bourgeoisie, its devotees continued to hold quite firmly to the group's values regarding heterosexual and male superiority (1989:53). According to Eckardt, it is ironic that the Black Power movement could transform the consciousness of an entire generation of black people on the question of black self-determination, yet fail so enormously in understanding the sexual politics of the movement and of black people across the board at the same time.

Black men and women were attempting to promote a new social agenda that often totally ignored their own gender differences. For example, the discussions and debates by white female feminists about terminology, political ideology, economics, and media images affecting women, regardless of ethnicity or race, were often devoid of any discussions about the issues facing black women and black men. On problems facing women in general, black women were chided for entering into allegiances with white women or other nonblack females. Eckardt writes that black women are subjected to double jeopardy—racism and sexism (1989:52). In her is wedded the high invisibility of a "woman of color." That is to say, black women are visible only when viewed as mothers to children or when functioning in traditional roles of helpers to males. As leaders, planners, initiators or promoters, black women remain largely invisible. Although black women have participated in such roles, leadership is predominantly a black male role. Indeed, to most black women, black liberation connotes power for men and women's liberation suggests power for women who are white. According to Diana Lewis (1988), black women have tended to see racism as a more powerful cause of their subordinate position than sexism, and they tend to view the women's liberation movement with considerable mistrust.

Added to these gender discussions are issues of sexuality, such as those related to problems of being a black homosexual in America. Discussions about black and gay issues were also part of the dialogue of the same ministers promoting women as helpmates to men, but not their leaders. The black gay rights struggle was not, and is not, a major part of the black civil rights struggle, but it has been the fuel for the gay rights debates that often came from the pulpits of black churches, the very places that provided the leadership for much of the civil rights movement. Many black ministers believe that women do not have a place as leaders in the church, citing biblical scripture to support their claims of the diminished role of women as leaders of the church or in the black home in general. These issues have only fueled further debate because a great many black women felt that their roles in the civil rights struggle had been reduced to playing supportive roles, instead of any real leadership roles. In their minds, there is no question that the civil rights movement was one of both black women and men playing key leadership roles. The dialogue, however, that supported the view of black women having only an expressive role, instead of an instrumental one, often came from male leaders in all spheres of the black civil rights movement. The issues that affected women were generally not part of the dialogue of discussions that placed ethnicity or being black as far more important. Gender in the post-civil rights era was, and is now, another major area of diversity for black Americans. Beverly Guy-Sheftall raises this question, "If women do form a distinct social group, how does one formulate a conceptual framework that takes into consideration race and its interactions with gender in the case of the black woman's experience" (1990:171)?

SUMMARY

Diversity has been the hallmark of the black population in the United States. Unfortunately, the overwhelming pervasiveness of the poverty, segregation, and isolation for hundreds of years presented a unified picture of the black population to both blacks and whites. To be sure, the experiences of poor blacks in the north, south, and west were different in terms of the availability of jobs, reaction to segregation, and/or their social structures, which developed to improve survival chances in these different areas of the United States. The struggles to bring an end to slavery, segregation, and isolation became the unifying theme for all blacks across all economic and social levels. The agreements on the question of race, however, overshadowed the issues of ideological differences, religious differences, gender issues, and sexuality questions.

The dawn of the civil rights movement lifted the veil of secrecy that covered and masked the underlying variability within the black population. To the community at large and other social groups and cultures (whites, Asians, Hispanics, and so forth), the black population appears as a huge monolithic society. Comedians continue to make jokes about black lifestyle as if there was such a thing that could apply to all blacks. The news media continues to report stories about blacks that present shallow images of the black population with the expected result—the perception that all blacks think alike and act alike. The media flashes images of welfare, and the images are of black people. There is a news story on crime; the images are of blacks. There is news of social disagreements, and a black social leader expresses himself as if he speaks for all blacks in America. The news media seek out the so-called black leaders for their opinions about various occurrences within black communities. Their utterances become the opinions of all blacks in American society. To be sure, many blacks may often agree with these utterances, but agreement on one aspect of black culture does not imply total agreement on all things. Skin tone makes segregation of ideas, actions, and lifestyles easier for a country that uses skin tone as a way of grouping, identifying, and segregating its citizens. Rarely, if ever, are the ideologies, habits, educational attainments, or economic achievements recognized as ways of distinguishing ethnic minorities, although such methods are frequently utilized to categorize one white or Asian person from another. The utterances of the white outcasts—skin heads, cultists, religious leaders, and such—are not taken as the views of all whites in America. Not even the views of the President of the United States, who is white, are reflections of the feelings and emotions of all Americans. For the majority of American society, it is easier to categorize minorities on the superficial level of skin tone than it is to make attempts at understanding the diversity within these populations.

CONCLUSION

For all ethnic minority populations, variety and diversity are the rule, not the exception. The key reason for examining diversity within population groups is to understand the impact that variety in thought and action has on social group behavior. Clearly, the demonstration of diversity among black Americans illustrates that this group is not a monolith. Such divergence in thought in key areas—political action, identification questions, or gender issues—points to the vast differences to be found among black Americans. For the public at large, outsiders to the ethnic minority populations, it is much easier to hold onto stereotypes, preconceived expectations, and prior single experience contacts to guide behavior toward a particular group. It is much harder to read about, go to a lecture on, or otherwise gain knowledge about a group. The limited knowledge that most Americans, and others, have about an ethnic minority population is fertile ground for discrimination on the basis of ethnicity, stereotyping based on single or limited experience, and racial hatred based on unfounded expectations.

The possibility exists that even within groups there is a lack of understanding of the differences between members. It is, therefore, extremely important that the concept of variety within populations gain a foothold among the population in general because, in many cases, ethnic minority groups are themselves surprised that when social or political activity is deemed an appropriate response to social change, not all members of that minority group are eager and willing to join some group activity. Indeed, during the civil rights movement itself, black American involvement ranged from those who wanted to maintain status quo, to those whose contributions were money not time, to those who were on the front lines of civil disobedience. Where the lack of knowledge exists among ethnic minority group members themselves, internal "cleansing" can lead to the same type of ostracism of a group member, which normally occurs outside of the group. In fact, ethnic minority group members have created categories for people who do not fit within group stereotypes of themselves. These categories usually take the form of name classification, as mentioned in this chapter—for example, *Uncle Tom* for black Americans, *coconut* for Hispanic Americans. These terms indicate that the person is not "one of us." Clearly, there is a need to understand that variety within a group is common, not exceptional. Not recognizing or accepting variety within the group by its own members or persons outside of the group is important. It determines the standard mode of social interaction within the group and provides for the overgeneralizations made by persons outside of the minority group.

REFERENCES

Anderson, E. 1990. *Streetwise: Race, Class and Change in an Urban Community*. Chicago: University of Chicago Press.

Asante, M. K. 1992. African-American studies: The future of the discipline. *The Black Scholar* 22(3):37–49.

Blumberg, R. 1988. *Civil Rights: The 1960's Freedom Struggle*. Boston: Twyane Publishers.

Clark, T. 1979. *Blacks in the Suburbs*. New Brunswick, NJ: Rutgers University Center for Urban Policy Research.

Clayborne, C. 1986. Civil rights reform and the black freedom struggle. In *The Civil Rights Movement in America*. Eagles, C. W. (ed). Jackson, MS: University of Mississippi Press.

Davis, R. 1997. *The Myth of Black Ethnicity*. Greenwich, CT: Albex Publications.

Early, G. 1996. Understanding Afrocentrism: Why blacks dream of a world without whites. In *The Best American Essays 1996*. Ward, G. C. (ed.). New York: Houghton Mifflin.

Eckardt, A. 1989. *Black-Woman-Jew*. Bloomington, IN: Indiana University Press.

Gibbs, T. 1997. Portrait of a minority. In *Cultural Diversity in the United States*. Naylor, L. L. (ed.). Westport, CT: Bergin & Garvey.

Guy-Sheftall, B. 1990. *Daughters of Sorrow*. Brooklyn, NY: Carlson Publishing.

Higham, J. 1997. *Civil Rights and Social Wrongs*. University Park, PA: Pennsylvania State University Press.

Kronos, S. 1971. *The Black Middle-Class*. Columbus, OH: Charles E. Merrill Publishers.

Lewis, D. 1988. A response to inequity: Black women, racism and sexism. In *Black Women in America*. Malson, M. (ed.). Chicago: University of Chicago Press.

Reed, E., Lawson, E., and Gibbs, T. 1998. *Afrocentricity in the 21st Century*. Forthcoming.

Young, W., Jr. 1964. Middle-Class Negroes and the Negro masses. In *Freedom Now*. Westin, A. (ed.). New York: Basic Books. pp. 315–317.

7

The Evolution of Ethnic (Ethnicity): Integrating Psychological and Social Models

Kimberly Porter Martin

INTRODUCTION

In the United States, the political, social, and psychological conflicts surrounding ethnicity focus the spotlight on this concept as one of the keys to the future of our society. Culture, race, and ethnicity have become inextricably intertwined in the American tradition, so much so that in everyday language, people interchange the terms as well as their meanings (Martin 1997). *Ethnicity* has emerged over the last decade as the politically correct term for labeling the racial and cultural diversity that is, at once, the greatest strength and the greatest challenge facing U.S. society today. In this chapter, *ethnic* or *ethnicity* will be defined as a social category based on varying combinations of criteria that may include racial, cultural, ancestral, and political characteristics.

Debates about the nature of ethnicity are important theoretically, but they are also crucial to the practical understanding and management of twenty-first century social issues. What will happen to ethnic categories and groups in the future? Will ethnicity continue to be the powerful organizing principle it has been in the past? How will cultural pluralism evolve around the world as advances in communication and transportation continue to shrink the world, throwing culturally, racially, and ethnically different people together face-to-face on a daily basis? How will the new global economy and the emergence of a global culture affect ethnicity?

This chapter cannot, of course, hope to address, much less answer, all of these questions. My intention is to introduce some theoretical materials that I have not seen integrated into the traditional approaches to the study of ethnicity and to explore some of the implications those materials might have for dealing with ethnicity nationally and globally in the future. The goals of this essay are fourfold: (1) to review a number of the theoretical approaches that have been used to study ethnicity; (2) to present two versions of an Ethnic Identity Development Model

(EIDM) drawn from counseling psychology; (3) to discuss the relationship between the EIDM presented and other theoretical models of ethnicity; and (4) to explore some of the possibilities for the future of ethnicity based on the analysis presented.

ETHNICITY AS ETHNIC IDENTITY

As Barth's classic work on ethnicity makes clear, the ecological context of ethnic groups varies widely, and the adaptive value of ethnicity in each instance is specific to the particular context of the group (1969). The enormous variability in how ethnicity is acted out in societies around the world makes the development of comprehensive models a daunting task. Ethnicity has been presented as states of being, doing, and knowing (Fishman 1980). It has been described as voluntary and involuntary. Its existence has been described as based in cultural traditions in social networks and institutions, in corporate action for special interests, in issues of personal identity (Spickard 1989), in symbolic systems (Gans 1979), and in the ecological context in which ethnicity exists (Reminick 1983). The actual formation, maintenance, evolution, and dissolution of ethnic groups have been investigated in ethnographies and in comparative research. The plethora of approaches to ethnicity provides a bewildering variety of possible perspectives on any given problem. Each approach addresses a different aspect of ethnicity, and each may or may not be relevant to any given ethnic group in a particular time or space.

Ethnic Identity

The common thread to all discussions of ethnicity is ethnic identity. An ethnic group cannot exist without individuals who identify with the group and participate as members in it, either symbolically or as part of a corporate group. Individuals identify with an ethnic group because of shared cultural patterns and traditions and they define group boundaries by participation in these patterns and traditions. Individuals use shared ethnic identity to create, utilize, and maintain the social networks and institutions that provide for their needs and structure their lives. They define themselves by membership in ethnic groups in order to obtain power and create opportunities for themselves and others who share the same identity. Thus, ethnic identity is a prerequisite for all psychological, structural, and functional explanations of ethnicity.

The roots of ethnic identity have been described as substitutes for or extensions of kinship, where kinship units based on biological or affinal relationships are too limited to be of any significance as social organizers. Kinship is a cross-cultural universal, one that varies widely in form, but that everywhere functions to locate an individual with regard to the social group into which he or she is born. Kinship, and by extension ethnicity, has been called primordial to convey the underlying biologically based ties to ancestry that form the most fundamental pattern of human relationships (Geertz 1963; Grosby 1994; Keys 1975; Nash 1989; Weber 1922). Van den Berge actually goes as far as to describe the concept of ethnicity, with its attendant ethnocentrism, as a kind of "biological nepotism" (1981:17).

In modern industrialized societies, the ties to extended family, and lately even to the nuclear family, are problematic. Yet children growing up need to develop identification with a group as well as to individuate. As access to the social anchor of kinship diminishes, the net is cast more widely in search of group identification. The logical progression moves from nuclear families to extended families to lineages to clans to ethnic groups, and finally to national identity, becoming less personal and, perhaps, less emotionally satisfying with each step. Identification with a group implies at least cognitive and emotional solidarity, a feeling of belonging. Beyond psychological benefits, kinship and ethnic groups are frequently the institutions through which corporate actions are taken and special interests are pursued. Access to a corporate action group with which one has primordial ties has the potential of satisfying needs at all levels: emotional, cognitive, social, economic and political. Ethnographies such as those done by Stack (1974) and Kornblum (1974) vividly depict how individuals from lower and working-class communities, who have ethnicity in common, form social networks to replace kin groups, using fictive kin terms to specify social distance within the network.

All social groups are defined by boundaries that create a we-they dichotomy. In kinship, the boundaries are drawn using sex, generation, collaterality, and marriage. In ethnicity, boundaries are made up of such raw materials as ancestry, places of origin, shared symbols, behavior patterns, beliefs, language differences, and power differences. Case studies done by Barth and Haaland, as presented in the classic work *Ethnic Groups and Boundaries* (1969), and Kandre (1967), made the point early on that the boundaries of ethnic groups are always permeable, allowing individuals to both join and leave the group. This particular insight has stood the tests of time and comparative research (Alba 1985; Goldberg 1995; Salamone 1997). The conditions for crossing the boundaries are as varied as the ecological, structural, and cultural factors that determine the existence of ethnic groups, but crossing ethnic boundaries always entails some adjustment to or abandonment of ethnic identity. Lyman and Douglas (1973) and Cohen (1978), extend the idea of permeability from permanent shifts in ethnic identity, to a kind of ethnic identity code-switching called situational ethnicity. As suggested by Salamone;

Situational ethnicity provides a means for managing multiple identities, for understanding that an individual has use of layers of personalities, each one activated according to purpose....it always must leave room for the strategizing individual who can and often does move from one identity and one group to another, changing "masks of identity" in the process (1997:120).

The fluidity of ethnicity is not only documented in the permeability of ethnic boundaries. In some cases, the nature of the boundaries and the content of the ethnic symbols and traditions that create ethnic identities exhibit enormous flexibility. Salamone (1997) summarizes the view that ideology tends to change as ecological factors change and that the only constant is the need to be distinctive from other groups. Such symbolic markers as hair styles and clothing change with time without undermining the ethnic group's boundaries; linguistic conventions and cultural traditions evolve and are, at times, even invented to create or perpetuate group integrity. At the heart of all of this seeming arbitrariness, the one constant is ethnic identity: the attachment of the individual to the idea of the group and to his or her membership in the group.

Because the investigation of ethnic identity focuses attention on the individual and the individual's perspective on the group, it would seem logical to seek insight from psychological models that address ethnicity, race, culture, or identity development. In fact, the traditional literature on ethnicity is primarily informed by the thinking of anthropologists, sociologists, and political scientists. Seldom are psychological models elicited to illuminate how and why ethnic groups form, operate, maintain themselves, and in some cases, dissolve. The emphasis on the social group rather than the individual begs important questions. Why do some individuals choose strong ethnic identities that are a major focus of how they view themselves? Why do others acknowledge their ethnicity but not emphasize that part of their identity in their everyday lives? Why do still others not find ethnicity to be meaningful at all in how they view themselves? What makes people activate their ethnicity? Conversely, what makes other people distance themselves from their ethnic group? How and why do some individuals shift their ethnic identity to suit the situation in which they find themselves?

One area of psychology in which much work on ethnicity has been done is the field of counseling. Here, professionals try to help individuals understand their ethnicity as it impacts their sense of self, their family and social relationships, and their world view. A number of theorists have worked on models that describe alternative modes of ethnic identification (Atkinson, Morten & Sue 1989; Carter & Helms 1987; Cross 1971; Hall, Cross, & Freedle 1972; Hardiman 1982; Helms 1984, 1985; Jackson 1975; Oler 1989; Parham 1989; Parham & Helms 1981; Ponteretto 1988; Sabnani, Ponterotto & Borodovsky 1991). For over twenty-five years, these attempts have been refined into two versions of a model (herein referred to as the EIDM) that addresses five stages of ethnic, racial, and/or cultural identity development, one for minority individuals and one for Euro-American members of the dominant social group (Sue & Sue 1990). One of the interesting things about both versions of this particular model is that the five stages in identity development seem to mirror the social and political evolution of American ethnicity in the past fifty or sixty years. As with the biological observation that "ontogeny recapitulates phylogeny," it can be argued that this model of how individuals perceive and utilize ethnic identity presents a microcosm of how ethnicity evolves in society, or at least how it has evolved in the American society. What follows is a description of the two versions of the EIDM and a discussion of their relevance for understanding ethnicity as a cultural, structural, and functional phenomenon. I propose that these models provide both literal and metaphorical insights on how the socially constructed phenomenon of ethnicity has developed in the United States, particularly in the past fifty years.

THE IDENTITY DEVELOPMENT MODEL

The Racial/Cultural Identity Development Model (R/CIDM) presents five stages of identity development for minority individuals. Corresponding stages of ethnic identity/awareness for whites are presented in the White Identity Development Model (WIDM). These models do not necessarily account for how ethnic, racial, or cultural identity develops during childhood and adolescence; instead, they tend to present a sequence of perspectives that an individual may or may not adopt during his or her lifetime. The developmental aspect of these models lies in the consensus of the various contributors that one perspective, or stage, logically grows out of the one preceding it. It is theoretically possible for an individual to be enculturated at a particular stage and to retain that perspective in his or her ethnicity for a lifetime. It is also theoretically possible for an individual to begin with a perspective and pass through each succeeding stage until he or she has reached the stage five perspective.

Stage One

Stage One in both versions of the EIDM is called Conformity. In this stage, the minority individual values and aspires to the dominant group culture and lifestyle. Self-esteem in individuals in Stage One is usually low because they do not like who they are. Their goal is to be less like themselves and more like dominant society members. Members of their own and other minority groups are likewise devalued because they too lack the appropriate qualities to join the dominant group.

The white individual at Stage One is extremely ethnocentric and, in many cases, racist. Being a member of the dominant society means that there is every reason to believe that the dominant group's culture and world view are superior to all others, and there is little reason to know or care much about the cultures of other groups. Sue and Sue describe the white person at this stage as being shaped by denial and compartmentalization (1990). This makes the avoidance of personal responsibility for systemic racism and ethnic discrimination possible (Katz & Ivey 1977). What the minority perspective and white perspectives in Stage One have in common is the glorification of the dominant group as the most desirable, the rejection of all things that do not reflect the dominant lifestyle and identity, and the commitment to full participation in the mainstream.

Stage One of the EIDM mirrors the status quo of the pre-civil rights 1940s and 1950s in the United States, where, for example, the goal of Negro soldiers returning from World War II was to be rewarded for their service by getting mainstream jobs and being more widely accepted into the mainstream society. It is also descriptive of the attitudes of many immigrants to the United States who have come seeking the American lifestyle and an American identity for themselves and their children. The expectation of assimilation that has shaped the way dominant society members view immigrants fits neatly into the parameters of this stage as well.

In the arena of social theory, cultural models of ethnicity help explain the implications of Stage One of the identity development model. Proponents of the view that ethnicity is primarily cultural see ethnicity as a manifestation of ongoing contact between groups with different cultural traditions. Different family structures, gender role expectations, communication patterns, world views, and values form the content of ethnicity when viewed from this perspective. The basic premise is that cultural differences create the ethnic boundaries that prevent the integration of groups who operate with different social, political, economic, religious, linguistic, and/or psychological templates.

One result of these boundaries can be structural, such as ethnic enclaves in industrialized societies or traditional territories maintained by tribal groups. These enclaves or territories act to maintain social distance that does not foster acculturation or assimilation. When groups are large enough, they can create and/or maintain parallel institutions to provide for the economic, religious, educational, political, and social needs of the group, further isolating them from contact with other factions within the society. Enclaves made up of large groups of immigrants sharing a distinctive language and culture will create businesses, schools, churches, and newspapers that function according to their own culture and use their own language. Such groups operate with limited kinds of interactions with the dominant society that do not encourage acculturation. Particularly for first- and second-generation immigrants, parallel institutions provide the best of both worlds—the improved economic status and lifestyle sought through emigration combine with the familiarity of language and cultural traditions to minimize culture shock. Chinatowns in major U.S. cities have been described as one example of these kinds of ethnic enclaves.

The goal for Stage One individuals, both minority and white, is to eliminate ethnic groups by accomplishing the full assimilation of all members of society to the mainstream culture. If the formation of ethnic groups results from cultural differences, then the breakdown of ethnic group boundaries requires reducing the cultural gap between groups. According to this perspective, ethnic groups should disappear over time, as constant contact causes change either in the cultural behavior of individuals or in the content of the cultures themselves.

For the Stage One immigrant, "becoming an American" means that the goal is to shed all accouterments of the old country. We see this reflected in the insistence of many first-generation immigrants whose children function in English and not in their language of origin. Even for those immigrants who insulate themselves in ethnic enclaves and parallel institutions, succeeding generations of children and grandchildren growing up in the United States generally do not confine themselves within the same boundaries. Full assimilation is said to take a minimum of three generations. Structural isolation may delay the process, but the evidence suggests that, for many second- and third-generation immigrants, being American is a high priority.

For Stage One dominant society members, both the existence of Stage One immigrants and their successful assimilation into mainstream culture reinforce ethnocentrism; the dominant culture must be the best culture if so many immigrants are willing to abandon their old-world lifestyles and conform to the American way of life. The course of events in their eyes is for the foreign to be transformed into the familiar. The immigrants they admire and hold up as exemplary are those immigrants who have Stage One attitudes and goals.

The cultural approach presents ethnicity as a phase that a pluralistic society such as the United States must pass through as it receives and assimilates immigrants from widely divergent backgrounds (Alba 1985). U.S. immigrant groups such as Italian, Jewish, Irish, and Polish Americans, whose gradual assimilation over several generations has made them virtually indistinguishable from the mainstream, are cited as models for immigrant attitudes and goals precisely because they are seen as abandoning strong ethnic identification. After assimilation, residual ethnic identity in individuals from these groups has been called symbolic (Gans 1979), or expressive (Alba 1985), when it does not play a major social, economic, or political force in people's lives. Again, this is the model for immigration and assimilation that Stage One dominant society members should logically embrace. It is the model that justifies their dismissal of minority ethnicity as an unimportant part of identity, necessary only as a crutch during the transition of acculturation. Ethnicity for the Stage One dominant society member is, and should be, secondary to one's loyalty to the dominant culture and group.

Up to this point, assimilation sounds as though it is a purely cultural matter, a matter of shedding the old ways and substituting the new. It is not so simple for some ethnic groups in the United States, however. For African-Americans, Native Americans, and Asian Americans, whose physical markers are frequently obvious and impervious to change, just adopting new behavior patterns, beliefs, and values does not guarantee that one will be allowed to assimilate. For these individuals, Stage One is a social and political "Catch-22." Like European immigrants, they also want access to mainstream culture, lifestyle, and economic status but are prevented from accomplishing their goals by the oppression and discrimination of the dominant society. A vicious cycle is set up whereby Stage One dominant society members denigrate minority group individuals for their cultural differences, while at the same time punish them when they try to participate as cultural equals in mainstream society. Here we must turn to political models of ethnicity that emphasize power imbalance between ethnic groups. The attitudes of Stage One are just the attitudes we would expect in a system that sees individuals who practice one culture as superior and worthy of privilege and individuals who practice alternative cultures as inferior and unworthy. Stage One dominant society members operationalize their ethnic identity with regard to minority ethnic groups through racism and oppression.

According to the WIDM, stage two dissonance for whites results in guilt about the way their group wields power over minority groups and about the way in which they and other whites benefit from a system that oppresses and exploits others. Their discomfort leads them to re-evaluate how they view members of other ethnic groups and to look with new eyes on the specific traditions, accomplishments and identities of minority individuals. Whites in this stage may envy those who have a strong ethnic heritage, and feel a sense of loss because their dominant status does not provide them with ethnic identification and solidarity within their own society. They will start to question the superiority of the dominant group, and to feel ambivalence about being a member of that group. Their ambivalence will lead to changes in how they view social and political issues, as well as how they deal with personal relationships.

Stage Two

Stage Two of the R/CIDM model is called Dissonance. In Dissonance, minority individuals begin to question themselves, their own inferiority, and they feel conflicted about whether they should seek to be like dominant society members. This is a transitional stage. On a social level, we can see this stage embodied in the early days of the civil rights movement during the 1950s. Negroes, particularly in the South, grew weary of segregation and injustice in the face of achievement and conformity to mainstream cultural values. They grew tired of the denigration of comfortable and time-honored traditions and lifestyles. They began to question whether they and their way of life were inferior and to embrace their own traits and traditions as worthy. As these feelings spread, the shift from cultural to political and structural ethnic content on the social level paralleled the shift on the part of individuals from seeking assimilation to the birth of ethnic pride and the embryonic beginnings of social action groups. Individuals at Stage Two of their lives are described as asking the kinds of questions that eventually gave birth to the civil rights movement, the Black Power movement, the Chicano movement, and the Native American and the Yellow Power movements.

Stage Two fits well with structural and political models of ethnicity. The shift in identity mode is consistent with frustration in the face of internally derived negative self-image and externally imposed discrimination and oppression. This stage is not about culture. It is about self-respect and political power. This is not a stage that is generally relevant to Euro-American immigrant groups. Through assimilation, Euro-American immigrants theoretically have the potential to escape discrimination and oppression because they have the potential to become indistinguishable from the mainstream, even if it takes several generations. As they assimilate, they can anticipate that their self-image, their social status, and their access to the goodies that society has to offer will improve as they become fully functional members of the dominant group.

Stage Three

Stage Three is called Resistance and Immersion. In this stage, minority individuals reject the dominant society, and all it stands for, and glorify minority traits, traditions, and values as superior to the mainstream. Individuals in Stage Three can identify with the experiences of other ethnic minority groups but emphasize the superiority of their own ethnicity over all others. In the White version of the model, we also see individuals elevating the culture, traditions, and solidarity of minority groups. Whites exhibiting the traits of Stage Three are ashamed of and self-abasing about the ways in which the dominant society has treated minority ethnic groups. They are frequently envious of the strong ethnic identity and pride that Stage Three minority individuals have and, in extreme cases, may even try to assimilate into a minority culture by adopting symbols, traditions, belief systems, and behavior patterns from that culture. Alternatively, they may try to revive or intensify their own ethnic identification in order to acquire group solidarity outside the mainstream culture and society.

In terms of social theory, Stage Three fits best with the view of ethnicity as a special interest or social action group. Ethnicity uses ancestry and cultural traditions as powerful symbols of unity that tie individuals into corporate groups. Particularly in conjunction with the economic oppression reflected in the *eth-class* model (Gordon 1964), ethnicity provides the most available and logical glue to hold oppressed working- or lower-class special interest groups together as they pursue political power, economic opportunity, and social justice (Alba 1990). Certainly the civil rights movement of the 1960s reflects the desperate need for civil action to dismember structural and ideological racism in our society. Ethnic identity and pride among black Americans were the building blocks for that movement, marshaling grief, despair, and anger and transforming them into action. The Chicano movement during the same period is another example of ethnicity as the major organizing principle for political action.

The importance of ethnic symbols as a force for creating corporate action groups can be seen in the shift in ethnic labels during the 1960s and 1970s. Here, the view that symbols constitute a central element in ethnicity is clearly supported. Negroes became blacks. Mexicans became Chicanos. Asians talked about Yellow Power. These name changes reflected the recognition of the potential of ethnicity to create social reform and were extraordinarily powerful symbols of the new purpose for which ethnicity was being rallied.

Symbolism is so powerful a force that new symbols are sometimes created to serve as unifying forces within ethnic groups. The African-American holiday *Kwanza* is a tradition filled with symbolic elements created for just such a purpose. African-Americans come from ancestry spanning dozens of tribal groups each with distinctive languages and cultures. In addition to the physical brutalization of African-American slaves, they were culturally raped, losing virtually all of their heritage. Kwanza is an American holiday, created as a symbol of the heritage of African-Americans here in the United States. Its sole purpose is to reinforce the unity of African-Americans as an ethnic group. The desire for solidarity and a sense of common heritage was what motivated the creation of this set of rituals and traditions.

Stage Four

Stage Four in the model is another transitional stage. In this Introspection stage, both minority and dominant society individuals begin to question the idea that any ethnic group is superior and to grow weary of having to represent and defend their group in everything they do and say. Sustaining the anger that fuels Stage Three is psychologically and emotionally draining for minority individuals. They begin to seek their own individuality beyond ethnic group membership. Likewise, whites undergo the same sorts of introspective re-evaluation in Stage Four. The shift of focus moves from group to individual and from hierarchically polarized designations of superior and inferior to more egalitarian and relative analyses in terms of similarities and differences.

Here is where the concept of situational ethnicity begins to be more relevant. Individuals at Stage Four see themselves as complex and multidimensional. They want to express themselves as individuals with many personas, roles, and identities, only one of which is ethnicity. They also want to experience others as individuals with many personas, roles, and identities and to relate to others in ways outside the limitations of ethnicity. At the same time, minority and white individuals alike feel guilt at abandoning the social and political causes that have mobilized, energized, and sustained minority ethnic groups. Here, there is conflict between two sets of values. The commitment to the cause of social, economic, and political justice wars with the need for individuality, personal expression, and self-determination in the face of group stereotypes.

Stage Five

The final stage, that of Integrative Awareness, is one in which minority and white individuals both find greater personal control and flexibility, allowing them to appreciate not only aspects of their own race and culture, but also those of other minority groups and of dominant society. In the words of Sue and Sue, "the person begins to perceive his or her self as an autonomous individual who is unique (individual level of identity), a member of one's own racial-cultural group (group level of identity), a member of a larger society, and a member of the human race (universal level of identity)" (1990:106).

Stage Five of the identity development model does not as easily evoke social parallels as the earlier stages do. Because it is the final stage in the developmental model, perhaps we have not yet fully experienced the social counterpart to this identity development mode. If this is the case, then we may not find full-blown social manifestations of this integrative stage. But we can look for trends that show the same sort of patterns as that proposed in the stages of the identity development model and that look like they are headed in the same direction.

One trend that seems to reflect the same pattern is the ever-increasing rate of intermarriage in the United States and around the world. One can assume that people who intermarry in the United States, where marriage is based on romantic love and personal relationships, relate to their spouses as individuals with many dimensions beyond ethnicity. Increases in intermarriage rates must, at some level, be based on Stage Five perspectives on ethnicity. In addition to how spouses relate to one another, intermarriage produces children who have the potential to draw on multiple ethnic backgrounds and identities.

For people of European-derived ethnicities, Alba states, "Among whites, a long-term trend of increasing intermarriage, which dates to the immediate post-World War II period and probably earlier, has made marriage across ethnic lines now the rule rather than the exception" (1990:12). Even with the racism and miscegenation laws that were intended to prevent intermarriage and sexual relations between people of different races, mixed-race labels such as *quadroon* and *octoroon* clearly demonstrate that interbreeding was quite common. Though children of mixed race parents were assigned to the lower-status group, some individuals succeeded in "passing" as members of the higher-status group, demonstrating that even under extreme conditions of oppression, race and ethnicity are sometimes personal options rather than givens. Spickard (1989) points to the activism of the post -civil rights era as a turning point for mixed-ethnic individuals and demonstrates that there is enormous variability in how intermarriage affects the offspring of mixed marriages.

As the demands of the Black Power Movement receded in the 1970s, mulattos began to have some access to their non-black side. In an age of relativism, ethnic identity, like other choices, became partly a matter of individual preference. One could not choose to identify oneself as something for which one's gene pool did not qualify, and the choice one made had enormous social and psychological implications, but if one came from multiple ethnic strains, increasingly one had the option of access to them all. A rising number of people chose biracial identities and successfully connected themselves to both parts of their heritage. Psychiatric authorities increasingly applauded this as the healthiest choice. What is most striking about the identity situation for mixed people in America is what did *not* happen. What began to happen in America in the 1970s was not the formation of such a separate group of mixed Jewish-Gentiles or mulattos or Eurasians. Rather it was the growth of an opportunity for individuals to resolve their personal identity dilemmas by embracing both halves of their inheritances—not as half-breeds, but as people entitled to identify fully with both (Spickard 1989:367).

Spickard (1989) argues that the impact of intermarriage has implications for all four of the theoretical arenas in which ethnicity is studied: retention of cultural traditions, participation in ethnic networks, commitment to, and participation in, group political action, social action, and personal identity. He emphasizes the importance not only of the personal attitudes and attributes of the individuals involved, but also the ecological contexts of specific ethnic groups and of the wider society. This is not a simple trend; however, the general direction of change is that of increased intermarriage between ethnic groups. Like the unilineal and multilineal evolutionists of the 1950s, we have an overall direction of change toward increased intermarriage, but with widely divergent pathways by which particular types of intermarriage are increasing. Certainly large numbers of individuals in American society today accept and sometimes embrace ethnic differences in their spouses, as well as cultivate multiple ethnic identities in their children and grandchildren. This movement toward equally valuing all of the heritages to which one and one's loved ones have claimed is consistent with the parameters of Stage Five, as is the development of individualized ethnic identities and behavioral sets based on these heritages.

Another trend that reflects increasing social acceptance of the individualization of ethnic identity is found in the ways in which race and ethnicity have been defined and counted in the U.S. census. Goldberg (1995) traces this process from 1790, when the census was initiated, to the present. In the beginning, there were no references to ethnicity, only to race. Here we see a pattern of increasing complexity in the way the census addresses the issue of diversity and a significant shift in who decides how individuals will be classified. During the first 100 years of the census, there were racial categories that were imposed by the all-knowing, all-powerful dominant group and its representatives. In the early twentieth century, simple racial categories proved unable to accurately portray the diverse population being profiled, and categories multiplied as authorities struggled to find the "right" set of labels. Self-identification was introduced in the 1960s and 1970s, at a time when empowerment and liberation from the oppression of the dominant group was a key cultural and political development. During this era, the idea of race gave way to the more complex concept of ethnicity, and the 1980 and 1990 censuses contained a proliferation of ethnic categories. Future censuses promise an open-ended ethnicity question that will allow a maximally individualized statement of ethnic identity. Individuals will be able to specify their own ethnic label using whatever criteria they choose. This pattern reflects the same sort of general progression seen in the identity development model, beginning with obsession with the dominant group and its standards and ending with self-determination and personalized identity, perhaps anticipating the next stage of ethnicity in the United States.

The next question revolves around how Stage Five is related to special-interest models of ethnicity. Ethnic solidarity provides social action in pursuit of the most fundamental of needs: economic sufficiency including food, shelter, and safety, followed by social and relationship needs. When issues of subsistence and safety are resolved, then work on social relationships and self-actualization becomes possible (Maslow 1968). The ability of individuals to identify with ethnicity in this way depends on the resolution of the problems and injustices that moved ethnicity beyond its role as a stage in the assimilation process to a role as a social change agent. As people are able to fulfill their economic and political needs, they are freed to focus on introspection and self-actualization. The need for solidarity is replaced by the desire for individuality in the Integrative Stage. Individuals exhibit a complex sense of self through which they are free to explore their own potential in any way they might choose. This is in stark contrast with Stage Three, where the commitment of the individual to the group is paramount, and the subordination of the self to group goals and perspectives is expected and admired.

Certainly we are far from economic and political equality in the United States. We have seen, however, great strides in the mobility of members of most, if not all, ethnic minority groups. The literature documents the increasing African-American middle class (Gibbs 1997) and the proliferation of Latino professionals (Cruz 1997) in the past three decades, demonstrating that even for the most oppressed of American ethnic groups, significant socioeconomic change has occurred. One interesting perspective on the relationship between socioeconomic class and ethnicity is presented by Van den Berge (1981), who outlines a schema with four types of society based on ethnic and social class mobility. Type A societies such as India are characterized by low ethnic mobility and low socioeconomic mobility. They are rigidly stratified, with occupational classes or castes that tend to be passed down in families. Although Type B societies are theoretically possible, Van den Berge can find no examples of this combination of low class mobility and high ethnic mobility. He explains this by postulating that changes in ethnicity need to be rewarded by such incentives as access to better jobs, political power, and economic resources. When low mobility blocks rewards, then there is no incentive to change ethnicity. Type D societies are typical in Latin America. They are characterized by high ethnic mobility combined with high socioeconomic mobility in systems where social class is highly associated with ethnicity. In order to change one's social and economic circumstances, one must change one's ethnicity. The fourth type of society, Type C, has high class mobility and low ethnic mobility. This category is represented by Switzerland, Belgium, and Nigeria. In such cases, intra-ethnic socioeconomic class structure mirrors that of the society as a whole, and one can change socioeconomic status without a change in ethnicity. As Van den Berge says, "There is no point in severing one's ethnic ties, unless this is the main (or, indeed, the only) way of improving one's position" (1981: 249). Here, one has the best of both worlds: a chance to achieve socioeconomically while retaining one's heritage and identity.

Van den Berge's model raises the question of whether we can achieve the kind of equality of opportunity for individuals regardless of ethnicity that characterizes Type C societies. We have made a beginning in breaking up the *eth-class* structures (Gordon 1964) in American society; the question is, can we follow through to their complete demise? This goal is consistent with the individualization and the de-emphasis of ethnicity that characterize Stage Five of the EIDM. It would seem that a Type C society would require Stage Five individuals who value their ethnicity, but do not depend on it for economic access, political power, and/or justice. Conversely, Stage Five individuals should thrive in a Type C society in which they are free to express themselves socially, economically, politically, and ethnically.

SOCIAL AND PSYCHOLOGICAL DESTINATIONS

Stage Five of the EIDM lays out a set of goals for self-actualization through the integration of ethnicity into a complex individualized personal identity. But what would the Stage Five counterpart look like at the societal level? Rex describes his idea of how ethnicity should be managed by society as egalitarian multiculturalism, which he describes as "not a flattening process of uniformity," but "cultural diversity coupled with equal opportunity, in an atmosphere of mutual tolerance" (1995:48). Interestingly enough, he uses the term "integration," the same term used to label Stage Five of the identity development model, to describe the moral basis for incorporating both "the recognition of cultural diversity and a fight for individual equality" (1995:48) that he sees as essential to a healthy society. His goals seem to closely reflect both a respect for ethnicity and the recognition of the individual that are essential to Stage Five of the EIDM.

Smooha and Hanf (1992) theorize four strategies for handling ethnicity and ethnic conflict in society: partition, ethnic democracy, consociational democracy, and liberal democracy. Partition requires the redrawing of political boundaries to reflect ethnic boundaries, spatially separating ethnic groups. Ethnic democracy is a system where one ethnic group has institutionalized dominance over all others. A consociational democracy views ethnic differences as permanent and pervasive and operates through a political system based on power sharing by all ethnic groups. Ethnic autonomy is maintained in a consociational democracy through localized parallel institutions run by individual groups, while national core values and institutions are shared by all. The fourth alternative, the liberal democracy, is similar to the consociational democracy; however, it uses the individual as its basic unit rather than the ethnic group. Ethnicity is ignored by the government, and individual rights are the focus of law and social policy. Ethnicity is "privatized" as an individual right.

Liberal democracy fosters civility, namely, a common domain of values, institutions and identity, at the expense of communalism. It equates nationalism with citizenship and the state with civil society. All citizens, irrespective of their national or ethnic origin, are considered equal nationals. Although subcultures are allowed within a common core-culture, liberal democracy has a clear bias toward ethnic integration and assimilation. It has better chances to succeed in an immigrant society where discontinuity with the past and willingness to trade culture and identity for social mobility are much greater than in a society composed of indigenous groups (Smooha & Hanf 1992:34).

In the history of the United States, slavery and segregation represent situations of modified partition. For much of its history, the United States has been engaged in an ethnic democracy, with the Euro-American/white group institutionalized as the dominant group over all other ethnic groups. During the 1960s, ethnic identity transformed from Stage One to Stage Three for many individuals in the United States. At the same time, the pressure grew to move from an ethnic democracy to a consociational democracy that would accommodate the ethnically based social action paradigms that were emerging as a way to seek equal rights for minority groups. Will we decide that the danger of regression to an ethnic democracy is too great and that ethnicity based on social action groups is fundamental to attaining and maintaining equal rights for individuals? If so, then can this combination of ethnic identification and sociopolitical configuration continue in the twenty-first century? The alternative is that we move away from consociational democracy and Stage Three ethnic identities toward the liberal democracy to which our core values say we should aspire. The evolution from ethnic group loyalty to individuation represented by Stages Four and Five of the EIDM fits well with the concept of liberal democracy. Will the ideals of the liberal democracy motivate increasing numbers of individuals to adopt Stage Five attitudes about ethnic identity? Or, as is implied by the developmental aspect of the EIDM, if increasing numbers of individuals adopt Stage Five attitudes about ethnic identity, will they work to move the society toward a liberal democracy?

In another analysis of how ethnicity and ethnic conflict can be managed, Chirot has identified five types of ethnic configurations in multi-ethnic nations (Paul 1998). Each of these five configurations is characterized by a different level of conflict and violence. The most violent of these stages is genocidal ethnic conflict that includes ethnic cleansing such as that occurring in Yugoslavia. Chirot cites Sri Lanka as an example of the second configuration. This is a multi-ethnic nation for whom ethnicity has triggered chronic warfare that has not escalated to the level of genocide and ethnic cleansing. Intermediate in the five configurations is South Africa, where ethnic conflict has erupted into violence leading to peaceful resolution through political channels. The fourth stage is a multi-ethnic society that has conflicts but in which those conflicts never reach the stage of war. Chirot classifies the United States in this category. Finally, Switzerland is an example of a society that is extremely multi-ethnic without serious conflict. By Chirot's reckoning, the United States is but one stage from managing its multi-ethnic nature without violence and conflict. Will we be able to move forward to Chirot's fifth stage, where acceptance of diversity and peaceful coexistence of ethnic groups emerges?

It should be obvious by now that theorists see ethnicity as a dynamic adaptive mechanism that, chameleon-like, changes its focus and impact on society and on the individual depending on the context in which it operates. Understanding the kinds of forms it takes and the contexts that shape those forms gives us some element of choice in the kind of ethnicity with which we live in our own society. I see the United States vacillating between a consociational democracy, in which ethnic identity as a social action tool remains strong and conflict will be present at mostly nonviolent levels, and a liberal democracy, in which ethnicity is not a political tool, but an important psychological and emotional component of personal identity and in which conflict between ethnic groups will not be necessary. If we choose the option of consociational democracy, then EIDM Stage Three ethnic identity should be the most adaptive personal perspective to take. If we choose the option of liberal democracy, then EIDM Stage Five ethnic identity should be the most adaptive personal perspective.

CONCLUSIONS

Anthropology has made its most fundamental contribution to knowledge in the understanding of the nature of culture and how it changes. Culture is abstract and yet is manifest in concrete behaviors. Culture change requires symbolic, cognitive, and emotional, as well as behavioral adjustments on the part of individuals as the basic cultural templates and patterns are revised, tested, and reinvented. Changes in the cultural rules and templates for how things ought to be done and how things ought to be perceived never change at the same rate as peoples' behavior. Cultural change must also spread through large proportions of the society before it becomes institutionalized. Ultimately, just as ethnicity depends on the commitment of individuals to the idea of an ethnic group and to participation in the group's activities, cultural change depends on the commitment of individuals to new ways of seeing and operating in the world. People change culture by changing their behaviors, even when the rules say they should not. If enough people join in a new behavior, then it becomes institutionalized into a new and changed cultural pattern. A cultural change can happen very slowly, or it can spread like wildfire.

Individualism is one of the strongest core values of American culture. One of the greatest challenges in American culture has always been the tension between the need to be an individual and the need to belong and to help and protect those close to us. As Geertz so eloquently stated twenty-five years ago:

The peoples of the new states are simultaneously animated by two powerful, thoroughly interdependent, yet distinct and often actually opposed motives—the desire to be recognized as responsible agents whose wishes, acts, hopes, and opinions "matter," and the desire to build an efficient dynamic modern state. The one aim is to be noticed: it is a search for an identity, and a demand that identity be publicly acknowledged as having import, a social assertion of the self as "being somebody in the world." The other aim is practical: it is a demand for progress, for a rising standard of living, more effective political order, greater social justice and beyond that of "playing a part in the larger arena of world politics," of "exercising influence among nations" (1963:40).

The United States is not a new nation in the sense that Geertz means, but it is continually a new nation in the sense that it is one of the most diverse and rapidly changing societies in the world today. The tension Geertz describes is the essential tension at least of our times and perhaps, in the bigger picture, the essential tension of human nature. It is manifest at this point in our history in the conflict between individual and ethnic group rights and responsibilities.

As long as there is a perception that an individual cannot obtain justice and equal opportunity on his or her own, then group solidarity based on ethnicity and EIDM Stage Three ethnic identity will remain the most practical option, even in the face of ideological dissonance. The emphasis on the ethnic group rather than the individual is based on a perceived imperative for social action. As long as the dominant social group refuses to share their power, wealth, and opportunity with members of other groups, that need will continue to be recognized, and ethnicity will remain a strong and pervasive social influence in American society, preventing a full commitment to the value of individualism. Conversely, as equal access to power, wealth, and opportunity increase, the social action imperative for ethnic solidarity will diminish significantly, shifting the ethnic focus to the psychological and emotional benefits that come from membership in a group. If most people in America choose Stage Three ethnic identities, then ethnic solidarity, ethnic boundaries, some level of ethnic conflict, and a consociational democracy are the likely result. If we choose to pursue true respect for individual, racial, cultural, ethnic and national differences based on real economic, political, and ideological opportunity for all individuals, then we can reduce the fear of injustice that fuels rigid ethnic boundaries and ethnic conflict, and a liberal democracy may evolve. Stage Five of the EIDM provides clues for what kinds of personal change will have to develop and spread, one person at a time, if a liberal democracy is the goal we choose.

REFERENCES

Alba, R. 1985. *Italian Americans: Into the Twilight of Ethnicity*. Englewood Cliffs, NJ: Prentice Hall.

Alba, R. 1990. *Ethnic Identity: The Transformation of White America*. New Haven, CT: Yale University Press.

Atkinson, D., Morten, G., and Sue D. 1989. A minority identity development model. In *Counseling American Minorities*. Atkinson, D., Morten. G. and Sue, D. (eds.). Dubuque, IA: W.C. Brown.

Barth, F. 1969. *Ethnic Groups and Boundaries: The Social Organization of Cultural Difference*. Boston: Little, Brown.

Carter, R., and Helms, J. 1987. The relationship between black value orientations to racial identity attitudes. *Evaluation and Measurement in Counseling and Development* 19:185–195.

Cohen, R. 1978. Ethnicity: Problem and focus in anthropology. *Annual Review of Anthropology* 7:379–403.

Cross, W. 1971. The Negro-to-Black conversion experience. Towards a psychology of Black liberation. *Black World* 20:13–27.

Fishman, J. 1980. Social theory and ethnography. In *Ethnic Diversity and Conflict in Eastern Europe*. Sugar, P. (ed.). Santa Barbara, CA: ABC-Clio.

Gans, H. 1979. Symbolic ethnicity: The future of ethnic groups and cultures in America. *Ethnic and Racial Studies* 2(1):9–17.

Geertz, C. 1963. The integrative revolution: Primordial sentiments and civil politics in the new states. In *Old Societies and New States*. Geertz, C. (ed.). New York: Free Press.

Gibbs, T. 1997. Portrait of a minority. In *Cultural Diversity in the United States*. Naylor, L. L. (ed.). Westport, CT: Bergin & Garvey.

Goldberg, D. 1995. Made in the USA: Racial mixing 'n matching. In *American Mixed Race*. Zack, N. (ed.). Lanham, MD: Rowman and Littlefield.

Gordon, M. 1964. *Assimilation in American Life*. New York: Oxford University Press.

Grosby, S. 1994. The verdict of history: The inexpungeable tie of primordiality—A response to Eller and Coughlan. *Ethnic and Racial Studies* 12(2):164–71.

Haaland, G. 1969. Economic determination in ethnic processes. In *Ethnic Groups and Boundaries: The Social Organization of Cultural Difference*. Barth, F. (ed.). Boston: Little, Brown.

Hall, W., Cross, W., and Freedle, R. 1972. Stages in the development of black awareness: An exploratory investigation. In *Black Psychology*. Jones, R. (ed.). New York: Harper and Row.

Hardiman, R. 1982. White identity development: A process oriented model for describing the racial consciousness of white Americans. *Dissertation Abstracts International* 43, 104A. Ann Arbor, MI: University Microfilms No. 82–10330.

Helms, J. 1984. Toward a theoretical explanation of the effects of race on counseling: A Black and white model. *The Counseling Psychologist* 5:153–165.

Helms, J. 1985. Cultural identity in the treatment process. In *Handbook of Cross-Cultural Counseling and Therapy*. P. Pedersen (ed.). Westport , CT: Greenwood Press.

Jackson, B. 1975. Black identity development. *Journal of Educational Diversity* 2:19–25.

Kandre, P. 1967. Autonomy and integration of social systems: The Iu Mien (Yao) Mountain People and their neighbours. In *Southeast Asian Tribes, Minorities and Nations*. P. Kunstadter (ed.). Princeton, NJ: Princeton University Press.

Katz, J., and Ivey, A. 1977. White awareness: The frontier of racism awareness training. *Personnel and Guidance Journal* 55:485–489.

Keys, C. 1975. Towards a new formulation of the concept of ethnic group. *Ethnicity* 3:202–13

Kornblum, W. 1974. *Blue Collar Community*. Chicago: University of Chicago Press.

Lyman, S., and Douglas, W. 1973. Ethnicity: Strategies of collective and individual impression management. *Social Research* 40:344–365.

Martin, K. 1997. Diversity orientations: Culture, ethnicity and race. In *Cultural Diversity in the United States*. Naylor, L. L. (ed.). Westport, CT: Bergin & Garvey.

Maslow, A. 1968. *Toward a Psychology of Being*. Princeton, NJ: Van Nostrand.

Nash, M. 1989. *The Cauldron of Ethnicity in the Modern World*. Chicago: University of Chicago Press.

Oler, C. 1989. Psychotherapy with black clients' racial identity and locus of control. *Psychotherapy* 26:233–241.

Parham, T. 1989. Cycles of psychological nigrescense. *The Counseling Psychologist* 17: 187–226.

Parham, T., and Helms, J. 1981. Influence of a Black student's racial identity attitudes on preference for counselor race. *Journal of Counseling Psychology* 28:250–257.

Paul, A. 1998. Psychology's own Peace Corps. *Psychology Today* 31(4):56–60.

Ponterotto, J. 1988. Racial consciousness development among white counselors' trainees: A stage model. *Journal of Multicultural Counseling and Development* 66:237–245.

Re Cruz, A. 1997. The Mexican American community in the United States. In *Cultural Diversity in the United States*. Naylor, L. L. (ed.). Westport, CT: Bergin & Garvey.

Reminick, R. 1983. *Theory of Ethnicity: An Anthropologist's Perspective*. Washington, DC: University Press of America.

Rex, J. 1995. Multiculturalism in Europe and America. *Nations and Nationalism* 1(2).

Sabnani, H. B., Ponterotto, J. G., and Borodovsky, L. G. 1991. White racial identity development and cross-cultural counselor training: A stage model. *The Counseling Psychologist* 19:76–102.

Salamone, F. 1997. The illusion of ethnic identity: An introduction to ethnicity and its uses. In *Cultural Diversity in the United States*. Naylor, L. L. (ed.). Westport CT: Bergin & Garvey.

Smooha, S., and Hanf, T. 1992. Conflict-regulation in deeply divided societies. In *Ethnicity and Nationalism*. Smith, A. (ed.). New York: E. J. Brill.

Spickard, P. 1989. *Mixed Blood*. Madison, WI: University of Wisconsin Press.

Stack, C. 1974. *All Our Kin: Strategies for Survival in a Black Community*. New York: Harper.

Sue, D., and Sue, D. 1990. *Counseling the Culturally Different: Theory and Practice*. New York: John Wiley & Sons.

Van den Berge, P. 1981. *The Ethnic Phenomenon*. New York: Elsevier Press.

Weber, M. 1978. Ethnic groups. In *Economy and Society*, Vol. 1. Roth, G., and Wittich, C. (eds.). Berkeley, CA: University of California Press. Originally published in 1922.

8

Cultural Diversity among Poor People

Norma Williams

One major social issue in contemporary society arises from the fact that there are so many poor people in a wealthy nation such as the United States. As a result of this situation, social scientists have for a number of decades been interested in the study of the poor. In this chapter, I shall review some of the research findings and examine some of the issues of diversity associated with socioeconomic classes discussed by sociologists, anthropologists, historians, and economists in their efforts to analyze the cultures of people who live in poverty. A major theme in this chapter is that we cannot understand the cultures of persons who live in poverty without also understanding the reactions of the more privileged sectors of society toward the poor. Thus, we cannot really understand the nature of the poor without discussing how they are defined and treated by those persons in more privileged positions in the society. The beliefs and perspectives of the privileged (especially the most powerful privileged) may often not be in keeping with the manner in which the poor define themselves.

I begin by discussing selected concepts and issues with respect to being poor. Second, I will examine the cultural patterns relating to poor people within the historical context. By considering how the poor were defined in the past in the United States, we can perhaps better understand the culture of the poor at the present time. Yet, U.S. society is today considerably different from what it was in the past. Third, I will consider the general characteristics of poor people in the United States in the latter part of the twentieth century. If social scientists are to understand the poor, we should keep in mind that poor (or near-poor) people are a diverse social category, particularly with respect to race, ethnicity, and gender; the poor are not culturally homogeneous. Further, the culture of the people who live in poverty today will be considered and the stereotypes that the more advantaged people hold about the poor will be thrown into question. Fifth, I consider the impact of race and ethnic discrimination on poverty. Sixth, I discuss the culture of the poor, in particular, how the cultural patterns of poor people differ from, and are similar to, people in the privileged sector. Seventh, I analyze the functions of poverty, and eighth, I will consider the present-day attacks against poor people and why many of the privileged sectors of U.S. society are hostile to people who live in poverty. Finally, I will focus on a brief examination of the future of the poor.

BASIC CONCEPTS AND ISSUES

Typically people who are poor are defined in terms of those who are privileged. Still, the federal government has, as we shall observe, seen fit to define a line below which people are deemed poor in that they do not have the income necessary to meet basic human needs with respect to food, clothing, and shelter. Most people understand when they lack adequate food and are hungry.

One of the problems in understanding poor people or the cultures of those who live in poverty is the danger of falsely stereotyping these people. Although the poor have their share of lazy people, laziness is not the cause of poverty. Most poor people, contrary to common stereotypes, work hard. They are poor because of the lack of equal social and economic opportunities. So, too, with respect to privileged persons, there are privileged people who are defined as successful not because they have worked hard but simply because they were born with special advantages (for example, they have inherited money).

In this chapter I touch upon only some of the major areas relating to the culture of poor people. There are several issues that I set to one side. One, for example, is homelessness, which has been studied by sociologists such as David Snow and Leon Anderson (1993) and Christopher Jencks (1994). Homelessness rose in the United States during the 1980s. In recent years, this social issue has received less attention than it did a decade ago, in part because the homeless have, as a result of urban social policies, become more invisible in large cities. The homeless have often been pushed from the main public spaces of urban centers and isolated from the view of the more privileged people.

I shall speak of the culture of poor people or the cultures of poor people, not "the culture of poverty," which the late Oscar Lewis (1968), an anthropologist, introduced in the 1960s. A number of scholars have criticized Lewis's conception, and I have avoided using the term "the culture of poverty" for several reasons. Lewis emphasized the idea that the culture of poverty has a life of its own independent of the structural constraints placed upon the poor. The research since the 1960s, however, has seriously challenged this conception of poverty. I also have avoided the concept of "underclass" (Wilson 1987) because it suggests that the poor are somewhat apart from the rest of the society. The term implies that poor people live apart from other social groups in the society. The so-called underclass, however, participates in a variety of complex ways in American society, especially in the context of their economic activities.

POOR PEOPLE IN A HISTORICAL CONTEXT

The issue of poverty is not a recent one. It can be argued that the plight of poor people is perhaps not as difficult in the late twentieth century as it was in earlier times in the United States. For instance, people today can expect to live longer than a few decades ago and considerably longer than they did a century ago. What is dramatic about the present is the existence of poverty in a society in which there is so much wealth.

Upon examining the history of poverty in the United States, we find that the more privileged sectors of the population have dealt with poor people in a variety of ways. Michael Katz (1996), a historian, has documented some of the history of poverty in the United States. Katz traces the problems relating to the poor (and welfare) back to colonial times. During that period, communities sought to cope with poor people mainly through programs of "outdoor relief." In outdoor relief, the poor remained at home, and members of the community helped the destitute in their homes. In modern times, we could speak of outdoor relief as a form of public welfare.

Although poor relief existed in the colonial period, I focus my attention on the practices during the nineteenth century in the United States because during that era four types of poor relief seem to have existed: outdoor relief, contracts, auctions, and poorhouses (or almshouses). The harshest of the practices with respect to the poor was the auction. Poor people who had become an economic and social burden upon the community were auctioned to the lowest bidder who then could treat the poor person in a harsh and cruel manner (Katz 1996:15). That some poor people were auctioned off as "merchandise" suggests that poor people were viewed as less than human during that period.

During the nineteenth century, poorhouses grew as communities sought to respond to the needs of the poor. These poorhouses were seen as organizations in which the poor could be, and were, forced to work. By being placed in poorhouses, the poor could be more readily disciplined and/or controlled. The more privileged members of the community assumed that the poor could, for instance, be socialized in these poorhouses not to drink. By placing people in poorhouses, children could be reared in such a way that they would be more useful to the community when they were adults. The poorhouses, however, did not function as originally planned. "Poorhouses not only failed to find work for their inmates; they did not even manage to reduce the expense of poor-relief" (Katz 1996:33). Yet, "fear of the poorhouse became the key to sustaining the work ethic" in the nineteenth century United States (Katz 1996:25). That is, persons would rather work than be sent to the poorhouse.

The patterns established during the nineteenth century were carried over into the twentieth century. During this period, efforts were made to change the treatment of the poor. During the Progressive Era at the turn of the century, there was a growing awareness of the issues associated with urbanization and industrialization. However, it was not until the Great Depression of the 1930s that fundamental changes were instituted with respect to programs for the poor. During the Great

Depression, the incidence of poverty grew to such an extent that it was no longer possible to rely upon local communities to care for the poor. It was during this period that the federal government became involved in assisting the poor. In the 1930s, the federal government experimented with a variety of programs for dealing with poverty. One of the lasting efforts of the social experiments of the New Deal was the passage of the Social Security Act of 1935, creating the Social Security Agency. This piece of legislation established three programs as entitlements: (1) Social Security, which was viewed as the nation's old-age insurance program, and it has done a great deal to help the elderly stave off poverty, (2) unemployment compensation for workers, and (3) Aid to Families with Dependent Children (AFDC). This program provided cash assistance to low-income single parents and their children; it excluded two-parent families because men were expected to support their families. Social Security was a national program and AFDC was administered at the state level (for further reading see Cherlin 1998).

POVERTY IN MORE RECENT TIMES

Although poverty is not something new, how it has been dealt with in more recent times differs considerably from how it was dealt with a century or more ago. The New Deal became the standard for efforts by the government to assist poor people. Neither the family nor the local community can effectively cope with poverty in a highly industrialized and urbanized society.

In the immediate post-World War II period of the 1940s and 1950s, the United States experienced a vast amount of industrialization and urbanization, which was accompanied by a great growth in wealth. The general standard of living for all American citizens was being raised, and this development set the stage for what happened during the 1960s. Although the general standard of living was raised considerably for the population as a whole, poverty remained a persistent problem. In the 1960s, the United States began to take seriously the issue of poverty. First, with President John F. Kennedy and later with President Lyndon B. Johnson and his Great Society, there was a major effort to address the problem of poverty. This "war on poverty" was characterized by the creation of programs such as Head Start. In this period, Medicare for older Americans and Medicaid health care for the poor were developed. In addition, the Food Stamp program greatly expanded upon a small program created during Roosevelt's New Deal to better serve the needs of the poor. Indeed, the Civil Rights Act of 1964 was the basis for extending political and social rights to racial and ethnic minorities.

During the 1960s, efforts were undertaken by the federal government to more accurately measure poverty. As a result, we have had, since that time to the present, an official measure of what it means to live below the poverty line. Many of the studies by social scientists have been based upon the data generated by the U.S. Bureau of the Census, as the government has sought to track patterns relating to the number of poor people in the United States. What is important to recognize is that an official measure of poverty exists in the United States which has been adjusted for changes in prices. What ten dollars can buy today is different from what it could buy in the 1960s. Although these official data are important, they must be supplemented by in-depth studies of poor people, for only then can we come to understand how poor people define and cope with the social situations in which they find themselves.

One advantage of the official poverty statistics is that we can trace the rise and fall of poverty over time. We discover that during the 1960s and early 1970s the poverty rate declined, increasing by the late 1970s. "The overall poverty rate actually increased after 1978 " (Wilson 1996:156). Some of this increase resulted from a significant restructuring of the industrial base in the United States during this period. As a result of the restructuring of industry, some of the better-paying jobs were eliminated through automation, and many industries shifted production overseas to take advantage of cheaper labor. This restructuring also has meant that education has become more significant than in the past. New professional and semi-professional positions, such as those associated with the use of computers, have been created; however, these require much more education than before. Persons with little or no formal education or skills, even persons who have only some high school education, are now more likely to fall into a poverty group. It seems that U.S. society is increasingly rewarding persons with formal educational credentials, as good-paying jobs require people with technical knowledge and credentials to prove it.

As poverty has increased since the late 1970s, it appears that privileged people in the United States have become less concerned (than they were in the 1960s, for instance) with issues relating to poverty. The elimination of poverty as such became a less popular topic for policy makers in the 1980s and 1990s. This issue is directly related to the war against the poor that characterizes the current political climate.

DIVERSITY AMONG THE POOR

From the research carried out by social scientists, it is clear that there is considerable diversity among poor people. We should remember that there are significant race, ethnic, gender, and age differences among poor people. The issue of race and ethnicity is especially pronounced in the study of poor people. Blacks or Hispanics have a much greater likelihood of becoming poor. This is not to suggest that there are no poor Anglos. The possibility of becoming poor, however, is greater if one is a member of an ethnic-minority group (Farley 1995). One reason that more blacks and Hispanics fall into poverty groups than do Anglos is tied to the existence of race and ethnic discrimination. Many blacks and Hispanics are excluded from full participation in society because of their cultural affiliation as minorities. As a result of discrimination, racial and ethnic minorities have fewer opportunities to succeed within society, economically, politically, or socially. This discrimination is reflected in the constant growth of large segregated areas in large metropolitan cities in the United States. These patterns are highlighted by the ghettos for the blacks and the barrios for Puerto Ricans and Mexican-Americans.

Paul Jargowsky, who has studied the racial and ethnic composition of high poverty areas in the U.S. metropolitan areas, writes:

One common impression of poor neighborhoods is correct: they are predominantly inhabited by members of minority groups. In 1990, nearly four out of five residents of high poverty neighborhoods were members of minority groups....Non-Hispanic blacks accounted for nearly half of the 8.4 million residents of these neighborhoods. Hispanics, primarily Mexicans and Puerto Ricans, accounted for nearly one-fourth, and a non-trivial number— nearly one-fourth of the total—were non-Hispanic whites (1997:61).

The proportion of white residents in these high poverty areas declines as one moves from the smaller to the larger metropolitan communities. It is in the large U.S. urban centers that the racial and ethnic minorities are most heavily concentrated in high poverty neighborhoods (Massey & Denton 1993). It is in these large cities that the contrast between the privileged and the poor minorities is the most visible.

There are several issues that require attention when discussing high poverty areas. Jargowsky observes that a few poor white areas (as defined in official statistics) include a number of college students, for their annual income is so low that many students fall into the category of the poor. It is also apparent, however, that most poor neighborhoods do not include college students.

Another problem that comes up when discussing high poverty neighborhoods is the labeling of Hispanics. Hispanics can include Mexican-Americans, Puerto Ricans, and Cubans, as well as Central and South Americans. It not only includes recent immigrants but also includes Mexican-Americans who trace their ancestry back to before the United States was established as a nation-state. The category of Mexican-American came into existence only after the signing of the Treaty of Guadalupe Hidalgo in 1848 (an agreement between Mexico and the United States). Mexican-Americans are the largest subgroup within the broad category of Hispanics; Mexican-Americans are now the second largest minority in the United States.

Because of historical circumstances and resulting cultural differences, blacks and Hispanics differ from one another. Joan Moore and Raquel Pinderhughes (1993) and the contributors to their volume have demonstrated that barrios are quite different from ghettos. As Hispanics (especially the Mexican-American population) become more visible, historic minority issues will undergo significant redefinition. This redefinition is well underway in California and Texas, and anyone seeking to understand poverty needs to pay special attention not only to majority-minority relations but also to relationships among and within minority groups. Minority group versus minority group relations within the context of Anglo social power and privilege will be one of the central issues of the twenty-first century, particularly as we attempt to comprehend poverty and how to cope with it.

In addition to the effect of race and ethnicity on poverty, we also should take into account gender and age. As for gender, the problems poverty poses for women are considerable. Women's wages typically have been considerably lower than those of men. In the late 1980s, however, women's wages became a little more like those for men, while at the same time, the inequality between the most advantaged and most disadvantaged groups was increasing. The wages of poorer women, however, became more like those of men, not because women's wages were rising but because of the deterioration of men's wages (Levy 1995:16). Thus, gender issues in relation to poverty can only be understood in terms of class and racial and ethnic differences.

Another aspect of poverty and gender needs to be mentioned—namely that relating to single-headed households (McLanahan & Sandefur 1994). The women who head these households are more likely to be poor than women in households that are relatively intact. This means that children of single-headed households are more likely to be poor. Yet, we must be careful when interpreting these data. We can assume that single-headed households cause poverty, for poverty may also disrupt family relationships and thus lead to single-headed households.

With respect to age, more young children are likely to be poor than are older people. In 1993, over one-fifth of children were officially classified as poor, the highest rate since the mid-1960s (Hernandez 1997). Although the rise of female-headed households has contributed to this rise of children in poverty, we also find that low wages for fathers contribute to this situation. One reason the elderly are somewhat shielded from the harshness of poverty is because of Social Security and very minimal health benefits. Many elderly however, still live in poverty because their Social Security benefits are very minimal.

RACIAL AND ETHNIC DISCRIMINATION AND POVERTY

I have assumed that racial and ethnic discrimination plays a role in poverty in U.S. society. Now I shall elaborate more fully on the name of this discrimination and how it relates to poverty.

Much of the older and starker forms of discrimination in U.S. society have disappeared. For example, there is no longer a Jim Crow system in place in the South in which blacks have to sit in the back of the bus or drink at separate drinking fountains. With the breakdown in the starker forms of legally based discrimination, however, more subtle forms of racial and ethnic discrimination have come into existence within U.S. society. Although many privileged Anglos see themselves as "color blind," they act in ways that keep blacks and Hispanics (or Latinos) in highly segregated and poverty-ridden sections of U.S. cities.

I have already suggested that segregation is related to poverty, and segregation is typically a result of discrimination. It is often recognized than blacks have been segregated. What is not as frequently discussed is the segregation of Hispanics. Orfield (1993), a prominent educator, has emphasized the growing segregation of Hispanics (especially the poor) in large urban centers.

But the next question is how this segregation is sustained. According to some scholars, Anglos have sought to sustain segregation in a variety of ways (Schrag 1998). In California, for instance, a series of statewide initiatives have been passed that serve to keep minorities, especially Hispanics, at the bottom of the social ladder. Schrag observes that Proposition 13, which limited the amount of taxes the privileged Anglos would pay, was a step in this direction. More recently, initiatives have been passed that serve to dismantle affirmative action and to undercut bilingual education. For the record, it should be observed that advocates of bilingual education have not reasoned that we should have two or more official languages in the United States. Instead, the evidence indicates that one learns more rapidly through, for example, Spanish (when that is spoken at home) than having to learn English from scratch. The more general point, following Schrag, is that various initiatives in California have been employed to deny minority children and youth an equal opportunity to get ahead. Thus, society is confronted today with indirect efforts to discriminate against racial and ethnic minorities.

But social scientists should not examine racial and ethnic discrimination only in macro terms. Discrimination is reflected in everyday life, especially in the schools. One of the ways in which minority children are discriminated against is through tracking (see Advisory Committee on Criteria for Diversity 1997). Racial and ethnic minorities who are poor are far more frequently tracked than are Anglos. A careful examination of tracking indicates that the privileged sectors of society are able to use their power and influence to keep their own children from being placed in educational tracks that are dead ends. These low-level educational tracks deprive many racial and ethnic minority children with an equal opportunity to succeed in the economic system.

Admittedly, these legal and organizational patterns are often reinforced by a set of beliefs. One of the beliefs that plays a prominent role in discrimination is the view that racial and ethnic minorities have lower Intelligence Quotients (IQs) than do Anglos. The popularity of the book on the bell curve by Hernstein and Murray (1994) attests to the fact that an influential segment of U.S. society believes that IQ tests actually measure innate intelligence, and thus, it is assumed that the tests demonstrate that Anglos are superior to blacks and Hispanics. What is overlooked is that these tests are biased against poor minorities, a fact well documented in a book by Claude Fischer et al. (1996).

THE CULTURE OF THE POOR

After the previous discussion, I can now consider how the culture of poor people is similar to (and different from) that of the privileged sectors of society. Scholars such as William Julius Wilson (1996) and Herbert Gans (1995) have observed that the values of poor people overlap with and are in many respects similar to people who are privileged. After studying poor people and people on welfare for about a decade, Mark Rank, a sociologist who teaches in a school of social work, has concluded that "These are people who work just as hard as the rest of us, care just as much about the future and their children's future, and hope to get ahead just as much as the next fellow. The difference lies not within them, but primarily within their position in relation to the larger forces found in our society" (1994:172). What we find among the poor is a day-to-day struggle to get by. It is frequently difficult for people in privileged positions to think about social situations in which people do not have the money to see a doctor if they have a serious illness, or in which people do not have enough money to pay for much-needed repairs on their dwelling, or in which people must stand in line for the limited services they receive. Many poor people are called upon to stand in line for a variety of services—for example, food stamps, medical care, and buses.

There is also a tendency in the literature to downplay suffering when talking about the poor. But the poor suffer from impaired health and from living in dilapidated apartments or houses. Most important of all, they suffer from the lack of food.

The problem of social suffering has received rather limited attention by social scientists. The issue of social suffering is raised by Arthur Kleinman and associates (1997). However, they devote relatively little attention to social suffering that results from poverty, and students of the poor seem to devote little attention to the social suffering by people who live in harsh circumstances, where they lack food, clothing, and shelter. The poor are not fools; they typically are humiliated from being labeled as poor.

In examining the problems faced by poor people, we need to look beyond their meager incomes. Immediately, we will find that the poor, who are the least able to afford various goods and services, may often pay more. Our knowledge about this issue dates back to the 1960s when David Caplovitz wrote the now classic book, *The Poor Pay More* (1963). If one has the opportunity to visit a grocery store that caters to the truly disadvantaged, one will find, on careful inspection, that many of the groceries are of an inferior quality. Note the breads, meats, and expiration dates on canned goods. Also, in recent years, journalists have documented how the poor pay more interest rates than do those who are privileged. From the perspective of the lender, the risks of lending to the poor are greater than lending to privileged clients. The poor work in unstable jobs at low wages, consequently they are often unable to repay loans. Nevertheless, the justifications that the lenders use for high interest rates reinforce the thesis that the poor pay more. Thus, people who are least able to pay high interest rates are the ones who must pay exorbitant rates. The fact that the poor pay more for goods and services and for borrowing money means that they are more disadvantaged financially than their incomes indicate.

Another aspect of the cultures of poor people relates to their cultural capital. Certainly the poor have created and have sustained highly complex cultural systems that include values, beliefs, and knowledge. The poor adopt a variety of ingenious ways of coping with their problems. In addition, we have learned that poor people often have created novel art forms and that they lack cultural capital or the lack knowledge about how activities are carried out by persons who work in powerful organizations. The poor have limited, if any, information about organizational rules and about the technical knowledge on which organizations are usually founded. In large part, this lack of knowledge results from the poor's limited education. Today, more than in the past, high school graduates may experience difficulty in securing good-paying jobs. High school dropouts and those persons with only grade school education are highly vulnerable to becoming poor. Moreover, formal educational measures do not fully capture the limitations of the formal educational knowledge of the truly disadvantaged. The poor attend schools with the least resources (such as computers), and their teachers seldom provide them with any understanding of the dominant organizations in society.

A careful examination of the issue of cultural capital will reveal that it has several dimensions. One is the technical knowledge loosely associated with formal education in "reading, writing, and arithmetic." Modern industrial societies have created a great amount of technical knowledge, and if one wishes to succeed in this complex society, one is called upon to master some of the knowledge associated with the "information age." One needs to acquire knowledge about the natural sciences, business and the law, and one also needs to acquire skills about how to transmit this information. With respect to acquiring the language skills associated with academic success, children of economically advantaged parents have a distinct advantage over economically disadvantaged children. Jay MacLeod in his book, *Ain't No Makin' It*, writes:

Upper-class students, by virtue of a certain linguistic and cultural competence acquired through family upbringing, are provided with the means of appropriation for success in school. Children who read books, visit museums, attend concerts, and go to the theater and cinema (or simply grow up in families where these practices are prevalent) acquire a familiarity with the dominant culture that the educational system implicitly requires of its students for academic attainment (1987:12).

There is not only the formal educational system but also the informal one. The educational system assumes that its students have acquired a great deal of background information and knowledge. Much of the knowledge teachers pass on to the students in the classroom requires knowledge about language (e.g., vocabulary), cultural values, and norms or rules that children learn not only in social interaction with their parents and siblings but also with members of their own culture, subgroup, or community.

Although knowledge about the rules of organizations are also transmitted in an informal manner, many of these rules are taught in classrooms (particularly in more privileged settings, e.g., in schools that are located in wealthy school districts and in private schools). Students learn to "beat" the standardized examinations, for example. They are frequently taught how to do well on these exams, and they often take these tests (or their equivalent) over and over again in order to master them. One reason the privileged gain admittance to college is that they have learned how to score well on standardized exams.

The organizational rules become more apparent when people apply for entrance into college. Knowledge about organizational rules are also significant in applying for jobs. We have only to walk around a large bookstore to find that there are numerous self-help books with respect to job interviewing. There are various subtle rules with respect to dress, answering questions in an interview, and so on. Knowledge about these rules is one reason that children of the privileged maintain their privilege, and the lack of this knowledge keeps people in their place. We must remember that if someone is, for instance, applying for unemployment insurance, they must be able to fill out forms (or have someone help them); otherwise they will never get the insurance. There are also all kinds of health forms that must be filled out. The kind of knowledge required to fill out complex forms is often taken for granted among the privileged sectors of the population. By not knowing about how to understand complex organizations, the poor are placed at a major disadvantage.

THE FUNCTIONS OF POVERTY

In keeping with a central theme of this chapter—namely that poor people cannot be understood except in relationship with people who have greater economic and political privilege—the following question must be raised: What are the "functions" of poverty within modern society? At first glance, it seems out of place to talk about the advantages of having poor people within a society. However, Gans (1995) has examined in some detail the functions of poverty. Relying on his writings, I can suggest some of the ways in which poverty serves the goals of the advantaged or privileged sectors of society. In examining the functions of poverty, I am emphasizing the perspective of the privileged, which differs considerably from the perspective of the truly disadvantaged (Williams & Sjoberg 1993).

One important function of poverty is economic. The poor provide privileged members of society with cheap and inexpensive labor. Although the privileged sectors often complain about how lazy the poor (or near-poor) are, the members of the upper and middle sectors of the society employ poor people to staff many positions in their businesses, to clean their homes, to baby-sit their children, and so on. The privileged may not want the poor (especially poor minorities) living next door, but they want the poor to do their dirty work for them.

But the economic functions of poor people go beyond cheap labor. Inasmuch as poor people are often seen as dangerous or morally inferior, their actions must be controlled or modified. This results in a considerable number of people being employed to staff the criminal justice system—police, judges, lawyers, court probation officers and others. Although not all violators of the law are poor, many who are arrested are poor. In addition, many middle-class people work in positions that are based on taking care of the welfare of poor people. Therefore, the existence of poor people makes it possible for a number of others to be employed in white-collar positions in U.S. society (for further reading see Gans 1971).

Gans also speaks of the "normative functions" of people in poverty. When poor people violate the cultural rules of the dominant sectors of society, they serve to reinforce the values and beliefs of the privileged. Rules are reinforced when those who violate the rules are punished for these violations. When the poor are defined as lazy, spendthrift, dishonest, or are criticized for refusing to take responsibility for their actions, the privileged sectors can more readily define themselves as meritorious and deserving of their advantaged position in society. The upper and middle classes come to define themselves not in terms of their own virtues, but in terms of how the poor act and behave. In practice, there is frequently one set of moral rules for the poor in contrast with another set of moral rules for the privileged group. Welfare mothers have been penalized if they live with a man, whereas many privileged persons today may live with one another (outside of the formal marriage arrangement), at least during part of their life, and this latter arrangement is socially acceptable.

A third group of functions associated with the existence of poverty are political in nature. One of these is scapegoating. If something goes wrong in the society, it is convenient for many politicians (as well as other privileged members of society) to blame the poor. The poor are seen as the ones who commit violent crimes, who fail to observe the law, and who are lazy. This scapegoating justifies the political and social controls within the society.

ATTACKS AGAINST THE POOR

Another aspect of the issue of poverty relates to the long-standing attacks against the poor, to what Gans (1995) labels "the war against the poor." In particular, after the Great Society was constructed in the 1960s, there have been sharp political and social criticisms of these programs, especially those related to welfare. This attack against welfare became very open during the 1980s, and it continued into the 1990s. President Bill Clinton in 1992 campaigned on a platform that called for changing welfare as we know it. Then, in 1996, the Republicans who controlled Congress mounted a well-organized attack against welfare legislation. This resulted in passage of a major bill that Clinton then signed into law. Katz has summarized principles of this legislation:

Together, Congress and the President ended the nation's sixty-one-year-old federal guarantee of poor assistance for its poorest families and gave states vast powers to run their own welfare and work programs. The legislation wove together the three major strands in recent welfare history—the attack on dependence, the devolution of authority to state governments, and the reliance on market models in social policy—into a powerful force that destroyed the meager entitlement of the poorest Americans to subsistence (1996:330).

In effect, what this legislation did was to abolish the Aid for Families for Dependent Children (AFDC) and replaced it with a program called Temporary Assistance for Needy Families (TANF). An important feature of TANF is that able-bodied welfare recipients should work after two years. Although states will have considerable freedom to define their own rules for the welfare programs they will administer, there are financial reasons for believing that current welfare programs will be far less supportive of the poorest families than was the old legislation. There will be great resistance by the privileged to any form of taxation that will assist poor people.

One reason the legislation abolishing the AFDC received such widespread political support was that it emphasized the need to work. Work has been a core value in U.S. society since the nation was founded. The idea that people would receive monies for which they did not work runs against the grain of many basic beliefs and values held by the public in the United States. Another reason for the attack against the welfare poor is that a large number have been members of minority groups. For at least a segment of the American population, the war against the poor has been one means for attacking racial and ethnic minorities (see Williams et al. 1993). While the repeal of AFDC has removed the issue of poverty from the headlines, the problem of poverty will not disappear from the public agenda (for further discussion see Cherlin 1998).

FUTURE SUPPORT FOR THE POOR

In the United States, the 1990s have been an era of prosperity. Yet, most social scientists and policy makers recognize that this prosperity has done little to raise the poorest sector of U.S. society.

What we have also learned in recent years is that the poverty line as stated by the federal government may underestimate the nature of poverty. Recently, Kathryn Edin and Laura Lein (1997) have published a detailed research report based on in-depth interviews with low-income single mothers in the late 1980s and early 1990s in Chicago, Boston, Charleston (South Carolina), and San Antonio. What they found is that official poverty statistics may underestimate the family budget for basic needs by perhaps as much as 25 percent. Although there is considerable individual variation with respect to the basic budget items for food, shelter, and clothing, the data collected by Edin and Lein indicate the problem of poverty may be greater than that reported by official statistics. (We also learn from this study that poor mothers, contrary to many stereotypes, are not spendthrifts. Instead, they stretch out their very meager incomes as far as possible.)

Even when the poor work hard, they may remain poor. What we must keep in mind is that income from low-paying jobs do not meet the needs of many families. Calling upon the poor to better themselves seems to be unrealistic unless they can secure a "living wage"—a wage that will support the workers and their families. We must remember that the children of the poor will encounter greater health problems and will secure limited education because they are poor, and they will be less capable of functioning effectively in a modern industrial society. Also, if a social order is to maintain some commitment to democratic beliefs of social justice, then we must concern ourselves with what the children of today will be like as adults tomorrow. A democratic society cannot totally abandon large elements of the society and still claim that it is democratic.

REFERENCES

Advisory Committee on Criteria for Diversity. 1997. Alternative diversity criteria: Analysis and recommendations. A report to the Texas Higher Education Coordinating Board, Austin, Texas.

Caplovitz, D. 1963. *The Poor Pay More.* New York: Free Press.

Cherlin, A. J. 1998. How will the 1996 welfare reform law affect poor families? In *Public and Private Families*. Cherlin, A. J. (ed.). New York: McGraw-Hill, pp. 120–127.

Edin, K., and Lein, L. 1997. *Making Ends Meet: How Single Mothers Survive Welfare and Low-Wage Work*. New York: Russell Sage Foundation.

Farley, R. (ed.). 1995. *State of the Union: America in the 1990s*. Vols. 1 and 2. New York: Russell Sage Foundation.

Fischer, C. S., Hout, M., Jankowski, M. S., Lucas, S. R., Swidler, A., and Voss, K. 1996. *Inequality by Design: Cracking the Bell Curve Myth*. Princeton, NJ: Princeton University Press.

Gans, H. 1971. The uses of poverty: The poor can pay all. *Social Policy*, July/August: 20–24.

———. 1995. *The War Against the Poor*. New York: Basic Books.

Hernandez, D. J. 1997. Poverty trends. In *Consequences of Growing Up Poor*. Duncan, G. J., and Brooks-Gunn, J. (eds.). New York: Russell Sage Foundation, pp. 18–48.

Hernstein, R., and Murray, C. 1994. *The Bell Curve: Intelligence and Class Structure in American Life*. New York: Free Press.

Jargowsky, P. A. 1997. *Poverty and Place: Ghettos, Barrios and the American City*. New York: Russell Sage Foundation.

Jencks, C. 1994. *The Homeless*. Cambridge: Harvard University Press.

Katz, M. B. 1996. *In the Shadow of the Poorhouse: A Social History of Welfare in America*. Revised ed. New York: Basic Books.

Kleinman, A., Dar, V. and Lock, M. (eds.). 1997. *Social Suffering*. Berkeley, CA: University of California Press.

Levy, F. 1995. Incomes and income inequality. In *State of the Union: America in the 1990s*. Vol. 1. Farley, R. (ed.). New York: Russell Sage Foundation, pp.1–58.

Lewis, O. 1968. The culture of poverty. In *On Understanding Poverty*. Moynihan, D. P. (ed.). New York: Basic Books.

MacLeod, J. 1987. *Ain't No Makin' It: Leveled Aspirations in a Low-Income Neighborhood*. Boulder, CO: Westview Press.

Massey, D. S., and Denton, N. A. 1993. *American Apartheid: Segregation and the Making of the Underclass*. Chicago: University of Chicago Press.

McLanahan, S., and Sandefur, G. 1994. *Growing Up with a Single Parent*. Cambridge: Harvard University Press.

Moore, J., and Pinderhughes, R. (eds.). 1993. *In the Barrios: Latinos and the Underclass Debate*. New York: Russell Sage Foundation.

Orfield, G. 1993. School desegregation after two generations: Race, schools, and opportunity in urban society. In *Race in America: The Struggle for Equality*. Hill, H., and Jones, J. E., Jr. (eds.). Madison, WI: University of Wisconsin Press.

Rank, M. B. 1994. *Living on the Edge: The Realities of Welfare in America*. New York: Columbia University Press.

Schrag, P. 1998. *Paradise Lost*. New York: The New Press.

Snow, D. A., and Anderson, L. 1993. *Down on Their Luck*. Berkeley, CA: University of California Press.

Williams, N., and Sjoberg, A. F. 1993. Ethnicity and gender: The view from above versus the view from below. In *A Critique of Contemporary American Sociology*. Vaughan, T. R., Sjoberg, G., and Reynolds, L. (eds.). Dix Hills, NY: General Hall, pp. 160–202.

Williams, N., Himmel, K. F., Sjoberg, A. F., and Torrez, D. J. 1995. The assimilation model, family life, and race and ethnicity in the United States. *Journal of Family Issues* 16(3):380–405.

Wilson, W. J. 1987. *The Truly Disadvantaged*. Chicago: University of Chicago Press.
——. 1996. *When Work Disappears*. New York: Random House.

9

X, Lies, and Social Signs: Defining Generation X

Beth Kaminow

Oftentimes, when one thinks of anthropologists, one thinks of people who study other cultures. Margaret Mead went to Polynesia, Bronislaw Malinowski went to the Trobriand Islands, and Clifford Geertz had his Balinese cockfights. But what of people who want to study groups within their own cultures? Certainly there is little definitional problem with the circumscribed study of a group that is located in a certain area; the Lubovitch Jews of Brooklyn, New York, for example. But what if an American wants to study a group that is spread out over the United States—one that is connected by something other than locality? This question was raised when I began researching certain aspects of that part of the American population frequently referred to as "Generation X."

The more I read in both the media and in quasi-academic texts, the more I began to realize that there is no clear definition of this group; that the phrase "Generation X" is merely a catch-all term for many different ideas. The main problem seems to be that the phrase either refers to an age group, as when authors such as Bill Strauss and Neil Howe (1993) or Susan Littwin (1986) use it, or it is used to describe people with certain attitudes, ideologies, or lifestyles, as when Douglas Rushkoff and various authors in his compilation *The Gen X Reader* (1994) use it. In this chapter, I will show that Generation X is a term that describes part, but not all of American youth culture. Although Strauss and Howe and others (Littwin 1986; Fenner 1994) try to make generalizations about American youth culture based on birth years, I believe that it is more useful to look at this group by examining different social signs that draw specific subgroups together. What follows is an overview of some of the ongoing debates about Generation X and its definition.

Since Douglas Coupland's novel *Generation X* was published in 1991, the term "Generation X" has been widely used throughout the popular press. The term is problematic because no one can seem to agree to what it means or which social group it encompasses. In *The Gen X Reader*, Rushkoff purports that "Generation X means a lot of things to a lot of people. We are a culture, a demographic, an outlook, a style, an economy, a scene, a political ideology, an aesthetic, an age, a decade, and a literature" (Rushkoff 1994:3). How, then, is one to analyze American youth culture or its parts? As Dick Hebdige (1979) points out, it is not constructive to look at "youth culture" as one group. In his book *Subculture: The Meaning of Style*, Hebdige discusses youth subcultures as arising because of various issues related to class but comments that these subcultures should also be looked at apart from adult class structure. In addition, groups that form youth culture arise from different reactions to the different social problems they face. Because of the way that society in America is formed, this necessarily means different subcultures within American youth culture.

Not all the commentators agree with the idea that American youth culture should be separated into groups. For example, Strauss and Howe write that stuck between the Boomers (another American subculture that is defined by age and that can be similarly deconstructed; however, it is not done so here) and the "Babies-on-Board youngsters are eighty million young men and women, ranging in age from eleven to thirty-one. They make up the biggest generation in American history; the most diverse generation—ethnically, culturally, economically, and in family structure; the only generation born since the Civil War to come of age unlikely to match their parents' economic fortunes; and the only generation born in this century to grow up personifying (to others) not the advance, but the decline of their society's greatness" (Strauss & Howe 1993:7).

In addition to the definitional problem already discussed, the population under examination in this chapter is known by many different names. In opposition to the "Boomers," whose birth years range from 1941–1964, they are referred to as "Busters" (Strauss & Howe 1993:16). In reference to their age they have been called "Twenty-somethings" (Rushkoff 1994:236). They also have been called the "Thirteenth Gen" (Strauss & Howe 1993) and are also defined by phrases like "The Lost Generation" (Rushkoff 1994:3), "The Postponed Generation" (Littwin 1986), and even "Slackers" (Rushkoff 1994:40). But perhaps the best known title of all is "Generation X."

But who is Generation X? What group of people are the commentators talking about? According to the dust jacket on the novel *Generation X*, the characters in the novel "are underemployed, overeducated, intensely private, and unpredictable. Like the group they mirror, they have nowhere to direct their anger, no one to assuage their fears, and no culture to replace their anomie" (Coupland 1991). For Strauss and Howe, the Thirteenth Gen (their name for Generation X and a title that, for them, names everyone born between the years 1961 and 1981) "aren't what older people wish they were, but rather what they themselves know they need to be: street smart survivalists clued into the game of life the way it really gets played, searching for simple things that work in a cumbersome society that offers little to them" (Strauss & Howe 1993:11). Andrew Levy explains that "the term Generation X can be applied mostly to certain white twentysomethings. Many black, Hispanic, and other minority people of a similar age would never consider themselves part of the same culture as their white counterparts" (1994:24).

Both the difficulty in defining who falls within the category of Generation X and the myriad of names for this group have caused problems for people who wish to understand this population. How can we understand Generation X without a clear definition? How can the term be seen from the perspective of those outside its boundaries and from its members' own perspectives? Who should be responsible for defining Generation X? Should it be defined by the members of the subculture themselves or social commentators looking from the outside in?

THE BOOMERS VERSUS THE XERS

Terms such as "The Slackers," "The Lost Generation," and "The Postponed Generation," which are used to name the group of young adults currently coming of age in America, are clearly negative. Who has chosen these unappealing titles? For the most part, it is the age group that precedes Generation X that has created and used these terms. The dichotomy between how the Boomers view Generation X and the way Generation X views itself is possibly due to a misunderstanding between generations (Strauss & Howe 1993). This misunderstanding is expressed negatively by David Martin, a self professed Boomer, when he explains that he is "fed up with the ceaseless carping of a handful of spoiled, self-indulgent, overgrown adolescents" (Rushkoff 1994:235). Indeed, Martin proposes calling America's youth the "Whiny" generation and ends his essay, which originally appeared in *Newsweek*, with these words of advice, "Move out of your parents' houses, start working, and for heaven's sake, stop whining" (1994:237).

Unlike Martin, who sees the Whiny Generation applying to a small part of this age group, Susan Littwin sees the problems discussed here as affecting the entire generation. Referring to the Postponed Generation, she writes, "Some of them feel entitled to good times, expensive equipment, and the kind of homes they grew up in. Others believe their rights include instant status, important, meaningful work and an unspoiled environment. *All* of them believe they have limitless choices, arrayed like cereals on the market shelves" (italics added) (Littwin 1986:16). Finally, Strauss and Howe discuss the negative attitudes faced by Xers. They tell their readers:

Adult Americans are by now of the settled opinion that 13ers are—front to back—a disappointing bunch....No one can blame them if they feel like a demographic black hole, a "thirteenth generation" curse on American history, whose only elder-anointed mission is to somehow pass through the next three quarters of a century without causing too much damage to their nation during their time (1993:24).

In direct rebuttal to discourse of this nature, Douglas Rushkoff (1994) and Eric Liu (1994) have compiled books of essays that attempt to show Generation X from its own perspective. Rushkoff explains that Boomers are "unable to see through the guise of apathy and anger worn by twentysomethings and [are] unable to understand what is beneath it" (Rushkoff 1994:4). Indeed, this seems to be the case even when authors such as Strauss and Howe (1993) and Littwin (1986) try to show sympathy for GenXers. Strauss and Howe seem to want to win the hearts of Generation X with their supposedly sympathetic acceptance of America's youth. "We understand you," they seem to be saying with a text replete with cartoons, marginal quotes, and intermittent dialogues on the Internet.

There are many issues in the Boomer authors' portrayal of this group that Xers take offense to. In his essay, Mark Saltveit argues that "you can't define this generation in a paragraph or an article" (1994:50). He goes on to say that the need to define is purely a Boomer trait and that GenXers wish only to define themselves experientially. As previously stated, authors such as Rushkoff make the case that members of Generation X are misunderstood by their older counterparts. He writes:

Although sociologists may have cast us as the despondent "thirteenth" generation—the hopeless mutant children of a society temporarily gone awry—we sure as hell are going to enjoy what's left of the cultural playground before our unemployment checks, parents' support, or Mcjobs give out. But our willingness to accept our inheritance—to enjoy the wasteland bequeathed to us—has brought members of Generation X under the critical scrutiny of those who created and now, ironically, reject us (1994:3).

It is clear that Generation X is perceived differently by these two groups. There is agreement, however, as to Generation Xers being raised in a time of turmoil.

Littwin says of Twentysomethings, "They put great emphasis on the self, dislike answering to others, believe that things will somehow work out for the best, that their fantasies will come true, and that the world they move in will be strung with safety nets" (Littwin 1986:15). She also describes America's youth as feeling entitled to a nice place to live, a high-paying job in their liberal arts fields, and happiness. David Martin (1994) claims that it is Generation X who blames the Boomers for their lack of success. I would suggest that it is more a case of the Boomers feeling guilty for making impossible promises to their young. Littwin, herself a Boomer, explains that this sense of entitlement occurs because of the delusion of middle-class Americans in the 1960s who are the parents of this current generation of young adults. According to her, in the early 1960s, when many Xers were born, things looked pretty rosy for America. There was money for education, housing was affordable for the young family, secure jobs could be gotten right out of high school, and one could stay with the same company for one's entire career.

With the turmoil of the late 1960s came social, financial, and political upheaval. Generation X was raised at the time of the Vietnam War and its detractors, with "I'm Okay, You're Okay," tied to the economic recession, and with a host of corrupt politicians. As Strauss and Howe describe it:

When they were born, they were the first babies people took pills not to have. When the 1967 Summer of Love marked the start of America's divorce epidemic, they were the wee kindergartners armed with latchkeys for re-entering empty homes after school. In 1974, they were the bell-bottomed seventh-graders who got their first real life civics lesson watching Nixon resign on TV (1993:13).

Jefferson Morley, a Generation X advocate, put it this way: "For us everything seemed normal" (1994:33).

Although Littwin sees the Postponed Generation as woefully lacking in many respects, her general thesis seems to attribute this lack to the parents of this population. A similar sense of guilt can be seen in Strauss and Howe. The authors write:

Born in the 1960s, Atari-waivers [their term for older 13ers] lie at the more abandoned, damaged, criticized, alienated end of their generation. These are Coupland's [the author of the novel *Generation X*] twentysomething's "Xers," who have suffered the most from the betrayed expectations of a youth world that went from sweet to sour as they approached it (1993:14).

These authors echo Littwin's notion that youth, and America, were spoiled by the time Generation X should have been able to enjoy it, and they all cite the Boomers as using up these resources. Despite the sense of guilt these authors note, they still see Generation X as failing; living in a fantasy world of high expectations and with a sense of entitlement without wanting to pay the price of hard work and self-denial. As Martin puts it, "Most people live lives of quiet desperation stuck in uninteresting jobs that they're afraid to lose" (1994:237), and Xers better get used to it.

Xers though, at least the ones who have written on the topic, see themselves in a different light. They often see themselves as possessing a "willingness to accept the inevitable aspects of [their] reality," along with the "unprecedented moral and intellectual courage to confront issues rather than cower before them" (Rushkoff 1994:8). Indeed, Rushkoff tells his Boomer counterparts, "We are not complaining, get it? Instead, we celebrate the recycled imagery of our media and take pride in our keen appreciation of the folds within the creases of our wrinkled popular culture" (1994:5).

Seemingly, the only thing Boomers and Xers can agree upon, then, is the idea that members of Generation X grew up in times of upheaval. The Boomers see Generation X as lacking in realistic life skills. Boomers also, at least to some extent, feel responsible for this supposed lack. On the other hand, members of Generation X see themselves as dealing with their new reality in a new way. Even Xers agree that this "new" reality is confusing. Boomers and Xers also agree that members of Generation X came of age in a time when social institutions were not as trustworthy as they had been in the past. The divorce rate rose to 50 percent. Parents were getting remarried, having second families. Blended families became common, as did single-parent households. Casual sex and drug use were celebrated on TV and in the movies, and scandals were considered newsworthy and worthy of the public's interest. Politicians were no longer considered America's heroes. With feminism came working mothers and questions about equality. Instead of easily defined social roles, Generation X was presented with so many choices that, to the Boomers, it seemed like they made no choices at all.

GENERATION X RE-(DE)FINED

As previously suggested, there is little else besides the backdrop for members of Generation X's youth that can be agreed upon by both Boomers and members of Generation X. There are some additional problems in defining this group. Some scholars see Generation X as a subculture of America, differentiated only by years. Others see it as only a subculture delineated by the actions, styles, and physical appearances of its members. But any definition of Generation X must account for both of these viewpoints. Generation X is better seen as a temporal subculture that is defined by social signs rather than by birth years. I use the term "social sign" to refer to the ways in which people communicate what they feel through what they actually do and how they physically express themselves. Rather than using the term "Generation X" to define an entire generation, it may be better to define it as a group connected by social signs. Instead of looking at all people born between the years 1965 and 1972 or 1961 and 1971 (Fenner 1994), it is more productive to look at people who are defined by the signs that members of Generation X and social commentators attribute to this population. The media and the literature about this social group provides some suggested social signs that can help to define this cultural group: black clothing; Grunge music and dress; movies such as *Slacker, Clerks,* and *Before Sunrise* in which members of this group are portrayed; dyed straight hair; a love of 1970s nostalgia; the popular magazine *'zines*; an interest in technology; and the prominence of permanent body adornment.

By looking at people who show these social signs, some distinctions can be drawn and conclusions reached regarding members of Generation X. For example, people who use these social signs are mostly white, between twenty-one and thirty-two, and from middle- or upper-middle class backgrounds. The conclusion is that "Generation X" is not a term that defines a generation, but is a subculture of youth differentiated by aspects of style. Rather than defining the group based on factors beyond their control (such as birth years and complexion), it might be better to look at people who, consciously or unconsciously, display certain social signs.

Generation X is a temporal subculture rather than a generational subculture because not all members of a generation respond to the same issues and problems in the same way. Levy, for instance, points out that someone raised in an urban environment and in a low-income family context will perceive the world differently that someone raised in a large house in the suburbs. This is why it may be more helpful to use the term "Generation X" to describe people who present themselves in a certain way rather than using age, socioeconomic background, or skin color to distinguish it and its members.

NEW REALITIES

In some ways this subculture responds to the "new" reality that all theorists agree is its legacy. Littwin talks about the Postponed Generation's lack of ability to commit to others. She explains:

Committed, lasting relationships are a critical aspect of maturity. Today's young adults are having more trouble with relationships than with almost any other area of their lives. They are having problems for two reasons: 1) They have trouble with commitment in general, and this is an echo, a subheading of their overall reluctance to define themselves. 2) The menu of choices makes life more confusing. It is different from the kind of lives their parents lived and have brought them up to expect. Once again, they are in unmapped territory, looking for trails and crumbs (1986:216).

On the other hand, the members of Generation X may not be committing to relationships in the same way as people have in the past, but they, nonetheless, commit. Books such as Coupland's *Generation X* and television shows such as *Friends*, which tend to depict characters who are not romantically involved yet are committed to one another, make a strong case for the ability of Xers to commit. While doing ethnographic work on Generation X, one informant told me, "Maybe people aren't finding husbands and wives but they're building families among their friends. I think that friends are a really strong social family." Another informant told me in reference to Generation X and her friends, "I couldn't believe there was a whole group of people...out there that felt the same way [I did]. That just named something that was unnamed." Another woman interviewed as part of a project about Generation X and tattoos explained that she got one of her tattoos as "a designation on [her] body that [she] is part of a tribe, whatever that tribe may be." In describing the home life of 13ers, Strauss and Howe write, "[Home is] a place where the daughters and sons of divorce can band together and invent their own fully functional surrogate families. A place where a generation raised to distrust everything can build small circles of total trust" (1993:205). What is confusing to Boomers is that these commitments do not look the same as the relationships of the past. Indeed, very little looks the same.

Another area of difference for Generation X lies in the realm of employment. Many articles in the popular press (Fenner 1994; Giles 1994; Dunn 1992) tell of the difficulty in finding jobs in the current market. There have been numerous references to Coupland's Mcjobs (Morley 1994; Strauss & Howe 1993), which are "Low-pay, low-prestige, low-dignity, low-benefit, no future job(s) in the service sector" (Coupland 1991:5).

Strauss and Howe use Boomers to offset a change in the way employment is viewed by young adults in America. They write:

[The late 1960s] was an era in which Kenneth Keniston, after interviewing hundreds of Boomer collegians, observed that he had "yet to find one who was worried about finding a job" and "relatively few who were worried about finding a *good* job." But 13ers look at work differently—as a means of survival, as an opportunity to prosper, as something that doesn't mean anything but just has to get done if anybody's going to get paid (1993:207).

But there is another side to this idea. Many recent articles have told of how Xers are prospering because of the computer boom, with which they were the first generation to grow up. Elizabeth Fenner writes in *Money* magazine that "many of these young people, far from living the reel of *Reality Bites*, are prospering. And, says Strauss, 'those who are doing well are doing very well'" (Fenner 1994:91). Littwin basically says that the only members of the Postponed Generation to succeed are the ones in the computer field. She writes:

Compared to their peers in other fields of endeavor, they seemed the soul of contentment. There is something about being valued, rewarded, sought after, courted, and treated well that tends to make people happy. When you throw in interesting work and considerable job independence, it is not a package that breeds misery (1986:166).

By looking at this population and their employment opportunities, we see that there are two sides to the story. There are people who "slack off" and get jobs in the service industry, and then there are those that have managed to jump on the technological band wagon. Are they all members of Generation X? If we go back to our definition—members of Generation X are people who display certain social signs—then members of both of these groups could possibly be considered Xers. However, it is not merely the fact that they fall within certain birth years that makes them members of Generation X. Not all people discussed by these authors would necessarily fall within the boundaries of our definition. This is an example of how difficulties may arise based on differing definitions of groups within the domain of popular culture.

A final example of the "changing landscape" that Generation X must adapt to comes with the growing idea of globalism. Through technology, various political and economic trends, and postmodern examinations of the "other," people in America and other Western societies have become more aware of, and have begun to use, other cultures' social signs. As with the popularity of Dashikis in the sixties, various styles of dress and hairstyle have inundated present-day American fashion. These styles always have contextual meaning. For example, the return of the Afro in black youth culture may be seen to represent a renewed vigor in "Black Power." The resurgence in the popularity in "hippie" garb may be perceived as a desire to return to a time of less complicated, purer activism.

Another way this examination of other cultures takes form is through an appreciation of multiculturalism and ethnicity, which are on the rise both politically and in the popular culture. Jeff Giles writes that "Xers may...be the least racist [generation]. 'We are the first generation to be born into an integrated society,' writes 25-year-old Eric Liu. 'We are accustomed to more race mixing than any generation before us. We started open-minded, and it's not too late for us to stay that way'" (1994:66).

XERS MARK THE SPOT

Tattoos are another of the social signs that characterize Generation X. In the 1960s, tattooing in the United States experienced a "renaissance" according to Clinton Sanders (1988, 1990), Spider Webb (1979), and other well-known tattoo experts. Sanders describes a "tattoo world" in which "younger tattooists, frequently with university or art school backgrounds and experience in traditional artistic media, have begun to explore tattooing as a form of expression" (Sanders 1988:19). Although this "renaissance" began in the 1960s, it can also be suggested that increased interest in tattooing in America is because it has become popular with members of Generation X. There are several possible interpretations of the use(s) of tattoos by members of this subculture.

Many social commentators who have written about Generation X have mentioned tattooing as a social sign that members of that subculture exhibit. For example, Strauss and Howe, in discussing members of this population write that "[they] are increasingly piercing, tattooing or otherwise disfiguring their bodies" (1993: 82). A *Washington Post* article discussing this aspect of the population states, "So X-Xers will stay babies, and mutilate themselves and tattoo their flesh" (Schillinger 1994:C1). Tattoos have long been associated with marginalized, deviant groups (Gell 1993; Sanders 1990). Despite this perception, members of Generation X may mark this type of sign on their bodies to represent displeasure and disillusionment with dominant society rather than representing their own deviance. In spite of Amy Krakow's blithe comment that "with all those tattooists working, tattooing has fast become at once a mainstream, *kinky*, fun form of body art and decoration that's also quite stately" (1994:32), tattoos are still seen as a deviant practice.

Albert Gell (1993) presents a discussion of the history of the pathology of tattooing, citing the work of criminal anthropologists Lombroso and Loos, who worked at the turn of the century and who suggested that tattoos, in conjunction with other social signs, reflect the moral deficiency of the wearer of the tattoo. Gell writes:

It is as true now as it was in Lombroso's time that criminals and the insane are very often tattooed, while criminologists, judges, and psychiatrists are not...the high incidence of tattooing among prisoners could hardly be regarded as a matter of chance. Neither may the content analysis [Lombroso] makes of criminal tattoos be dismissed simply as a projection of class prejudice. In tattooing slogans like 'born to be hanged' or the insignia of commorist gangs on their bodies, Lombroso's criminals appear to have played deliberately into his hands. They have biologized their criminality, stigmatized themselves (1993:13).

Although Gell is arguing in part that the criminality associated with tattoos comes from the choice of what is marked onto the flesh, it is the actual mark that is perceived as the deviant social sign. As he writes, "Criminals and the insane are very often tattooed, while criminologists, judges and psychiatrists are not" (1993: 13). Personal choice of tattoo aside, one popular perspective of tattoos in the West is that they show a moral deviance or a disposition toward criminal activity. Sanders tells us that:

Early in the twentieth century tattooing began to lose favor among the American elite and increasingly came to be seen as the vulgar affectation of the unsavory types who frequented the Bowery and similarly disreputable urban areas....Additionally, it came to be seen as a deviant practice because heavily tattooed men and women were commonly exhibited as curiosities in circuses and side shows. P.T. Barnum displayed tattooed dwarfs, tattooed wrestlers, tattooed ladies, and entire tattooed families. The Depression spurred the definition of the tattooed-person-as-freak as unemployed men and women became heavily tattooed in order to find some means of earning a living (1990:18).

Criminality and side-show freak are two of the prevailing ideas that members of Western cultures hold about members of its own society who wear the social marks of tattoos. A third image held by some members of the dominant society associates tattooing with the image of the "bad boy/biker." As Jane and Michael Stern tell us:

The question of skin prejudice notwithstanding, the acquisition of a brazen tattoo, or even better, many tattoos, is a surefire strategy to violating most people's idea of good taste. Unlike other forms of rebellious behavior, a tattoo is permanent; it shows serious commitment to the cause of blasphemy....in the modern world it is not the beautiful people who get tattooed: it's skinheads, heavy-metal rock groups, and motorcycle outlaws (1990:283).

What are members of Generation X actually saying by adopting tattooing as a social sign? Some answers to this question may be gleaned by looking at tattoos in relation to three ideas that Hebdige discusses. First is the idea that style or social signs reflect dominant society. The second idea revolves around the notion that social signs are a response to dominant society. Lastly, the idea of style is a form of refusal. Although Hebdige (1979) wrote about the punk movement in Great Britain in the 1970s, which encountered different social problems than members of Generation X, his ideas can be applied here. He explains, "The punks were not only directly *responding* to increasing joblessness, changing moral standards, the rediscovery of poverty, the Depression, etc., they were *dramatizing* what had come to be called 'Britain's decline'" (1979:87).

In a similar way, the social signs that members of Generation X adopt can be seen as reflecting difficulties that affect them. During Generation X's short history, there has been a sense of ubiquitous, low-grade criminality present in the United States. The following passage by Ian Williams describes America during the 1970s.

I recall huge cars, gas lines, bad music, silly hair cuts. In first grade I remember being dragged from the tether ball court to see the president resign on TV. A few years later, I often watched "Saturday Night Live" when my parents were out to dinner and sat quizzically through jokes about drugs and boobs. My friends and I bought tickets to the "PG" version of *Saturday Night Fever* and then sneaked into the "R" version playing next door; there we marveled at all the incredible wanton fun those guys and girls fifteen years older were having on the dance floor and in the back seats of cars (1994:176).

Although this is a rather amusing recounting of Williams's youth, the tone is one of banal complacency in relation to the ebbing morality he senses. People drove big cars despite the oil crisis. He was interrupted from a childhood game to hear the president resign. He watched as issues about sex and drugs were made humorous on late-night television. He snuck into the "R" version of *Saturday Night Fever* to see "wanton fun." One possibility for the popularity of tattooing among members of Generation X is as a reflection of the moral attitudes held by, and actions of the people in power during their youth and continuing through today.

Another way to view this social sign is to see it as a response to the ills of the society. Social commentators and theorists (Littwin 1986; Strauss & Howe 1993; Morley 1994; Rushkoff 1994) agree that the backdrop of Generation X's youth was peppered with impermanence. They were born right after (or were babies) when John F. Kennedy and Martin Luther King, Jr., were assassinated. The divorce rate rose steadily during their youth. Because of this, many Xers were raised in single-parent families or "blended" families. The women's movement gave rise to new definitions of gender roles, and education began to deteriorate (Strauss & Howe 1993). If we look at the tattoos of Generation X in this light, we can see it as a dramatic, permanent response to the lack of permanence they felt as a group as they were growing up and that continues to the present day.

Tattoos can also be seen as a form of refusal. By looking at tattoos with their deviant connotations, members of Generation X are in some ways refusing to enter into dominant society. Littwin sees this refusal as a postponement. She writes, "It now takes another decade to grow up in our culture. While we can dither about definitions of maturity, most of us know what we mean by it. We mean having meaningful work and committed relationships, being part of a community, and assuming responsibility. We mean paying your own way, carrying your weight in the world" (1986:245). One problem with Littwin's thesis is that it remains to be seen whether this subculture will, by her definition, "grow up" in ten years. The social climate, as previously suggested, is a changing one. What is a "committed relationship" to people who have witnessed the divorce rate rise to affect three in five marriages? What does "meaningful work" mean to people who have watched the work place become rapidly changed by technology to the point where people are being replaced by computers, where the very notion of "workplace" has been changed drastically by technology? What does "community" mean to people who are living in the most mobile and transient America to date? It is suggested that with the changing landscape of America, members of Generation X are challenging Littwin's notion of "growing up" by using certain social signs such as the tattoo.

Social signs can be seen as a way for subcultures to evoke discourse with dominant society. Having provided some interpretations of what Generation X might be "saying" with its use of tattoos, it is now possible to turn to the ways that dominant society often "replies" to the "conversation(s)" subcultures begin. Dominant society responds to subcultures such as Generation X by co-opting the signs they use and incorporating them back into the realm of "acceptability." This is done through the media and through marketing the signs of subcultures as "fashionable." Hebdige writes:

The emergence of a spectacular subculture is invariably accompanied by a wave of hysteria in the press. This hysteria is typically ambivalent: it fluctuates between dread and fascination, outrage and amusement. Shock and horror headlines dominate the front page while, inside, the editorials positively bristle with "serious" commentary and the center spreads or supplements contain delirious accounts of the latest fads and rituals (1979: 93).

It must be remembered that Hebdige talks primarily about punks in Great Britain who were responding much more violently to a more violent situation than members of Generation X. The "hysteria" in the press at the height of the punk movement can be seen as analogous to, but not quite the same as the "barrage of essays, op-ed pieces and feature articles blaming us baby boomers for the sad face of the twentysomething's generation" (Rushkoff 1994:235). After all, the signs the punks employed and the ones Generation X use are different. The punks were characterized by angry music, violence, and ripped clothing held together by implements of torture and bondage, while Generation X is characterized by apathy, "grunge" and nostalgia. Yet, there appears to be the same sense of urgency in the press to define this subculture, to explain it, and contain it. There is the exact same feeling of dread and fascination associated with the punk movement and Generation X. Joel Achenbach writes:

Generation X is nothing less than a genetic disaster, a freak mutation of Western Civilization, so decrepit in its values and so retarded in its social skills that America as we know it is in danger, that our society may be nearing the threshold beyond which extinction is inevitable, that we must summon the will to take this legion on the face of humanity, this pustulate generational whitehead, between our fingers and squeeze. Metaphorically speaking (1994: B4).

Here, clearly, is an example of the dread that dominant society feels about Generation X. Because "young people are too full of irony, sarcasm, detachment, [and] moral flinching" (Achenbach 1994:B4), they are a threat to our very lives.

There are many more articles that seem to show a fascination with Generation X and its "latest fads and rituals." Several articles have appeared discussing places where Generation X "hangs out" (Schillinger 1994; Sherrill 1995; Span 1995), what movies they go to see (Bellafonte 1995), and their love of 1970s nostalgia (Bonastia 1995). Through these articles in the popular press, subcultures such as Generation X become demystified. Their signs and passions are explained away, and ultimately, they, like most subcultures, are "just like you and me." This media coverage is one way dominant society brings subcultures and their signs back into the acceptable boundaries of society. Another way is through marketing.

To the business world, "Generation X" is a demographic group to be sold and catered to. Its signs are just so many things to be sold to others. As Hebdige tells us, "The creation and diffusion of new styles is inextricably bound up with the process of production, publicity and packaging which must inevitably lead to the delusion of the subculture's subversive power....Each new subculture establishes new trends, generates new looks and sounds which feed back into the appropriate industries" (1979:95).

With the rise in popularity of body adornment among members of Generation X, one can see tattoos on models and on rock and roll stars (in fact, there is now an entire magazine devoted to pictorial essays about popular bands and the tattoos they sport). As tattoos became more visible and, indeed, more acceptable through their increased visibility in the media, marketers happily began selling temporary tattoos of college and sport-team insignias, "tribal" designs, and even dinosaurs to appeal to an even younger demographic group. These temporary tattoos give the wearer the image of being "with it" or "in the know" without having to go through the ritual of being marked or the consequence of having the design on his or her body permanently. In this way, the people responsible for marketing temporary tattoos take all the "sting" out of the adornment, thus changing the meaning of tattoos again by slightly altering the product. Because temporary tattoos are easily marketable and wash off, they are much closer to Krakow's "mainstream, kinky, fun form of body art and decoration" (1994:32). They are also the easiest way for the marketing industry of the dominant society to co-opt this social sign brought to the forefront by members of Generation X.

Through their use of social signs, subcultures can begin a discussion with dominant society, usually about the displeasure or disillusionment members of that subculture feel about the order of things. Tattoos of Generation X can be seen as a form of reflection, response, and ultimately a refusal or challenge to the order of dominant society. As with most "conversations," this one is not one-sided, for dominant society "responds." I have suggested that the response comes in the form of a co-option of the sign and that, in the end, the boundaries of what is acceptable in dominant society are broadened to include the signs of the subculture, although in a softened, "watered-down" version.

CONCLUSION

"Generation X" is a phrase used to describe a group of Americans coming of age in the late 1980s and early 1990s. Can we really lump this entire group together using birth years alone? With this chapter, I have shown that grouping people together using only age as a factor may not be the most constructive way to go about defining a population for ethnographic use. Despite the difficulties involved, I believe it is useful to use social signs to define who members of "Generation X" are. It is nearly impossible to make any sort of generalizations based on age alone. Instead, we need to look at subcultures based on the way in which people define themselves. In their new choices of committed relationships, employment, attitudes toward other cultures, and uses of body modification, members of Generation X have begun dealing with adult issues in a "changing landscape." These examples do not show any kind of postponement in attaining adulthood, only reactions to different situations. I have shown some of the difficulties of defining this group and how this may create a misinterpretation of the actions of this subculture.

REFERENCES

Achenbach, J. 1994. Putting all the X in one basket. *The Washington Post*, April 27, B1 and B4.
Bellafonte, G. 1995. Generation X-cellent. *Time*, February 27, 62–64.
Bonastia, C. 1995. Sucking in the '70s. *The New Republic,* January 30, 11.

Coupland, D. 1991. *Generation X: Tales for an Accelerated Culture.* New York: St. Martin's Press.

Dunn, W. 1992. Hanging out with American youth. *American Demographics* 14:24–35.

Fenner, E. 1994. Generation X strikes back. *Money* 23:6, 90–97+.

Gell, A. 1993. *Wrapping in Images:Tattooing in Polynesia.* Oxford: Clarendon Press.

Giles, J. 1994. Generalization X. *Newsweek*, June 6, 62–72.

Hebdige, D. 1979. *Subculture: The Meaning of Style.* London: Methuen.

Krakow, A. 1994. *The Total Tattoo Book.* New York: Time Warner.

Levy, A. 1994. Looking for Generation X. *Division and Diversity* 3(3):24–26.

Littwin, S. 1986. *The Postponed Generation: Why American Youth Are Growing Up Later.* New York: William Morrow Press.

Liu, E. 1994. *Next: Young American Writers on the New Generation.* New York and London: W. W. Norton and Company.

Martin, D. 1994. The whiny generation. In *The Gen X Reader.* Rushkoff, Douglas (ed.). New York: Ballantine Books, pp. 235–237.

Morley, J. 1994. Twentysomething. In *The Gen X Reader.* Rushkoff, Douglas (ed.). New York: Ballantine Books, pp. 30–40.

Rushkoff, D. (ed.). 1994. *The Gen X Reader.* New York: Ballantine Books.

Saltveit, M. 1994. Whatever. In *The Gen X Reader.* Rushkoff, D. (ed.). New York: Ballantine Books, pp. 50–53.

Sanders, C. 1988. Marks of mischief: Becoming and being tattooed. *The Journal of Contemporary Ethnography* 16(4):395-432.

———. 1990. Memorial decoration: Women, tattooing, and the meanings of body alteration. *Michigan Quarterly Review.*

Schillinger, L. 1994. Adventures in babyland. *The Washington Post,* December 18, C1 and C2.

Sherrill, M. 1995. The neo-martini. *The Washington Post,* March 10, C1 and C4.

Span, P. 1995. Lounge-itude: Mood music swings back. *The Washington Post,* March 10, C1 and C4.

Stern, J., and Stern, M. 1990. *The Encyclopedia of Bad Taste.* New York: HarperCollins.

Strauss, B. ,and Howe, N. 1993. *13th Gen: Abort, Retry, Ignore, Fail?* New York: Vintage Books.

Webb, S., and Vassi, M. 1979. *Pushing Ink: The Fine Art of Tattooing.* New York: Simon and Schuster.

Williams, I. 1994. Trash that baby boom. In *Next: Young American Writers on the New Generation.* Liu, E. (ed.). New York: W. W. Norton and Company.

10

Culture in Conflict: Rugged Individualism and Educational Opportunity in a Diverse Society

Patrick James McQuillan

In the Declaration of Independence, our forefathers stated succinctly: "We believe that all men [*sic*] are created equal." This belief in the fundamental equality of all people is a cornerstone to our nation's political, economic, and social institutions. Americans are also firmly committed to the idea of "rugged individualism": Each person "controls his [*sic*] own destiny, and...does not need help from others" (Hsu 1983:4). Validation for this conviction is embodied in the lives of Americans as diverse as Abraham Lincoln and Rocky Balboa, Harriet Tubman and Madonna. Although both views are central to American society (Bellah et al. 1985; Fine & Rosenberg 1983; MacLeod 1987; McQuillan 1998; Spindler & Spindler 1987a, 1987b), these beliefs are not always compatible. As George and Louise Spindler maintained, Americans typically frame their most emotional social debates in terms of key cultural values, oftentimes placing these values in opposition to one another:

We claim that there is an American culture because since pre-revolutionary times we have been dialoguing about freedom and constraint, equality and difference, cooperation and competition, independence and conformity, sociability and individuality, Puritanism and free love, materialism and altruism, hard work and getting by, and achievement and failure....It is not because we are all the same, or that we agree on most important matters, that there is an American culture. It is that somehow we agree to worry, argue, fight, emulate, and agree or disagree about the same pivotal concerns. Call them values, value orientations, cultural foci, themes, whatever. They are pivotal, and they are arranged in oppositional pairs (Spindler & Spindler 1987b:152).

With the tensions inherent to American culture in mind, I examine the matter of educational opportunity from the cultural point of view, juxtaposing our faith in rugged individualism with our commitment to individual equality, in this case, equality of educational opportunity. In doing so, some critical questions arise, questions that seem fundamental to our diverse society: If everyone is equal, why should anyone be accorded special treatment? Or, is equality of opportunity linked to race and ethnicity, such that certain groups, because of being historically disadvantaged through discrimination, need special treatment? Can we assume that treating everyone "equally" constitutes equality of opportunity?

In our increasingly pluralistic society, we should realize that in confronting these questions people will filter their understandings of such pivotal ideas as equity and educational opportunity through prevailing cultural beliefs. These values will then influence what issues are deemed important and relevant; they will provide a language with which to debate these ideas, and they will shape how the outcomes of these debates are understood. Such discussions can have a profound impact on American society as they impact decisions regarding when to reach out to those less advantaged, as well as when we define something as an individual, not societal, responsibility.

Moreover, in these debates that help shape our social policy agendas, both sides often feel wholly justified. With a logic founded on cultural beliefs, which, by definition, are broadly shared (although interpretations can differ markedly, as this chapter will reveal), neither side believes its stance is extreme. Both sides can view their arguments as reasonable and appropriate. Perhaps because of a perceived moral superiority, such certainty can lead opposing sides to demean and insult one another, intentionally and unintentionally, thereby further polarizing the two sides and undermining efforts at finding a mutually satisfying compromise. This trend has been evident in the ongoing battles that surround our nation's dialogue on abortion rights, prayer in school, and gun control.

Following discussions of culture and educational opportunity in contemporary U.S. society, I look at a controversy that arose in the spring semester of 1998 at the University of Colorado regarding the rights of a coalition of students of color and gay, lesbian, bisexual, and transgendered (GLBT) students to petition the university for what some considered "special privileges." To explore how this controversy played out, I rely extensively on letters to the editor in the campus newspaper, the *Colorado Daily*, analyzing them in terms of how they used American cultural beliefs to inform their reasoning. To expand this cultural analysis of educational opportunity further, I offer a case study of one urban high school, Russell High (pseudonym). Framing the school's experience in terms of American cultural values, I argue that relying on the assumptions of individual autonomy that closely entwine with American views of rugged individualism clouds our ability to look critically at the various issues of equity (Bellah et al. 1985). Stepping back from the individualist assumptions of personal autonomy that inform much of our understanding of educational opportunity, I discuss how the collective nature of the Russell student population undermined the education students received in ways that were largely outside the power of individual students to remedy, making the issue of educational opportunity problematic.

This chapter is explicitly evaluative. I argue that our cultural values can sway public opinion and disadvantage certain segments of our population. Nonetheless, in making this argument, I have tried to be inclusive, to represent the relevant perspectives on the topics I examine (although I certainly do not do full justice to the complexity of these matters). In many cases, issues of diversity are framed in terms of "diverse" populations, making a heretofore unheard voice explicit, but with limited attention to the larger context within which this new voice arises. For cultural debates to move beyond this tendency, more voices should be heard and understood, not just the voices of our diverse populations. Sound, democratically based decision making requires this.

With this guideline in mind, I present multiple sides to the controversy at the University of Colorado, and in looking at Russell High, I note why the individualist lens offered such a compelling way to understand educational opportunity, as well as why this view ultimately disadvantaged certain students. In our nation's debates on diversity, we need rich understandings and clear pictures. We must know not only why one view wins favor, but also why another view proves limited. The dialogue must continue and deepen for people to believe that justice is being served.

WHAT IS CULTURE?

Culture is a social phenomenon that informs much of our lives. As Clifford Geertz writes, it is "the framework of beliefs, expressive symbols, and values in terms of which individuals define their world, express their feelings, and make their judgments" (1973:144–45). In Geertz's view, culture is interpretive. It does not determine one's actions; rather, it offers a way in which people "make sense" of their world (see Brightman 1995 for a comprehensive assessment of how the concept of culture has recently been subjected to scrutiny and criticism). Thus, our cultural beliefs can shape our conceptions of beauty, our attitudes toward violence, and our views of logic and common sense. Yet people are often unaware of how cultural values influence their lives. Margaret Mead noted that if humans were fish, the last thing they would discover would be water—that is, our most intimate and fundamental values can be so much a part of our lives that the degree to which they shape our perceptions and attitudes become invisible and unquestioned (Spindler & Spindler 1982). Mead's concern is critical because culture is never value-free. All culture promotes valuing some things and devaluing others—the individual perspective over the collective, strict child-rearing practices over permissive ones, innovation over continuity, and so on. Speaking to this issue, Ray McDermott and Hervé Varenne discuss the "disabling" potential of culture:

Culture is generally taken to be a positive term...but every culture, we must acknowledge, also gives...a blind side, a deaf ear, a learning problem, and a physical handicap. For every skill that people gain, there is another that is not developed; for every focus of attention, something is passed by; for every specialty, a corresponding lack. People use established cultural forms to define what they should work on, work for, in what way, and with what consequences....Being in a culture may be the only road to enhancement; it is also very dangerous (1995:331–332).

In a related vein, because cultural values encourage people to interpret their worlds in particular ways, they also serve to "hide from us other ways of thinking....[such that certain cultural beliefs] come to seem 'inevitable,' 'natural,' 'normal,' 'practical,' 'common sense'" (Gee 1990:91–92). Thus, while cultural values represent what society has deemed valid and legitimate, these values can serve the interests of some but not others (Bellah et al. 1985). This matter is at the heart of this chapter, as our views of equity and educational opportunity, beliefs fundamental to our democratic society, are shaped by our cultural ideals.

THE QUESTION OF EDUCATIONAL OPPORTUNITY

For many Americans, educational opportunity is an unquestioned reality. Through much of our history, public education has been portrayed as playing a vital role in helping empower students with the skills and knowledge that allowed them to succeed. As Diane Ravitch, assistant secretary of education for the Bush administration, observes in *The Schools We Deserve*:

For most of our history, penniless immigrants have streamed through our port cities; their transition from poverty and illiteracy into the vast American middle class owes much to the public schools....Sometimes crudely, but almost invariably with remarkable success, the public schools made them Americans and taught them the language and ideas with which they could later demand equality and justice (1985:8–9).

According to the "22nd Annual [1990] Gallup Poll of the Public's Attitudes Toward the Public Schools," many Americans shared this view. In response to the question, "Do black children and other minorities in this community have the same educational opportunities as white children?" some 79 percent of the total sample answered "Yes"; while only 15 percent said "No" (Elam 1990). Summarizing the many national reports on American schools that followed publication of *A Nation at Risk*, the landmark critique of the American system of schooling, Jeannie Oakes found much the same attitude prevailed: "[Even though] schools fail to serve all students equally well...[They] are seen as essentially neutral...as color-blind and affluence-blind....All children are seen as entrants in an equal, fair, and neutral competition" (1986:63).

That educational opportunity is viewed as largely unproblematic can be seen in the many and varied ways in which our schools, courts, and school systems have abandoned efforts once seen as critical to preserving educational opportunity for all students. The cities of Denver, Oklahoma City, and Norfolk, Virginia, for instance, all abandoned their efforts at busing to promote school integration, a policy shift embraced by whites and persons of color (Orfield et al. 1996; Donato & McQuillan 1997). Bilingual programs have been dismantled or converted to English-as-a-second-language programs, even though most researchers and school personnel consistently endorse such efforts (Soto 1997). Various challenges to affirmative action initiatives have been upheld by our courts. As Gary Orfield and his colleagues argue: "Most courts have been passive in enforcing [integration] orders....Only in the face of flagrant violations do courts do anything to justify the claim that they are 'running the system.' Our study indicates that courts rarely act to assure benefits and often require no serious accountability" (1996:349).

In the landmark *Brown vs. Board of Education* ruling, our Supreme Court ruled that those who had been disadvantaged for generations through such things as segregated schooling, inequitable funding, and being defined as socially and academically inferior to others needed assistance to establish a foothold in our society. Yet increasingly, American society and the institutions it created to promote educational opportunity no longer question the reality of educational opportunity—even though American schools are now more segregated than they were when our courts initiated school busing to promote integration. Quotas are now defined as discriminatory, rather than ameliorative. Bilingual education is divisive, not a sound approach to learning a second language. The playing field is assumed to have been leveled, at least enough that urban students (who are mainly students of color) warrant less concern.

Even though such views of educational opportunity have been popular in the 1980s and 1990s, these beliefs often differ among racial and ethnic groups. In the Gallup Poll cited earlier, people of color felt very differently from whites:

Whites [83 percent of survey respondents] in America seem convinced that, on the whole, blacks and other minority children have the same educational opportunities as whites. This conviction has not changed since 1975, when the question was first asked in these surveys. But nonwhites (who make up 14 percent of the sample in the [1990] poll) have a considerably different view. A disturbing 38 percent see inequality of opportunity in education (Elam 1990:4).

Moreover, for people of color, this view seems quite reasonable. Educational disjunctures within American society along the lines of race/ethnicity and socioeconomic status did grow increasingly pronounced during this time (U.S. Bureau of the Census 1990). Schools serving low-income and minority students often had less per capita funding (Kozol 1991; Orfield et al. 1996). A "report card" on the performance of American high school students issued by the Department of Education reported that even though "the achievement of minority students has improved over the years...the gaps between minority and white students are still large [even though] the performance of white students has remained stagnant over nearly two decades" (*Los Angeles Times* 1990). Moreover, enrollments in higher education during the 1980s suggest that the disadvantages experienced by many in high school affected college attendance as well. Although the number of African-American and Hispanic students (the two largest groups of color in the United States) attending American colleges increased by 10.5 and 61 percent, respectively, during the 1980s, the college-going rates of eighteen- to twenty-four-year-old African-American and Hispanic high school graduates remained unchanged. In effect, increases in the number of people of color going to college paralleled increases in their numbers in the larger population. In contrast, the college-going rate for white youths increased from 33 percent in 1981 to 40 percent in 1989 (U.S. Department of Education 1992).

This disjuncture between how Americans perceive the educational opportunity and the educational experience of many low-income people and people of color raises a disturbing question: How can some students be apparently disadvantaged while much of society feels that equality of opportunity really exists? One way to understand this development is to examine our cultural values. Social researchers and social theorists have offered various explanations for the relatively poor performance of students of color and low-income people in formal schooling (e.g., Bourdieu & Passeron 1977; Bowles & Gintis 1977; Ogbu 1974, 1987; Willis 1977). I consider my ideas on this issue as complementary to these other points of view, for as James Gee writes, "In any society, various cultural models...will share certain basic assumptions. These shared assumptions form what we might call 'master myths' in a society. These master myths are frequently associated with certain characteristic metaphors or 'turns of phrase and thought' in which society encapsulates its favored wisdom" (1990:91–92). In American society, many of these myths promote a commitment to individualism in which one "can achieve success if he or she works hard enough and...can improve social status because the social structure is open and hard work will get you there" (Spindler et al. 1990:23).

Faith in the power of individual achievement often begins young in America. In outlining why he thought American schools would soon regain their international prominence, for example, Lamar Alexander, secretary of education in the Bush administration, spoke to this conviction: "This is the country that grew up reading *The Little Engine that Could*" (Klein 1991:5), the children's story about a train that overcame great obstacles through dogged perseverance. Indeed, if as Daniel Shanahan asserts, "Humankind lives by its myths" (1992:10), it is no surprise that tales of Horatio Alger, Ben Franklin, Jackie Robinson, and Andrew Carnegie "which repeated over and over again the American doctrine that any boy [sic] who was poor, honest, industrious, and ambitious was 'bound to rise'" (Warner et al. 1944:46), have proven so enduring.

In the area of education, consider how Americans often draw on classic notions of rugged individualism to portray urban education. The film *Stand and Deliver*, for instance, focused on an inner-city Los Angeles math teacher, Jaime Escalante, whose entire class, mostly Latino, passed the advanced placement calculus test even though the testing agency accused his students of cheating and required them to re-take the exam. *Dangerous Minds*, a recent Hollywood portrayal of urban schooling, featured Michelle Pfeiffer promoting individual autonomy to her students: "There are no victims in this classroom!"—the implication being that you are a victim only if you allow yourself to be one. *Small Victories*, by Samuel Freedman (1990), celebrated the efforts of an English teacher at a New York City high school ranked among the worst 10 percent in the state—which nonetheless had 92 percent of its graduates go on to higher education. In Patterson, New Jersey, the singular efforts of Principal Joe Clarke drew an onslaught of public attention: the cover of *Time* magazine, a television movie, and a job offer from President Ronald Reagan. With a bull horn in one hand and a Louisville slugger in the other, Clarke offered a compellingly American image: an urban John Wayne prepared to single-handedly remedy a system out of control. With no intention of demeaning these stories or their messages, one can acknowledge that they are optimistic—told to people who already believe that effort will be rewarded. These stories fit our cultural expectations and are therefore inherently credible.

Moreover, American faith in the power of individuals to act on their own behalf has implications for how society views the related concept of responsibility. In brief, if individuals largely control their fate, the responsibility for success and failure lies with the individual. The featured speaker at a Russell High assembly (the school discussed in depth later in this chapter), the only African-American fighter pilot in the navy at one time, told his audience: "If you don't make it, there is no excuse! If you don't make it, it's because you didn't work hard enough to get it! If you don't make it, it has nothing to do with your financial background, or your parents or anybody else. If you don't make it, it's because you didn't care enough about yourself." The final remarks from *A Nation at Risk*, addressed specifically to students, reflected many of the same assumptions: "In the end it is *your* work that determines how much and how well you learn. When you work to your full capacity, you can hope to attain the knowledge and skills that will enable you to create your future and control your destiny. If you do not, you will have your future thrust upon you by others" (NCEE 1983:35–36).

In part, this emphasis on the power of the individual in American society explains why some students can have markedly different educational experiences than others, while much of society is unconcerned with issues of educational opportunity. Many people continue to believe that realizing educational opportunity is an individual matter and that those failing to capitalize on this opportunity have only themselves to blame. For some people this is true, but not for all.

RACIAL AND ETHNIC TENSIONS AT
THE UNIVERSITY OF COLORADO

During the spring semester of the 1997–1998 academic year, a Native American organization at the University of Colorado submitted a list of demands to the school administration. Shortly thereafter, an African-American group did the same. Following these actions, representatives from various student groups—including other ethnically affiliated associations and GLBT persons—formed a coalition that staged a protest by occupying the office of the vice chancellor for student affairs and submitting a list of collective demands to the university administration. Adopting a cultural perspective that frames this controversy in terms of conflicting beliefs and values, I examine how the ensuing dialogue regarding the rights of students of color and GLBT students on campus was informed by assumptions of individual autonomy.

To understand this controversy, it helps to first consider the list of demands submitted to the administration by the coalition (*Colorado Daily* 1998f:1, 5). These included:

(1) That the University implement in-state tuition for all Native Alaskan, Native Hawaiian,

and Native American students, along with free tuition for the Southern Ute and Mountain Ute in Colorado.

The students' rationale for this demand stemmed mainly from a desire to redress historic inequities that had been perpetrated by the U.S. government in its treatment of native peoples.

(2) That the university provide administrative support for removing the Board of Regents' [the state governing board of the university] prohibition on the use of general funds for GLBT concerns, including the funding of the GLBT Resource Center and domestic partner benefits for GLBT staff and faculty.

In making this demand, students noted that the GLBT Resource Center was the lowest funded "center" on campus. In addition, they maintained that denying domestic partner benefits to GLBT staff meant that employees of the institution were unable to provide medical and other insurance to their life partners, unlike their heterosexual colleagues, a discrepancy that kept GLBT students, staff, and faculty "underfunded, unprovided for, and marginalized financially, socially, and politically."

(3) That the university create a more specific "diversity" definition and enforce mandatory diversity training for all staff and faculty.

Students felt that even though the university required each campus unit to develop and implement specific diversity plans, there was no mechanism to promote accountability for such undertakings. In addition, the vague definitions of what constituted diversity further undermined any effort at holding campus units accountable for promoting a diverse work force.

(4) That the University broaden its racial and ethnic categories to be more inclusive of the students that attend CU Boulder.

This demand stemmed from the coalition's sense that statistics on recruitment and retention of students of color are marred when students must check "other" as their racial/ethnic identification. Their needs can go unnoticed because they are neither targeted nor monitored. By expanding its categories, students felt that the university could provide better services to all students and honor the true diversity students bring to campus.

(5) That the University lift its prohibition on the use of administrative funds for speakers and increase funding to Latino Advocacy, Black Advocacy, Asian American Committee on Education, and American Indian Advocacy.

Three years earlier, the chancellor revoked the use of administrative funds for student-generated speakers, a result of a controversial Muslim speaker being invited to campus. Students wanted to end what they viewed as a silencing of student-identified speakers who "carry important and valid messages of experience and truth to the student body." Further, students argued that the activities of their various constituent organizations were underfunded.

(6) That the University create Program Directors for the Native American, Latina/o, African-American and Asian American communities to supplement the current work of the Cultural Unity Student Center [a campus support organization that worked extensively with students of color].

In stating this demand, the coalition noted that during the 1960s and 1970s the university had race-specific programs, counselors, and resources that helped students adjust to university life and that sponsored various events. As the positions were consolidated, these student groups felt they suffered from overload—having full academic schedules and working jobs while organizing events, meetings, and actions within their organizations. As the students wrote, "Other schools have shown higher recruitment and retention rates when this burden is lifted by the implementation of a program director, counselor and one support staff for each student population."

(7) That all university committees that affect student life include a representation by diverse and inclusive students.

This demand was rather straightforward in that students simply wanted to ensure the various campus committees involved with programs and policies related to student life include at least 75 percent students.

In many respects, the coalition's demands were intended to promote greater equality among student groups on campus. Native peoples had been cheated, lied to, and disenfranchised by the American government. Tuition adjustments were a reasonable means for redressing such inequities. In the same vein, the coalition argued that GLBT students and employees should receive the same benefits as their heterosexual counterparts. Doing otherwise constituted discrimination and unequal treatment.

The coalition's request that the university implement mandatory diversity training was also linked to equality, in this case creating an environment equally supportive of GLBT students and students of color as mainstream students. The following demand, that the university broaden its racial and ethnic categories, reflected a similar assumption: If the university ignored the true diversity among its students, some students remained institutionally invisible. So how could the university treat them equitably? The request for race-specific program coordinators reflected a similar belief: To be treated equitably, students needed to be understood by those who are charged with supporting them. Race-specific coordinators would most be able to accomplish this end. Implicit in these demands was the assumption that white students and heterosexual students already enjoyed many of the benefits the student coalition sought to achieve. There was no need for special training to deal with white students nor for race-specific coordinators for white students, since most university personnel were white. By virtue of prevailing demographics, the university already accommodated its mainstream white students.

In concluding its list of demands, the student coalition noted, "These demands are serious yet extremely feasible. They either exist at other institutions in the state or other universities in the nation. Many arise from programs that once existed here at CU." As with many arguments based on cultural rationales, students felt justified in what they perceived as "extremely feasible" demands. They were merely seeking equality, a foundational American value.

The ensuing series of editorials in the *Colorado Daily*, a widely distributed university publication, touched upon a range of themes linked to American culture, both supporting and criticizing the students' actions. Two prominent themes that regularly arose in critical editorials centered on rugged individualism and equality. Speaking to the value of rugged individualism, for instance, a community member wrote:

Why is it that when we argue against increasing entitlement packages as a solution to the persistent devil of racism, we are vilified as "racists" by those with whom we disagree? Why is there nothing white people can do, short of sacrificing the shirts off our backs, to "stand and be counted?" Why should regular folks pursuing their lives and trying to make ends meet be accused by the self-righteously indignant?

I'll tell you why. It is because it is far too easy to feel sorry for oneself and to project blame onto others than to accept responsibility for one's own destiny. It is because those of you on the Crusade are ideologically frozen, unwilling and unable to think about anything other than a hand-out as a solution. Without the psychology of victimization, you run the risk of an intellectual void. No longer able to define yourselves by what you are not, you are forced to discover who you truly are. That can be scary, but it is what living is all about *(Colorado Daily* 1998d:6).

A self-identified "American Asian" student who could have taken "the self-serving view and support[ed] racial preferences" offered his reactions to the coalition's demand, another endorsement of rugged individualism:

I am American-Asian, not Asian-American. I'm half Japanese. Born in Japan I am immensely proud of my heritage. But I'm first and foremost an American since I live here, work here, pay taxes here. I could take the self-serving view and support racial preferences. I won't. If discrimination is wrong then it is always wrong.

I'm a firm believer that America should discard its ugly and divisive prejudices as we move into the next millennium. A color-blind society if you will. We cannot achieve that goal if we perpetuate "unequal treatment of people" by categorizing everyone by gender, sexual preference and skin color as liberals would have us do.

Equal rights for all . . . special rights for nobody *(Colorado Daily,* 1998c:9).

As this American Asian student stated in conclusion, many editorials said that since all Americans are equal, there is no need for special privileges. Indeed, such privileges constitute inequitable opportunity. As one student wrote:

Perhaps affirmative action isn't the real issue. The real issue seemed to be the racial diversity of institutions of higher learning. In that case, why not work for a program that wouldn't base enrollment on race at all. A simple idea may be to apply by Social Security number (instead of name, so race can't be told by an applicant's last name), and there would be no questions regarding race on the application. Then enrollment would be based strictly on merit....Could this be a better idea than affirmative action? (*Colorado Daily* 1998a:6)

On this same issue questioning whether the students' requests constituted special privileges, another student wrote:

I am writing this letter in objection to the list of demands placed by the students who are fed up with the CU administration's lack of services provided for minority and gay students. I am all for equal opportunity and rights, but one must question whether this list of demands does, indeed, strive for equality....If this group wants to be viewed as equal to everyone else, then why do they insist that CU train its employees to learn about diversity? If everybody is equal, then diversity should not exist. Because of the bias outlined in the list of demands, I hope that the administration is not taking it seriously. It seems that as this group strives for equal opportunity, they demand special favors that will keep them separate from the majority (*Colorado Daily* 1998f:6).

As the controversy continued, there were responses to earlier editorials. One editorial in particular, which argued that those "not actively working to end social injustice...are one of its causes," generated a number of reactions. Again, reader responses consistently portrayed the students' demands as actually undermining true equality:

In her 3/6 column, Pamela White exhorts all of us whites to "stand up and be counted, or shut the hell up," because, "If you are not actively working to end social injustice, then you are one of its causes." OK, I'll stand and be counted.

In the same column, Ms. White calls it an "unreasonable demand" for whites to ask not to be "reminded" of their "connect[ion]" to their ancestors' "murder[ing], rap[ing], and pillag[ing]." That is absurd. I'm not sure that any of my ancestors did any of those things, and, if they did, I do not inherit any guilt, just as I do not inherit special merit for any noble actions taken by my ancestors. The goodness, or evil, of my life springs from my own actions, no one else's. I will stand alongside Ms. White in racial hatred. Such acts diminish the soul of the perpetrator and add anguish to all of society.

Yet, does not Ms. White herself advocate the use of racial classifications to promote racial preferences? Does she not wish to *expand* the use of such preferences whenever she feels that some kind of statistical numbers aren't to her satisfaction? Does she not explicitly repudiate the idea that we should always do our best to make decisions without regard to color?

I call that stand "the promotion of social injustice," and I accuse Ms. White of being "one of its causes." Before she lectures the rest of us, Ms. White should put her own house in order (*Colorado Daily*, 1998g:10).

An emeritus professor joined the debate and, in challenging the coalition's demands, expressed a similar sense of injustice:

In a letter to the *Colorado Daily,* CU-Boulder's Chancellor expresses outrage at what he calls "hate messages" allegedly addressed to the Black Student Alliance and Oyate (Native Americans on campus)....He writes: "[W]e condemn any expression of racism and bigotry directed at any persons or group on the Boulder campus."

Hmmm. Have to think about that a minute, my dear chancellor? "Any expression of racism," did you say? And against "any person or group" on campus, did you say? Well, uh, what about your student admission policies which are patently based on race? [The University of Colorado at Boulder's admission policies state that the University considers a wide range of student characteristics in making admission decisions, including race and ethnicity.] And, uh, what about personnel decisions for both faculty and staff? Aren't many of them based on race—perhaps not primarily but often to a decisive extent?

What do you call the university's practice of racial and gender preferences, which you euphemistically or hypocritically (choose either adverb) call "diversity," if not "an expression of racism"? Is your condemnation of "racism" on campus not rather selective? Is it not possible for white heterosexual males to be discriminated against? In student admissions to the university? In faculty and personnel decisions?...Are you promoting "racial diversity" at the expense of equal opportunity for all regardless of race?

I trust, dear Chancellor, that you have read the recent Center for Equal Opportunity's...study of "Racial Preferences in Colorado Higher Education?" The CEO study conclusively demonstrates that the university is guilty of quiet institutional racism exercised behind closed doors against non-minority males (and some Asians minorities). CU-Boulder rejected a number of non-minority applicants with substantially higher qualifications (based on objective test and grade-point averages) than those submitted by some minority applicants (except Asians). Are you forgetting that for each unqualified minority admitted to CU in recent years, one qualified non-minority was rejected?

I call CU's admission policies institutional racism. What do you call them? I call the white applicants who were rejected by the better universities because of their lack of skin color...today's "invisible people."...Is racism OK with you so long as it is not exercised against members of the four racial or ethnic groups with political clout, the "protected" groups?...If writing such messages is racism (and it is), so is your institution's own practice of racism in a different sense—a more serious one that doesn't just offend some people but deprives them of their right to "equal protection under the law" (*Colorado Daily*, 1998b:12–13).

While the two themes I presented and analyzed, rugged individualism and equality, were far from the only issues raised in these editorials, they were popular and emotional topics. The question of individual responsibility and whether making adjustments for the university's students of color and GLBT students actually constituted unequal treatment for the rest of the university were regularly debated. These were cultural matters, at least in part, and people reacted strongly to this debate. In addition, it seems both ironic and revealing that those opposed to the coalition's demands also framed their arguments in terms of equality. In this case, opponents of the coalition contended that there was no need for special treatment for anyone. For them, American society, including the University of Colorado, was essentially equal and just. This view is typical in the United States. Those from the mainstream, mainly whites, often see educational opportunity as unproblematic (consider the Gallup Poll cited earlier), while persons of color view the situation quite differently (McQuillan 1998).

Further, the sense of polarization that was probably inherent to this debate was surely heightened by the language used by those writing editorials, for both sides. Authors charged that the opposition was "ignorant," denied any "personal responsibility," "avoid[ed] logic and reason," and so on. In one case, a student who wrote that the demands submitted by the African-American student group were "ludicrous" received over 1,500 e-mail messages from one student who blocked her or his return address. This person even found the author's grade point average and address and threatened him by saying he or she "knew" about him.

Regardless of one's stance on the coalition's demands, it is unlikely that either side in this debate will achieve its ends by the power of its insults or threats. But when the logic of a debate is for some so self-evident, the logic of one's strategies for promoting that point of view may become counterproductive. At this time, the university administration has considered the students' demands and is working with the student coalition. As of June 1998, no official action has been taken on the students' demands. I, too, offer no solution to this debate. It is a complex issue that will require dialogue. What is key is that this debate reveals how we talk about educational opportunity. The critical issue arises in the next section when I discuss how similar assumptions of educational opportunity and individual autonomy influenced what occurred in one urban high school.

EDUCATIONAL OPPORTUNITY AT RUSSELL HIGH SCHOOL

While the language of the Colorado student coalition and many editorials spoke to the need for equality of opportunity for all, the following discussion of schooling at Russell High, an urban high school where I conducted a five-year ethnographic study, presents a different picture of educational opportunity. Overall, the school's predicament was depressing. Student failure was rampant. The drop-out rate was consistently over 40 percent. Attendance was quite poor. The school enrolled a highly mobile student population, far more so than other city schools. Teacher morale was horrendous. But educational opportunity was not a particular concern within the city's school department or general populace. These outcomes were seen as deserved, reasonable, and essentially just. Yet in the same school system, the college preparatory school, Latin High, graduated virtually its entire student body each year. Attendance was not an issue, neither was student mobility. The school had the highest Metropolitan Achievement Test scores in the state. (Russell had the lowest.) In 1989, Latin High students averaged a combined score of 1028 on the SAT. (Russell students averaged 679.)

SCHOOLING AND INDIVIDUALISM

For me, these marked differences in student achievement represent educational inequality. The general indifference to these developments can be understood, at least in part, by the fact that, as occurred at the University of Colorado, people see educational opportunity in mainly individual terms. This is not surprising since many aspects of our schooling system reinforce this point of view (Henry 1965; McQuillan 1998). For instance, since all students are individuals with particular needs and interests, schools have developed a "shopping mall" of offerings that acknowledge this diversity and seek to meet the needs of many unique individuals (Powell et al. 1985). Most student work is done individually and assessed in individual terms, not collective terms (Kohn 1992). The common practice among American teachers of rewarding individual efforts also bespeaks a commitment to the idea of individualism. As Phillip Jackson observes, teachers systematically reward individual effort, even in the face of academic failure:

Consider...the common teaching practice of giving a student credit for trying. What do teachers mean when they say a student tries to do his work? They mean, in essence, that he...does his homework...he raises his hand during class discussion...he keeps his nose in the book during free study period....He is, in other words, a "model" student, though not necessarily a good one. It is difficult to imagine any of today's teachers...failing a student who tries, even though his mastery of course content is slight (1968:34).

A commitment to such conceptions of individualism was not only commonplace in the structures and practices of Russell High, but this value was extolled in school assemblies as well—through what was said as well as by who said it. Featured speakers at these assemblies not only affirmed the value of individual effort in their remarks, but they embodied this ideal through what they had accomplished in life (McQuillan 1998). Every speaker had attained some measure of "success" in American society—business people, prominent educators, and politicians. Many were people of color—the star of a popular television program, the only African-American fighter pilot in the U.S. Navy, the creator of an innovative career resource program.

Moreover, the speakers consistently addressed the value of individual effort. As the fighter pilot told his student audience in the student assembly noted previously:

I learned from being a little boy I don't quit anything. Why do you think I'm a pilot? Do you think in the projects my father had an airplane and he used to come up to me and say, "Come on son, let's take a little spin?" Why do you think I'm a pilot?...I joined the Navy and I studied I studied I studied I studied I studied. I didn't even know how to spell "aerodynamics" when I got in the Navy. I knew *nothing* about flying. But I studied hard....I now am an airline pilot...and the only reason I'm an airline pilot is because I never quit!

In the same spirit, a motivational speaker (also a well-to-do businessman) explained his success in the same assembly: "Hey folks, excuses are for losers! Losers need excuses to justify why they fail everyday!...The only limitations that exist, in terms of your potential for success, are the limitations that are self-imposed....No one can hold you down!"

In that same assembly as she concluded her remarks, the director of a career resource program reflected on failures in her life and told students to avoid similar mistakes:

I gave up on me and it took me a long time to recover and realize that I could do something about what happened to me. And I'm here to help you to not give up on yourselves. But you have got to seize the opportunities wherever you get them....For Heaven's sakes, wake up and realize that you are in charge of yourselves!...You are not going to do anything with your lives until you realize this!

For these assembly speakers, Russell students were autonomous individuals largely in control of their lives. The key point was that students should realize the value of this insight and act accordingly.

Media representations of Russell High also accorded with and promoted the ever popular American conceptions of individualism and individual achievement. Two "specials" on Russell High, the most extensive examples of media coverage of the school during my research, are revealing in this regard. The first was a television news program that presented an overview of Russell High and the city school system. The second was a feature in the Sunday newspaper that examined a school reform program at Russell. Although both presentations covered a range of topics, one theme was common to both: Readers and viewers met a number of people who were "succeeding," evidence that, regardless of the obstacles, some people were making it (McQuillan 1998, in particular, chapter 7). The TV special spoken of in that chapter introduced two African-American students, fraternal twins—one, the senior class president; the other one, an all-state basketball player—who were "planning to leave their inner-city neighborhood for college." Each discussed his social and moral development. The basketball star commented, "I see people stealing and stuff like that. I was a part of that when I was small, but I grew up to know that was wrong." His brother, the class president, noted how he had grown apart from some of his friends who had chosen different directions in their lives: "As time moved on, people's morals and values changed. They became...lower [for some of my friends] and they stopped dreaming. I still love all my friends and stuff, but there comes a time when people move on."

The newspaper article also introduced a number of Russell High "successes," including Celeste Robinson, a student for whom a school reform program "has been a lifesaver." Although personal problems interfered with Celeste's academic performance, her teachers' support and her own hard work got her back on track. Reflecting on her experience, Celeste explained, "Everyone thought I was dumb and an air head. I wanted to prove to myself and to them that I wasn't. So this year, when I did good, everyone was surprised. They all said, 'Oh my God, Celeste got an A!'" By stressing that students who wanted to succeed could do so and by saying virtually nothing about the school's dropout or failure rates and never introducing any Russell High "failures," these media representations helped preserve a view of society as equitable and full of opportunity for those willing to work.

SCHOOLS AS COLLECTIVE INSTITUTIONS

While Americans often explain educational achievement in individual terms, schools, the primary means by which we try to realize our nation's commitment to educational opportunity, are collective institutions, and should be understood from that point of view as well. As James Coleman observed over thirty years ago:

The higher achievement of all racial and ethnic groups in schools with greater proportions of white students is largely, perhaps wholly, related to effects associated with the student body's educational background and aspirations. *This means that the apparent beneficial effect of a student body with a high proportion of white students comes not from racial composition per se, but from the better educational background and higher educational aspirations that are, on the average, found among white students.* The effects of the student body environment upon a student's achievement appear to lie in the educational proficiency possessed by that student body, whatever its racial or ethnic composition (1990:92–93; emphasis added).

To appreciate how the nature of the student population Russell High enrolled influenced students' educational experience, it helps to examine the structure of the school system and compare Russell High's population with other high schools. For instance, Russell High enrolled more students of color, averaging between 80 and 85 percent during my research, than any other school in the city, public or private. (Latin High enrolled around 25 percent students of color during this same time.) Because of the close link between race/ethnicity and socioeconomic status, this meant that Russell enrolled a disproportionate number of low-income students (Orfield et al. 1996). In fact, Russell had the greatest percentage of students that qualified for the free/reduced lunch program in the city, over 60 percent of the student body. (About 12 percent of Latin High's students qualified for free/reduced lunch.) Also, about 6 percent of Russell students were designated "special education," and one-quarter of the student body was enrolled in ESL courses. (Latin had no special education or ESL students.) The parents of Russell students had relatively low incomes, and only 10 percent had earned college degrees. In sociological terms, these developments correlated with low "cultural capital" (Coleman 1990), which translates as one's economic well-being as well as the degree to which one has internalized various aspects of social life—the speech, dress, and behavioral norms of the dominant group(s), for instance. Schools with high percentages of students with low cultural capital often do poorly, in part, because of the attitude students bring to school as well as how the institution responds to them.

Juxtaposed with the value of individual effort extolled by Russell's assembly speakers as well as those writing in the *Colorado Daily*, it helps to consider how the collective nature of the Russell student population influenced students' educational opportunity—in ways that were beyond the ability of most students to change. In one of my first conversations with Russell's principal, for instance, he reflected on his initial efforts at a school that had seen twelve principals in thirteen years and which had the reputation of enrolling a disruptive student population: "My first priority was discipline—'to secure the perimeter' as they say in the military....I had to get students into classrooms and keep disruptive outsiders out of the school." During my research, which began three years into the principal's tenure, controlling students and keeping the building orderly continued to be high priorities. Throughout the school day, administrators carried walkie-talkies so they could communicate with one another at any time and address problems as soon as possible. When students passed between classes, all three principals were generally in the halls. Both assistant principals had secretaries whose entire responsibilities entailed processing the passes, lists, and disciplinary forms the assistant principals generated—work consistently so time-consuming that student assistants were recruited to help.

Early in their high school careers, Russell students heard that order was a prime concern of the school's administration. As an assistant principal remarked during a ninth grade "orientation" assembly on the first day of school in September 1987:

Welcome to Russell High. I need to make a few things clear to you so let me run them down quickly: No one gets into the building until 8:15, unless you're in the breakfast program. [Russell had a government-subsidized breakfast program for eligible students.] You have to be in your home room by 8:15 and it's better to be on time than staying for [the other assistant principal] for an hour. If you're a chronic late student, [the other assistant principal] will deal with you in other ways....People who don't "sign in" to the late room are suspended....We don't like to see people in the corridor. We expect you to show us your pass. We won't accept the excuse that you're late to school. Be on time. Be where you belong at all times, and you'll be fine.

When administrators focus on order, three developments, with implications for students' educational achievement, are common. First, administrators have less time to be educational leaders. During my five years at Russell, I never saw or heard of a principal or assistant principal who visited a teacher's classroom. Administrators seldom participated in professional development work or reform efforts undertaken by the school. Second, when administrators make discipline and control top priorities, teachers often adopt a similar outlook. As Phil Cusick found, in schools where this occurred, "it was more important to keep [students] in school, in class, and in order than to teach them something and see that they learned it" (1983:39). From a similar vantage point, Linda McNeil spelled out the implications for student learning: In such settings "the strategies for instruction are quite similar: control students by making work easy" (1986:184).

Third, to ensure order, schools tend to restrict students' free time and access to extracurricular activities. At Russell, there were no free periods, study halls, or activity periods. During my research, the school sponsored no after-school dances and few after-school events. There was even a proposal to end school at one o'clock so as to avoid having a lunch period, a time perceived by many faculty and administrators as disruptive to the peace of the school. All these efforts sought to restrict the amount of free time students spent with one another, thereby limiting the likelihood of problems. An unintended effect, however, was that teachers, administrators, and students had few opportunities in which to evolve a sense of community that could make the school a desirable place to be. Considering the limited involvement by Russell students in extracurricular activities, seeing the daily attendance sheet, or watching the number of students who regularly skipped classes to hang out in a nearby commercial district suggested that many students felt little commitment to a school community.

The collective nature of the student population also influenced the work done by the school guidance department. For example, the school enrolled a highly mobile student population—more so than any other secondary school in the city (McQuillan 1998, in particular, chapter 3). Therefore, guidance counselors spent substantial amounts of time processing students—into and out of the school. One guidance counselor, new to Russell at the time, noted that her colleagues referred to the school as the "revolving door." She quickly found out why: Because of the number of students who transferred into and out of Russell during the summer, she spent the entire first quarter of the school year settling student schedules. To keep up with her work, she seldom took lunch or had a free period. Even so, she spent relatively little time with individual students discussing anything other than schedule changes. Another guidance counselor described his work much the same:

I don't really spend that much time at all with individual students. Most of that I do during students' home room period....I try to see all the students in my class [he had tenth graders that year] but I never make it through to seeing every student. Sometimes kids are absent so they miss the meeting. It just hasn't seemed to work to set individual times to meet with students. When I schedule meetings with individual students, I usually only end up getting to see about one of five students.

Given this situation, most Russell students met with guidance counselors only if they had schedule problems, if their parents called the school and intervened, or if the student had the personal initiative. For other students, an individual meeting with a guidance counselor was a luxury. At other city schools, with less mobile student populations, guidance counselors had time for concerns other than settling student schedules.

That Russell enrolled a disproportionately disadvantaged student population had consequences for faculty as well. A small minority of teachers were blatant about the consequences for them: They had given up and did little substantive in their classes, mainly because they decided that most students were unconcerned about their education. But this was a handful. Still, even well-intentioned and hard-working teachers were affected by the challenges they faced. A science teacher who had taught for thirteen years at Russell High described the tension generated by her desire to push students and the students' ensuing resistance: "It kills me to see kids sleep in class. They'll just say: 'I'm tired,' or 'This is boring,'or 'Leave me alone.' They resent you when you try to get them to participate in class. This past year, the apathy and hostility were the worst. My kids get angry and resent me because I truly want them to be students."

An English teacher with over fifteen years experience at Russell discussed how the collective nature of his students led him to lower his standards: "You can't assign homework in books with my [lowest-track] students because the books that go out of the school disappear. We have large numbers of books missing. And the budget just gets to a point where you can't afford to replace the books anymore. You can give homework to the [school's top track] but not with [the lowest track]."

Another English teacher who had recently transferred to Russell from Latin High compared the school to his previous one, in particular, to the increased demands he felt teaching at Russell:

You're still teaching but you face more kinds of problems. That's why it's so exhausting. Not only are you a teacher but you're a social worker. At times I have offered students medical advice. To reach some of these students it's not enough just to disseminate information in class. You need to really get to know the students. And *that* takes its own toll. *That's* why it's so exhausting. And then it becomes very hard to leave school and make the night yours—because you either have work to do or you are thinking about your students. Here are some kids that I know I can't reach. And I do think about that....It's tiring.

Although all three teachers were, in my observations and in the opinions of many of their colleagues, exemplary, their teaching was influenced by the collective nature of their students. In fact, two of the teachers eventually transferred to other city schools because of the demands and tensions they experienced at Russell.

What I describe of Russell High is fully consistent with what other researchers have found in similar urban schools: teaching strategies that compromise academic standards in the interests of order and control; a comparable emphasis on control and order by administration officials, with less concern for academic matters; disproportionate numbers of low-income, special education, and limited-English proficient students; disproportionately high dropout rates, failure rates and rates of student turnover; and demoralized teachers. Perhaps more importantly, as long as schools continue to understand educational achievement (or the lack thereof) of its students in individual terms, faculty and administrators will continue to attempt to resolve the challenges they face by focusing on individual students rather than the collective nature of their student populations. As Jeannie Oakes notes in *Keeping Track: How Schools Structure Inequality:*

In our search for the solution to the problems of educational inequality, our focus was almost exclusively on the characteristics of the children themselves. We looked for sources of educational failure in their homes, their neighborhoods, their language, their cultures, even in their genes. In all our searching we almost entirely overlooked the possibility that what happens *within* schools might contribute to unequal educational opportunities and outcomes. We neglected to examine the content and processes of schooling itself for ways they might contribute to school failure (1985:xiv).

SUMMARY

Listening...requires not only open eyes and ears, but open hearts and minds. We do not really see through our eyes or hear through our ears, but through our beliefs. To put our beliefs on hold is to cease to exist as ourselves for a moment—and that is not easy (Delpit 1988:501).

Lisa Delpit's statement goes to the heart of what this chapter is about. First, our beliefs predispose us to see the world in particular ways, and second, this tendency is difficult to overcome. Reflecting both trends, a contentious dialogue centered on issues of diversity and equity at the University of Colorado was itself insulting and divisive (at least as evidenced by the editorials). Yet to resolve the issues raised by the student coalition in a manner satisfying to both sides, there seemed to be a need for people to understand the whole picture, to consider the experiences and views of those who both supported and challenged the coalition's proposals. But this will not be easy, especially when people are so certain of their beliefs that they ignore the insults that accompany their discussions. In fact, this public debate seemed ironic in that those who supported the student coalition, as well as those who saw no need for "special privileges," all based their arguments, to some degree, on issues of equality.

To promote effective dialogue, we must keep in mind that the United States is a very divided country, a reflection of what Andrew Hacker (1992) termed our "residential apartheid." Having productive discussions across social, educational, economic, and neighborhood divides is difficult. Indeed, these divisions help explain why whites and people of color in this country can see educational opportunity so differently—because it often is very different. For dialogue to be educational, people must keep in mind that most whites do not know what it is like to be a person of color in our country, and the two worlds can be quite different. Reflecting on her own education, Peggy McIntosh aptly noted that, like our cultural beliefs, "white privilege" is a largely unexamined phenomenon for most white people: "My schooling gave me no training in seeing myself as an oppressor, as an unfairly advantaged person....I was taught to see myself as an individual whose moral state depended on her individual moral will" (1989:10).

While I propose no solution to the Colorado controversy, I do believe that ongoing dialogue, leading to increased understanding, is critical to finding any satisfying resolution. Furthermore, insults will not bring about change, but they likely will harden people in their existing position. In such dialogues, the goal is not to blame or insult but to educate.

While there was no acrimonious debate on educational opportunity at Russell High, this was not a positive development. The lack of attention to this concern suggested that people were confident in their beliefs. Educational opportunity was being realized; there was no need to disrupt the system. But I have argued that this complacency reflected a naive faith in the individual autonomy of Russell students. The school system and general public were seeing opportunity from an individual, not a collective, point of view. Shifting the focus, as I attempted to do, created a very different picture, one in which educational opportunity became problematic. Revealing the power of our cultural beliefs to hide and distort, it is disturbing that the structure of the school system worked to the advantage of the upper-income white students in the city (given Latin's enrollment pattern) and to the disadvantage of the diverse student body at Russell.

In closing, I recall the words of W. Lloyd Warner, who observed over forty-five years ago that issues of educational opportunity are not only a concern for urban students, they are intimately entwined with the social fabric that holds our nation together, that makes the United States what it is:

The most significant characteristic of the American class system—and the reason Americans think of it as being democratic—is the firm belief that there must be equality of opportunity for all and a chance for everyone to have his turn at bat. Such a belief means that the system must provide for the rise of men and their families from lower to higher levels....They believe that a man [sic], by applying himself, by using the talents he has, by acquiring the necessary skills, can rise from lower to higher status....The opportunity for social mobility for everyone is the very fabric of the "American Dream." *The American Dream is not a mere fantasy that can be dismissed as unimportant to those who think realistically, for...it is the basic, powerful, motivating force that...makes all Americans partners in the well-being of each, since each feels that, although he is competing with the rest, he has a stake in the common good.* When the principles of social mobility in the United States are not operating, there are troubles ahead not only for those who do not experience mobility but for every American (1953: 29–30; emphasis added).

REFERENCES

Bellah, R., Madsen, R., Sullivan, W., Swidler, A., and Tipton, S. 1985. *Habits of the Heart.* New York: Harper and Row.

Bourdieu, P., and Passeron, J. C. 1977. *Reproduction in Education, Society, and Culture.* London: Sage.

Bowles, S., and Gintis, H. 1977. *Schooling in Capitalist America.* New York: Basic Books.

Brightman, R. 1995. Forget culture: Replacement, transcendence, reflexification. *Cultural Anthropology* 19(4):509–546.

Coleman, J. S. 1990. *Equality and Achievement in Education.* Boulder, CO: Westview Press.

Colorado Daily. 1998a. All white people racist? Now hold on, there. March 4, 5–6.

———. 1998b. Chancellor endorses another institutional racism. April 3, 12–13.

———. 1998c. I don't support racial preferences. March 16, 9.

———. 1998d. I'm an awful racist, and other rhetorical triumphs. March 12, 6.

———. 1998e. I object to the list of demands. March 9, 6.

———. 1998f. Protesters ponder next step. February 26.

———. 1998g. White should put her own house in order. March 16, 10.

Cusick, P. 1983. *The Egalitarian Ideal and The American High School.* New York: Longman.

Delpit, L. 1988. The silenced dialogue: Power and pedagogy in educating other people's children. *Harvard Educational Review* 58(3):280–298.

Donato, R., and McQuillan, P. J. 1997. Latino school resegregation. Paper presented at The Latino Civil Rights Crisis sponsored by the Harvard Civil Rights Project and the Tomas Rivera Policy Institute, Los Angeles, CA, December.

Elam, S. 1990. The 22nd annual Gallup poll of the public's attitudes toward the public schools. *Phi Delta Kappan* 72(1):41–55.

Fine, M., and Rosenberg, P. 1983. Dropping out of high school: The ideology of school and work. *Journal of Education* 165:257–272.

Freedman, S. 1990. *Small Victories: The Real World of a Teacher, Her Students, and Their High School.* New York: Harper and Row.

Gee, J. P. 1990. *Social Linguistics and Literacies: Ideology and Discourses.* New York: Falmer Press.

Geertz, C. 1973. *The Interpretation of Cultures.* New York: Basic Books.

Hacker, A. 1992. *Two Nations: Black and White, Separate, Hostile, Unequal.* New York: Charles Scribner's Sons.

Henry, J. 1965. *Culture Against Man.* New York: Vintage Books.

Hsu, F. 1983. *Rugged Individualism Reconsidered*. Knoxville, TN: University of Tennessee Press.

Jackson, P. 1968. *Life in Classrooms*. Chicago: University of Chicago Press.

Klein, E. 1991. We're talking about a revolution. *Boston Globe Parade Magazine*, August 25, 5.

Kohn, A. 1992. *No Contest: The Case Against Competition*. Boston: Houghton Mifflin.

Kozol, J. 1991. *Savage Inequalities*. New York: Crown Publishing.

Los Angeles Times. 1990. U.S. students' performance: Low and stagnant. September 27, C1.

MacLeod, J. 1987. *Ain't No Makin' It: Leveled Aspirations in a Low-Income Neighborhood*. Boulder, CO: Westview Press.

McDermott, R., and Varenne, H. 1995. Culture as disability. *Anthropology and Education Quarterly* 26(3):324–348.

McIntosh, P. 1989. White privilege: Unpacking the invisible knapsack. *Peace and Freedom*, July–August, 10–12.

McNeil, L. 1986. *Contradictions of Control*. New York: Routledge.

McQuillan, P. J. 1998. *Educational Opportunity in an Urban American High School: A Cultural Analysis*. Albany, NY: State University of New York Press.

National Commission on Excellence in Education (NCEE). 1983. *A Nation at Risk: An Imperative for Educational Reform*. Washington, DC: U. S. Department of Education.

Oakes, J. 1985. *Keeping Track: How Schools Structure Inequality*. New Haven, CT: Yale University Press.

———. 1986. Tracking, inequality, and the rhetoric of reform: Why schools don't change. *Journal of Education* 168(1):60–80.

Ogbu, J. 1974. *The Next Generation*. New York: Academic Press.

———. 1987. Variability in minority school performance. *Anthropology and Education Quarterly* 18(4).

Orfield, G., Easton, S., and the Harvard Project on School Desegregation. 1996. *Dismantling Desegregation*. New York: The New Press.

Powell, A., Farrar, E., and Cohen, D. 1985. *The Shopping Mall High School*. Boston: Houghton Mifflin.

Ravitch, D. 1985. *The Schools We Deserve*. New York: Basic Books.

Shanahan, D. 1992. *Toward a Genealogy of Individualism*. Amherst, MA: University of Massachusetts Press.

Soto, L. D. 1997. *Language, Culture, and Power*. Albany, NY: State University of New York Press.

Spindler, G. and Spindler, L. 1982. Roger Harker and Schoenhausen: From the familiar to the strange and back again. In *Doing the Ethnography of School: Educational Anthropology in Action*. Spindler, G. (ed.). Prospect Heights, IL: Waveland Press.

———. 1987a. Cultural dialogue and schooling in Schoenhausen and Roseville. *Anthropology and Education Quarterly* 18(1):3–16.

———. 1987b. Ethnography: An anthropological view. In *Education and Cultural Process*. Spindler, G. (ed.). Prospect Heights, IL: Waveland Press, pp. 151–156.

Spindler, G., Spindler, L., Trueba, H., and Williams, M. 1990. *The American Cultural Dialogue and Its Transmission*. New York: The Falmer Press.

U.S. Bureau of the Census. 1990. *Census Code Book*. Washington, DC: U.S. Government Printing Office.

U.S. Department of Education. 1992. *Trends in Racial/Ethnic Enrollment in Higher Education: Fall 1980 Through Fall 1990*. Washington, DC: Office of Educational Research and Improvement.

Warner, W. L. 1953. *American Life: Dream and Reality*. Chicago: University of Chicago Press.

Warner, W. L., Havighurst, R., and Loeb, M. 1944. *Who Shall Be Educated?* New York: Harper and Brothers.

Willis, P. 1977. *Learning to Labour*. Westmead, England: Saxon House.

Postscript

When all is said and done, America's diversity comes from many quarters, some recognized and some not. The constituent cultures that make for the diversity of America come from the specific beliefs and practices shared by groups of people, while differentiating them from other groups learning different things. In many ways, all the constituent groups of America are special-interest groupings, created out of a need for people who share something to respond to the circumstances in which they find themselves. Such groupings provide individuals with guidance for living out their daily lives, pursuing the goals of the group that come from the circumstances within which they find themselves. Some of these groups are identified as ethnic cultural groupings, since they distinguish the unique cultural constructs of groups that developed around people who have moved from one nation-state to another and must adjust to the new context. In reality, the use of the term *ethnic* is primarily for self-identification of members of such groupings, identifying their common cultural origins and unique creation within the nation-state. For America, there are many such groupings that reflect the people who have come to America from throughout the world. Special-interest groups can be found with every organizational activity of the United States and all manner of specific purpose groupings made up of people who share similar thoughts on some aspect, part, or question of American living.

As long as Americans categorize people according to the mythological concepts of race or ethnicity that they create and recognize, the problems of discrimination and prejudice that accompany cultural diversity in America will continue and only get worse. Perhaps Harley et al., are right in suggesting that the only way racism and discrimination can disappear is when the bigots and racists are "lobotomized and their seed sterilized." These things will surely never happen. More importantly, virtually every constituent cultural group found in America has been the focus of prejudice and discrimination. It is not a malady that afflicts only categories of people grouped according to some physical characteristic, because they speak a language other than English, or come from some other region of the world, it afflicts everyone. Thus, Americans are faced with the task of finding another way to deal with the problem. Learning to be a little less ethnocentric and a little more aware of, and sensitive to, others who are not bad because they are different, they are just different, is clearly the place to begin.

With all these diverse groups making up the United States, the main question is how to resolve the problems of diversity when there are so many different views as to what needs or should be done. Even within well-identified groupings, there is variation. That these groups are competing for prominence, status position, and limited resources only makes for continuing conflict between them. Cultures represent "truths," and members of each of the constituent cultural groups of America know that their culture is the real truth. Admitting that someone else's truth may be more true than yours is not part of believing in one's truth. This introduces a cultural stalemate in the United States, a stalemate between competing truths. While one can pass laws and legislate a particular brand of truth, that does not mean it will be accepted by everyone. Everyone believes that if it would just be done "my way" everything would be fine. The major thrust of every cultural group is to change the way of believing and acting of other cultural groups. The debates surrounding every major social issue of America reflect America's diversity. The pursuit of political power reflects the drive of individual groups to assume the power to impact their own lives and those of everybody else. With power, the group invariably attempts to impose its will (truth) on everybody else. Prejudice and discrimination are the consequences of competing and conflicting truths, part of the process of getting ahead or overpowering those other truths. In a land that values the individual, diversity, freedom, and conformity, the only real truth is the stalemate between cultural groupings and their truths. Individualism for oneself is demanded. Others should conform. Freedom to be different is demanded for self, not necessarily given to other. If one's group is in any way different, diversity for the group is okay, but not for others. Conformity is valued in America, but this really means others should (or must) conform to the thinking of the specific group—my group (depending on the individual and the group). Stalemate means to reach deadlock, to reach a standstill. Resolving the problems of cultural diversity has reached such a stalemate because there is no one to tell Americans which of the truths are the real ones except all the constituent groups of America that already possess it.

Bibliography

Achenbach, J. 1994. Putting all the X in one basket. *The Washington Post,* April 27, B1 and B4.

Advisory Committee on Criteria for Diversity. 1997. Alternative diversity criteria: Analysis and recommendations. A report to the Texas Higher Education Coordinating Board. Austin, TX.

Agar, M. 1994. *Language Shock: Understanding the Culture of Conversation.* New York: William Morrow.

Alba, R. 1985. *Italian Americans: Into the Twilight of Ethnicity.* Englewood Cliffs, NJ: Prentice-Hall.

————. 1990. *Ethnic Identity: The Transformation of White America.* New Haven, CT: Yale University Press.

Alston, R. J., Russo, C. J., and Miles, A. S. 1994. Brown v. Board of Education and the Americans with dis-abilities act: vistas of equal educational opportunities for African Americans. *Journal of Negro Education* 63(3):349–357.

Althan, G. 1988. *American Ways: A Guide for Foreigners in the United States.* Yarmouth, MA: Intercultural Press.

American Forces Information Service. 1995. *Defense 94.* Vol 5. Alexandria, VA: U.S. Department of Defense.

Anderson, E. 1990. *Streetwise: Race, Class and Change in an Urban Community.* Chicago: University of Chicago Press.

Arensberg, C. M., and Niehoff, A. H. 1971. *Introducing Culture Change.* Chicago: Aldine.

Asante, M. K. 1992. African-American studies: The future of the discipline. *The Black Scholar* 22(3):37–49.

*Associated Press.*1998. Hundreds mourn man dragged to his death in Texas. June 14, 16.

Atkinson, D., Morten, G., and Sue, D. 1989. A minority identity development model. In *Counseling American Minorities.* Atkinson, D., Morten, G., and Sue, D. (eds.). Dubuque, IA: W. C. Brown.

Atkinson, D. R., and Hackett, G. 1998. *Counseling diverse populations.* Boston, MA: McGraw-Hill.

Barth, F. 1969. *Ethnic Groups and Boundaries: The Social Organization of Cultural Difference*. Boston: Little, Brown.

Bell, D. A. 1992. *Faces at The Bottom of the Well: The Permanence of Racism*. New York: Basic Books.

Bellafonte, G. 1995. Generation X-cellent. *Time*, February 27, 62–64.

Bellah, R., Madsen, R., Sullivan,W., Swidler, A., and Tipton, S. 1985. *Habits of the Heart*. New York: Harper and Row.

Benokraitis, C., and Feagin, J. R. 1978. *Affirmative Action and Equal Opportunity: Action, Inaction, Reaction*. Boulder, CO: Westview.

Blackwell, J. 1988. Dynamics of minority education: An index to the status of race and ethnic relations in the United States. *Trotter Institute Review* 2:5–13.

Blassingame, J. W. 1972. *The Slave Community: Plantation Life in the Antebellum South*. New York: Oxford University Press.

Bloom, A. 1997. *The Closing of the American Mind*. New York: Simon & Schuster.

Bluestone, B., and Harrison, B. 1982. *The Deindustrialization of America*. New York: Basic Books.

Blumberg, R. 1988. *Civil Rights: The 1960's Freedom Struggle*. Boston: Twayne Publishers.

Bobo, L. 1988. Group conflict, prejudice, and the paradox of contemporary racial attitudes. In *Eliminating Racism*. Katz, P., and Taylor, D. (eds.). New York: Plenum, pp. 85–114.

Bodnar, J. W., and Dengler, R. n.d. The emergence of a command network at the national level. Unpublished manuscript.

Bonastia, C. 1995. Sucking in the '70s. *The New Republic,* January 30, 11.

Bonvillian, N. 1993. *Language, Culture and Communication: The Meaning of Messages*. Englewood Cliffs, NJ: Prentice-Hall.

Bourdieu, P., and Passeron, J. C. 1977. *Reproduction in Education, Society, and Culture*. London: Sage.

Bourgois, P. 1995. *In Search of Respect: Selling Crack in El Barrio*. Cambridge, MA: Cambridge University Press.

Bowles, S., and Gintis, H. 1977. *Schooling in Capitalist America*. New York: Basic Books.

Brightman, R. 1995. Forget culture: Replacement, transcendence, reflexification. *Cultural Anthropology* 19 (4):509–546.

Campbell, D. 1984. *Women at War with America: Private Lives in a Patriotic Era*. Cambridge: Harvard University Press.

Caplovitz, D. 1963. *The Poor Pay More*. New York: Free Press.

Carmichael, S., and Hamilton, C. V. 1967. *Black Power: The Politics of Liberation in America*. New York: Random House.

Carter, R., and Helms, J. 1987. The relationship between black value orientations to racial identity attitudes. *Evaluation and Measurement in Counseling and Development* 19:185–195.

Cherlin, A. J. 1998. How will the 1996 welfare reform law affect poor families? In *Public and Private Families*. Cherlin, A. J. (ed.). New York: McGraw-Hill, pp. 120–127.

Chicago Tribune. 1993. Civil wrongs: As blacks go house hunting, too often the door is closed. November 14, C1.

Clark, T. 1979. *Blacks in the Suburbs*. New Brunswick, NJ: Rutgers University Center for Urban Policy Research.

Clayborne, C. 1986. Civil rights reform and the black freedom struggle. In *The Civil Rights Movement in America*. Eagles, C. W. (ed). Jackson, MS: University of Mississippi Press.

Cohen, R. 1978. Ethnicity: Problem and focus in anthropology. *Annual Review of Anthropology* 7:379–403.

Coleman, J. S. 1990. *Equality and Achievement in Education.* Boulder, CO: Westview Press.

Collins, S. M. 1983. The making of the black middle class. *Social Problems* 30:369–381.

Colorado Daily. 1998a. All white people racist? Now hold on, there. March 4, pp. 5–6.

———. 1998b. Chancellor endorses another institutional racism. April 3, 12–13.

———. 1998c. I don't support racial preferences. March 16, 9.

———. 1998d. I'm an awful racist, and other rhetorical triumphs. March 12, 6.

———. 1998e. I object to the list of demands. March 9, 6.

———. 1998f. Protesters ponder next step. February 26.

———. 1998g. White should put her own house in order. March 16, 10.

Cortese, A. J. 1992. Affirmative action: Are white women gaining at the expense of black men? *Equity & Excellence* 25(2–4):77–89.

Cose, E. 1993. *The Rage of a Privileged Class: Why Are Middle-Class Blacks Angry? Why Should America Care?* New York: HarperCollins.

———. 1997. *Color-Blind: Seeing Beyond Race in a Race-Obsessed World.* New York: HarperCollins.

Coupland, D. 1991. *Generation X: Tales for an Accelerated Culture.* New York: St. Martin's Press.

Cox, G. O. 1974. *Education for the Black Race.* New York: African Heritage Studies Publishers.

Crosby, F., Bromley, S., and Saxe, L. 1987. Recent unobtrusive studies of black and white discrimination and prejudice. *Psychological Bulletin* 87:546–563.

Cross, W. 1971. The Negro-to-Black conversion experience: Towards a psychology of Black liberation. *Black World* 20:13–27.

Cusick, P. 1983. *The Egalitarian Ideal and the American High School.* New York: Longman.

Dalton, H. L. 1995. *Racial Healing.* New York: Doubleday.

Davis, A. Y. 1981. *Women, Race, & Class.* New York: Vintage Books.

Davis, R. 1997. *The Myth of Black Ethnicity.* Greenwich, CT: Albex Publications.

Delpit, L. 1988. The silenced dialogue: Power and pedagogy in educating other people's children. *Harvard Educational Review* 58 (3):280–298.

Donato, R., and McQuillan, P. J. 1997. Latino school resegregation. Paper presented at The Latino Civil Rights Crisis sponsored by the Harvard Civil Rights Project and the Tomas Rivera Policy Institute, Los Angeles, CA, December.

Dovidio, J. 1993. The subtlety of racism. *Training & Development* 47(4):51–57.

Du Bois, W. E. B. 1962. *Black Reconstruction in America 1860–1880.* New York: Atheneum.

Dunn, W. 1992. Hanging out with American youth. *American Demographics* 14:24–35.

Dunnigan, J. F., and Nofi, A. A. 1990. *Dirty Little Secrets: Military Information You're Not Supposed to Know.* New York: Quill/William Morrow.

Early, G. 1996. Understanding Afrocentrism: Why blacks dream of a world without whites. In *The Best American Essays 1996.* Ward, G. C. (ed.). New York: Houghton Mifflin.

Eckardt, A. 1989. *Black-Woman-Jew.* Bloomington, IN: Indiana University Press.

Edin, K., and Lein, L. 1997. *Making Ends Meet: How Single Mothers Survive Welfare and Low-Wage Work.* New York: Russell Sage Foundation.

Ehrlich, H. J. 1990. *Campus Ethnoviolence and the Public Options.* Baltimore, MD: National Institute Against Prejudice and Violence.

Elam, S. 1990. The 22nd annual Gallup poll of the public's attitudes toward the public schools. *Phi Delta Kappan* 72 (1):41–55.

Essed, P. 1991. *Understanding Racism.* Newbury Park, CA: Sage.

Farley, R. (ed.). 1995. *State of the Union: America in the 1990s.* Vols. 1 and 2. New York: Russell Sage Foundation.

Farley, R., and Allen, W. R. 1987. *The Color Line and Quality of Life in America.* New York: Russell Sage Foundation.

Feagin, J. R., and Feagin, C. B. 1996. *Racial and Ethnic Relations.* 5th ed. Upper Saddle River, NJ: Prentice-Hall.

Feagin, J. R., and Hahn, H. 1973. *Ghetto Revolts.* New York: Macmillan.

Feagin, J. R., and Sikes, M. 1994. *Living with Racism: The Black Middle Class Experience.* Boston: Beacon Press.

Feagin J. R., and Vera, H. 1995. *White Racism: The Basics.* New York: Routledge.

Fenner, E. 1994. Generation X strikes back. *Money* 23:6, 90–97+.

Fine, M., and Rosenberg, P. 1983. Dropping out of high school: The ideology of school and work. *Journal of Education* 165:257–272.

Fischer, C. S., Hout, M., Jankowski, M. S., Lucas, S. R., Swidler, A., and Voss, K. 1996. *Inequality by Design: Cracking the Bell Curve Myth.* Princeton, NJ: Princeton University Press.

Fischer, L. 1989. Equality: An elusive ideal. *Equity & Excellence* 24(2):64–71.

Fish, S. 1994. *There's No Such Thing As Free Speech.* New York: Oxford University Press.

Fishman, J. 1980. Social theory and ethnography. In *Ethnic Diversity and Conflict in Eastern Europe.* Sugar, P. (ed.). Santa Barbara, CA: ABC-Clio.

Fiske, S. T. 1993. Controlling other people: The impact of power on stereotyping. *American Psychologist* 48(6): 621–628.

Freedman, S. 1990. *Small Victories: The Real World of a Teacher, Her Students, and Their High School.* New York: Harper and Row.

Gaines, S. O., and Reed, E. S. 1995. Prejudice: From Allport to DuBois. *American Psychologist* 50(2):96–103.

Gans, H. 1971. The uses of poverty: The poor can pay all. *Social Policy* (July/August): 20–24.

———. 1979. Symbolic ethnicity: The future of ethnic groups and cultures in America. *Ethnic and Racial Studies* 2(1):9–17.

———. 1995. *The War Against the Poor.* New York: Basic Books.

Gapasin, F. E. 1996. Race, gender and other problems of unity for the American working class. *Race, Gender, & Class* 4(1):41–62.

Gee, J. P. 1990. *Social Linguistics and Literacies: Ideology and Discourses.* New York: Falmer Press.

Geertz, C. (ed.). 1963. *Old Societies and New States.* New York: Free Press.

———. 1973. *The Interpretation of Cultures.* New York: Basic Books.

Gell, A. 1993. *Wrapping in Images: Tattooing in Polynesia.* Oxford: Clarendon Press.

Gibbs, J. T. 1985. Can we continue to be color-blind and class-bound? *Counseling Psychologist* 13:426–435.

Gibbs, T. 1997. Portrait of a minority. In *Cultural Diversity in the United States.* Naylor, L. L. (ed.). Westport, CT: Bergin & Garvey.

Giles, J. 1994. Generalization X. *Newsweek,* June 6, 62–72.

Goldberg, D. 1995. Made in the USA: Racial mixing 'n matching. In *American Mixed Race.* Zack, N. (ed.). Lanham, MD: Rowman and Littlefield.

Goodenough, W. 1990. Evolution of the human capacity for beliefs. *American Anthropologist* 92(3):597–612.

Gordon, M. 1964. *Assimilation in American Life*. New York: Oxford University Press.

Grosby, S. 1994. The verdict of history: The inexpungeable tie of primordiality—A response to Eller and Coughlan. *Ethnic and Racial Studies* 12(2):164–171.

Guy-Sheftall, B. 1990. *Daughters of Sorrow*. Brooklyn, NY: Carlson Publishing.

Haaland, G. 1969. Economic determination in ethnic processes. In *Ethnic Groups and Boundaries: The Social Organization of Cultural Difference*. Barth, F. (ed.). Boston: Little, Brown.

Hacker, A. 1992. *Two Nations: Black and White, Separate, Hostile, Unequal*. New York: Charles Scribner's Sons.

Hall, E. T., and Hall, M. R. 1990. *Understanding Cultural Differences*. Yarmouth, MA: Intercultural Press.

Hall, W., Cross, W., and Freedle, R. 1972. Stages in the development of black awareness: An exploratory investigation. In *Black Psychology*. Jones, R. (ed.). New York: Harper and Row.

Hardiman, R. 1982. White identity development: A process oriented model for describing the racial consciousness of white Americans. *Dissertation Abstracts International* 43. 104A. Ann Arbor, MI: University Microfilms.

Healey, S. 1993. The common agenda between old women, women with disabilities and all women. *Women & Therapy* 14(3/4):65–77.

Hebdige, D. 1979. *Subculture: The Meaning of Style*. London: Methuen.

Helms, J. 1984. Toward a theoretical explanation of the effects of race on counseling: A black and white model. *The Counseling Psychologist* 5:153–165.

———. 1985. Cultural identity in the treatment process. In *Handbook of Cross-Cultural Counseling and Therapy*. Pedersen, P. (ed.). Westport, CT: Greenwood Press.

Henry, J. 1965. *Culture Against Man*. New York: Vintage Books.

Hernandez, D. J. 1997. Poverty trends. In *Consequences of Growing Up Poor*. Duncan, G. J., and Brooks-Gunn, J. (eds.). New York: Russell Sage Foundation, pp.18–48.

Hernstein, R., and Murray, C. 1994. *The Bell Curve: Intelligence and Class Structure in American Life*. New York: Free Press.

Higham, J. 1997. *Civil Rights and Social Wrongs*. University Park, PA: Pennsylvania State University Press.

Holzer, H. J. 1994. Black employment problems: New evidence, old questions. *Journal of Policy Analysis and Management* 13(4):699–722.

Hsu, F. 1972. *Psychological Anthropology*. Cambridge, MA: Schenkman, pp. 241–262.

———. 1983. *Rugged Individualism Reconsidered*. Knoxville, TN: University of Tennessee Press.

Jackson, J. 1975. Black identity development. *Journal of Educational Diversity* 2:19–25.

———. 1988. The program for research on black Americans. In *Advances in Black Psychology*. Jones, R. (ed.). Richmond, CA: Cobb & Henry, pp. 38–40.

Jackson, P. 1968. *Life in Classrooms*. Chicago: University of Chicago Press.

Jargowsky, P. A. 1997. *Poverty and Place: Ghettos, Barrios and the American City*. New York: Russell Sage Foundation.

Jencks, C. 1994. *The Homeless*. Cambridge: Harvard University Press.

Jones, E. 1986. What it is like to be a black manager. *Harvard Business Review* 64:39–43.

Kandre, P. 1967. Autonomy and integration of social systems: The Iu Mien (Yao) Mountain People and their neighbours. In *Southeast Asian Tribes, Minorities and Nations*. Kunstadter, P. (ed.). Princeton, NJ: Princeton University Press.

Katz, J., and Ivey, A. 1977. White awareness: The frontier of racism awareness training. *Personnel and Guidance Journal* 55.

Katz, M. B. 1996. *In the Shadow of the Poorhouse: A Social History of Welfare in America.* Revised. New York: Basic Books.

Kearney, M. 1984. *World View.* Novato, CA: Chandler and Sharp.

Keys, C. 1975. Towards a new formulation of the concept of ethnic group. *Ethnicity* 3:202–213.

King, J. E. 1991. Dysconscious racism: Ideology, identity, and the miseducation of teachers. *Journal of Negro Education* 60(2):133–146.

Klein, E. 1991. We're talking about a revolution. *Boston Globe Parade Magazine*, August 25, 5.

Kleinman, A., Dar, V., and Lock, M. (eds.). 1997. *Social Suffering.* Berkeley, CA: University of California Press.

Knight Ridder News Service. Illinois teen's attack resembles fatal dragging of Texas man. June 14.

Kohn, A. 1992. *No Contest: The Case Against Competition.* Boston: Houghton Mifflin.

Kornblum, W. 1974. *Blue Collar Community.* Chicago: University of Chicago Press.

Kozol, J. 1991. *Savage Inequalities.* New York: Crown Publishing.

Krakow, A. 1994. *The Total Tattoo Book.* New York: Time Warner.

Kronos, S. 1971. *The Black Middle-Class.* Columbus, OH: Charles E. Merrill.

Kuper, A. (ed.). 1977. *The Social Anthropology of Radcliffe-Brown.* Boston: Routledge and Kegan Paul.

Langer, E. 1990. The American neo-Nazi movement today. *Nation*, July, 82.

Lawson, E., and Thompson, A. 1995. Black men make sense of marital distress and divorce: An exploratory study. *Family Relations* 44:213–218.

Levy, A. 1994. Looking for Generation X. *Division and Diversity* 3(3):24–26.

Levy, F. 1995. Incomes and income inequality. In *State of the Union: America in the 1990s.* Vol. 1. Farley, R. (ed.). New York: Russell Sage Foundation, pp. 1–58.

Lewis, D. 1988. A response to inequity: Black women, racism and sexism. In *Black Women in America.* Malson, M. (ed.). Chicago: University of Chicago Press.

Lewis, O. 1968. The culture of poverty. In *On Understanding Poverty.* Moynihan, D. P. (ed.). New York: Basic Books.

Littwin, S. 1986. *The Postponed Generation: Why American Youth Are Growing Up Later.* New York: William Morrow.

Liu, E. 1994. *Next: Young American Writers on the New Generation.* New York and London: W. W. Norton and Company.

Los Angeles Times. 1990. U.S. students' performance: Low and stagnant. September 27, C1.

Lyman, S., and Douglas, W. 1973. Ethnicity: Strategies of collective and individual impression management. *Social Research* 40:344–365.

Mack, W. P., USN (Retired Vice Admiral), and Paulsen, T. D. USN (Captain). 1983. *The Naval Officer's Guide.* 9th ed. Annapolis, MD: Naval Institute Press.

MacLeod, J. 1987. *Ain't No Makin' It: Leveled Aspirations in a Low-Income Neighborhood.* Boulder, CO: Westview Press.

Mandela, N. 1991. Poster. Corte Monterrey, CA: Cortal Publishing.

Marable, M. 1983. *How Capitalism Underdeveloped Black America: Problems in Race, Political Economy and Society.* Boston: South End Press.

Martin, D. 1994. The whiny generation. In *The Gen X Reader.* Rushkoff, Douglas (ed.). New York: Ballantine Books, pp. 235–237.

Martin, K. 1997. Diversity orientations: Culture, ethnicity and race. In *Cultural Diversity in the United States.* Naylor, L. L. (ed.). Westport, CT: Bergin & Garvey, pp. 75–89.

Maslow, A. 1968. *Toward a Psychology of Being.* Princeton, NJ: Van Nostrand.

Massey, D. S., and Denton, N. A. 1993. *American Apartheid: Segregation and the Making of the Underclass*. Cambridge: Harvard University Press.

McConahay, J. B., and Hough, J. 1976. Symbolic racism. *Journal of Social Issues* 32:38–50.

McDermott, R., and Varenne, H. 1995. Culture as disability. *Anthropology and Education Quarterly* 26(3):324–348.

McIntosh, P. 1989. White privilege: Unpacking the invisible knapsack. *Peace and Freedom*, July–August, 10–12.

McLanahan, S., and Sandefur, G. 1994. *Growing Up with a Single Parent*. Cambridge: Harvard University Press.

McNeil, L. 1986. *Contradictions of Control*. New York: Routledge.

McQuillan, P. J. 1998. *Educational Opportunity in an Urban American High School: A Cultural Analysis*. Albany, NY: State University of New York Press.

Middleton, R. A., Harley, D. A., Rollins, C. W., & Solomon, T. n.d. Affirmative action, cultural diversity, and disability policy reform: Foundations to the civil rights of persons with disability. *Journal of Applied Rehabilitation Counseling*. Forthcoming.

Mitchell, E. 1991. Do the poor deserve poor schools? *Time,* October 14, 60.

Moore, J., and Pinderhughes, R. (eds.). 1993. *In the Barrios: Latinos and the Underclass Debate*. New York: Russell Sage Foundation.

Morley, J. 1994. Twentysomething. In *The Gen X Reader*. Rushkoff, D. (ed.). New York: Ballantine Books, 30–40.

Morris, A. 1984. *The Origins of the Civil Rights Movement*. New York: Free Press.

Myers, L. J., et al. 1991. Identity development and worldview: Toward an optimal conceptualization. *Journal of Counseling & Development* 70:54–63.

Nash, D. 1993. *A Little Anthropology*. 2nd ed. Englewood Cliffs, NJ: Prentice-Hall.

Nash, M. 1989. *The Cauldron of Ethnicity in the Modern World*. Chicago: University of Chicago Press.

National Commission on Excellence in Education (NCEE). 1983. *A Nation at Risk: An Imperative for Educational Reform*. Washington, DC: U. S. Department of Education.

National Opinion Research Center. 1994. *General Social Survey*. New York: National Opinion Research Center.

Naylor, L. L. 1998. *American Culture: Myth and Reality of a Culture of Diversity*. Westport, CT: Bergin & Garvey.

———. (ed.). 1997. *Cultural Diversity in the United States*. Westport, CT: Bergin & Garvey.

Nichol, B., and Lee, C. 1998. Jasper scarred but healing, Jackson tells mourners. *Dallas Morning News*, June 14, 1A, 38A.

Oakes, J. 1985. *Keeping Track: How Schools Structure Inequality*. New Haven, CT: Yale University Press.

———. 1986. Tracking, inequality, and the rhetoric of reform: Why schools don't change. *Journal of Education* 168(1):60–80.

Ogbu, J. 1974. *The Next Generation*. New York: Academic Press.

———. 1987. Variability in minority school performance. *Anthropology and Education Quarterly* 18(4).

Oler, C. 1989. Psychotherapy with black clients' racial identity and locus of control. *Psychotherapy* 26:233–241.

Orfield, G. 1993. School desegregation after two generations: Race, schools, and opportunity in urban society. In *Race in America: The Struggle for Equality*. Hill, H. and Jones, J. E., Jr. (eds.). Madison, WI: University of Wisconsin Press.

Orfield, G., Easton, S., and the Harvard Project on School Desegregation. 1996. *Dismantling Desegregation*. New York: The New Press.

Parham, T. 1989. Cycles of psychological nigrescense. *The Counseling Psychologist* 17: 187–226.

Parham, T., and Helms, J. 1981. Influence of a Black student's identity attitudes on preference for counselor race. *Journal of Counseling Psychology* 28:250–257.

Paul, A. 1998. Psychology's own Peace Corps. *Psychology Today* 31(4):56–60.

Pettigrew, T. F., and Martin, J. 1987. Shaping the organizational context for black American inclusion. *Journal of Social Issues* 43(1):41–78.

Pierce, B. 1998. Benefits in unskilled jobs erode along with pay. *Dallas Morning News*, June 14, 11A.

Pinkney, A. 1968. *The Committed: White Activists in the Civil Rights Movement*. New Haven, CT: College and University Press.

———. 1993. *Black Americans*. 4th ed. Englewood Cliffs, NJ: Prentice-Hall.

Ponterotto, J. G. 1988. Racial consciousness development among white counselors' trainees: A stage model. *Journal of Multicultural Counseling and Development* 66:237–245.

Powell, A., Farrar, E., and Cohen, D. 1985. *The Shopping Mall High School*. Boston: Houghton Mifflin.

Powers, W. 1994. It don't mean a thing. *The Washington Post*.

Rank, M. B. 1994. *Living on the Edge: The Realities of Welfare in America*. New York: Columbia University Press.

Ravitch, D. 1985. *The Schools We Deserve*. New York: Basic Books.

Re Cruz, A. 1997. The Mexican American community in the United States. In *Cultural Diversity in the United States*. Naylor, L. L. (ed.). Westport, CT: Bergin & Garvey.

Reed, E., Lawson, E. and Gibbs, T. 1998. *Afrocentricity in the 21st Century*. Forthcoming.

Reminick, R. 1983. *Theory of Ethnicity: An Anthropologist's Perspective*. Washington, DC: University Press of America.

Rex, J. 1995. Multiculturalism in Europe and America. *Nations and Nationalism* 1(2).

Reynolds, A. L., and Pope, R. L. 1991. The complexities of diversity: Exploring multiple oppressions. *Journal of Counseling & Development* 70(1):174–180.

Ricks, T. 1995. New marines illustrate growing gap between military and society. *Wall Street Journal*, July 27.

Rudofsky, B. 1974. *The Unfashionable Human Body*. New York: Anchor Books.

Rushkoff, D. (ed.). 1994. *The Gen X Reader*. New York: Ballantine Books.

Sabnani, H. B., Ponterotto, J. G., and Borodovsky, L. G. 1991.White racial identity development and cross-cultural counselor training: A stage model. *The Counseling Psychologist* 19:76–102.

Salamone, F. 1997. The illusion of ethnic identity: An introduction to ethnicity and its uses. In *Cultural Diversity in the United States*. Naylor, L. L. (ed.). Westport CT: Bergin & Garvey.

Saltveit, M. 1994. Whatever. In *The Gen X Reader*. Rushkoff, D. (ed.). New York: Ballantine Books, 50–53.

Sanders, C. 1988. Marks of mischief: Becoming and being tattooed. *The Journal of Contemporary Ethnography* 16(4):395–432.

———. 1990. Memorial decoration: Women, tattooing, and the meanings of body alteration. *Michigan Quarterly Review*.

Schillinger, L. 1994. Adventures in babyland. *The Washington Post,* December 18, C1 and C2.

Schmidt, P. 1996. An end to affirmative action? Californians prepare to vote. *Chronicle of Higher Education*, October 25, A32–34.

Schrag, P. 1998. *Paradise Lost*. New York: The New Press.

Schuman, H., Steeth, C., and Bobo, L. 1985. *Racial Attitudes in America*. Cambridge, MA: Harvard University Press.

Shanahan, D. 1992. *Toward a Genealogy of Individualism*. Amherst, MA: University of Massachusetts Press.

Sherrill, M. 1995. The neo-martini. *The Washington Post*, March 10, C1 and C4.

Sigelman, L., and Welch, S. 1991. *Black Americans' Views of Racial Inequality*. New York: Cambridge University Press.

Sleeter, C. E. 1994. A multicultural educator views: White racism. *The Education Digest* 59(9):33–36.

Smooha, S., and Hanf, T. 1992. Conflict-regulation in deeply divided societies. In *Ethnicity and Nationalism*. Smith, A. (ed.). New York: E. J. Brill.

Snow, D. A., and Anderson, L. 1993. *Down on Their Luck*. Berkeley, CA: University of California Press.

Soto, L. D. 1997. *Language, Culture, and Power*. Albany, NY: State University of New York Press.

Sowell, T. 1981. *Ethnic America*. New York: Basic Books.

Span, P. 1995. Lounge-itude: Mood music swings back. *The Washington Post*, March 10, C1 and C4.

Spickard, P. 1989. *Mixed Blood*. Madison, WI: University of Wisconsin Press.

Spindler, G., and Spindler, L. 1982. Roger Harker and Schoenhausen: From the familiar to the strange and back again. In *Doing the Ethnography of School: Educational Anthropology in Action*. Spindler, G. (ed.). Prospect Heights, IL: Waveland Press.

———. 1987a. Cultural dialogue and schooling in Schoenhausen and Roseville. *Anthropology and Education Quarterly* 18(1):3–16.

———. 1987b. Ethnography: An anthropological view. In *Education and Cultural Process*. Spindler, G. (ed.). Prospect Heights, IL: Waveland Press, pp. 151–156.

Spindler, G., Spindler, L., Trueba, H., and Williams, M. 1990. *The American Cultural Dialogue and Its Transmission*. New York: The Falmer Press.

Spradley, J. P., and Rynkiewich, M. A. (eds.). 1975. *The Nacirema: Readings on American Culture*. Boston: Little, Brown.

Stack, C. 1974. *All Our Kin: Strategies for Survival in a Black Community*. New York: Harper.

Staples, R. 1982. *Black Masculinity: The Black Male's Role in American Society*. San Francisco, CA: The Black Scholar Press.

———. 1985. Changes in black family structure: The conflict between family ideology and structural conditions. *Journal of Marriage and Family* 53:221–230.

Steffan, J. 1992. *Honor Bound: A Gay American Fights for the Right to Serve His Country*. New York: Villard Books.

Stern, J., and Stern, M. 1990. *The Encyclopedia of Bad Taste*. New York: HarperCollins.

Strauss, B., and Howe, N. 1993. *13th Gen: Abort, Retry, Ignore, Fail?* New York: Vintage Books.

Sue, D., and Sue, D. 1990. *Counseling the Culturally Different: Theory and Practice*. New York: John Wiley & Sons.

Swinton, D. H. 1988. Economic status of blacks, 1988. In *The State of Black America*. Jacob, J. E. (ed.). New Brunswick, NJ: Transaction Books, pp. 129–152.

Terborg, J. R. 1977. Women in management: A research review. *Journal of Applied Psychology* 62:647–664.

Thompson, C. E., & Jenal, S. T. 1994. Interracial and intraracial quasi-counseling inter-actions when counselors avoid discussing race. *Journal of Counseling Psychology* 41(4):484–491.

Tiersky, E., and Tiersky, M. 1975. *The U.S.A.—Customs and Institutions: A Survey of American Culture and Traditions.* New York: Regents Publishing Company.

Triandis, H. 1989. The self and social behavior in differing cultural contexts. *Psychology Review* 96:506–520.

Turner, M. A., Fix, M., and Struyk, R. 1991. *Opportunities Denied: Discrimination in Hiring.* Washington, DC: Urban Institute.

U.S. Bureau of the Census. 1990. *Census Code Book.* Washington, DC: Government Printing Office.

———. 1995. *Census Code Book.* Washington, DC: Government Printing Office.

———. 1996. *Statistical Abstract of the United States.* Washington, DC: Government Printing Office, pp. 229–231.

U.S. Bureau of Labor Statistics. 1991. *Employment and Earnings.* Washington, DC: U.S. Government Printing Office.

U.S. Department of Commerce. 1994. *Statistical Abstract of the U.S., 1994.* Washington, DC: U.S. Government Printing Office.

U.S. Department of Education. 1992. *Trends in Racial/Ethnic Enrollment in Higher Education: Fall 1980 Through Fall 1990.* Washington, DC: Office of Educational Research and Improvement.

———. 1994. *The Condition of Education, 1994.* Washington, DC: U.S. Government Printing Office.

———. 1995. *The Black Population in the United States: March 1994 and 1993*; Current Population Reports P-20 (420). Washington, DC: U.S. Government Printing Office.

———. 1996. *School Enrollment: Social and Economic Characteristics of Students.* Current Population Reports, Series P-22. Washington, DC: U.S. Government Printing Office.

Van den Berge, P. 1981. *The Ethnic Phenomenon.* New York: Elsevier Press.

Walters, R. 1996. The criticality of racism. *The Black Scholar* 26(1):2–8.

Warner, W. L. 1953. *American Life: Dream and Reality.* Chicago: University of Chicago Press.

Warner, W. L., Havighurst, R., and Loeb, M. 1944. *Who Shall Be Educated?* New York: Harper and Brothers.

Webb, S., and Vassi, M. 1979. *Pushing Ink: The Fine Art of Tattooing.* New York: Simon and Schuster.

Weber, M. 1922. Ethnic groups. In *Economy and Society,* Vol. 1. Roth, G., and Wittich, C. (eds.). Berkeley, CA: University of California Press.

———. 1929. *The Protestant Ethic and the Spirit of Capitalism.* New York: Charles Scribner.

Weisbard, E. 1994. Sucking in the '70s. *Spin,* 30.

Wellman, D. 1997. *Portraits of White Racism.* Cambridge, MA: Cambridge University Press.

West, C. 1993. *Race Matters.* Boston: Beacon Press.

Wilcox, D. M. 1998. *Alcoholic Thinking: Language, Culture, and Belief in Alcoholics Anonymous.* Westport, CT: Praeger.

Wilkinson, D. 1977. The stigmatization process: The politicization of the black male's identity. In *The Black Male in America.* Wilkinson, D., and Taylor, R. (eds.). Chicago: Nelson-Hall, pp. 145–158.

Williams, I. 1994. Trash that baby boom. In *Next: Young American Writers on the New Generation*. Liu, E. (ed.). New York: W. W. Norton and Company.

Williams, N., Himmel, K. F., Sjoberg, A. F., and Torrez, D. J. 1995. The assimilation model, family life, and race and ethnicity in the United States. *Journal of Family Issues* 16(3):380–405.

Williams, N., and Sjoberg, A. F. 1993. Ethnicity and gender: The view from above versus the view from below. In *A Critique of Contemporary American Sociology*. Vaughan, T. R., Sjoberg, G., and Reynolds, L. (eds.). Dix Hills, NY: General Hall, pp. 160–202.

Willis, P. 1977. *Learning to Labour*. Westmead, England: Saxon House.

Wilson, W. J. 1987. *The Truly Disadvantaged*. Chicago: University of Chicago Press.

———. 1996. *When Work Disappears*. New York: Random House.

Yates, D., and Pillai, V. 1992. Public policy and black inequality: A critical review of the 1980s. *Indian Journal of American Studies* 22:23–31.

Young, W., Jr. 1964. Middle-Class Negroes and the Negro masses. In *Freedom Now*. Westin, A. (ed.). New York: Basic Books, pp. 315–317.

Zimmerman, J. 1995. *Tail Spin: Women at War in the Wake of Tailhook*. New York: Doubleday.

Index

About the Contributors

CLEMENTINE K. FUJIMURA is an associate professor of language and culture studies at the U.S. Naval Academy, Department of Language Studies. She received her Ph.D. in anthropology from the University of Chicago. Besides teaching Russian, German, and anthropology, her research focuses on education and subculture studies. She has published on the subjects of children's culture, orphans and street children, and Russian culture.

TYSON GIBBS is an associate professor of anthropology at the University of North Texas. He received his Ph.D. in anthropology (medical) from the University of Florida. During his career, he has served as the director of programs, Geriatric Center, Emory University, and as program director of the Gerontology Program, West Georgia College. He has authored *A Guide to Ethnic Health Collections in the United States* (Greenwood 1996).

DEBRA A. HARLEY is an associate professor of rehabilitation at the University of Kentucky. She received her Ph.D. in special education from Southern Illinois University, Carbondale. Her research interests include cultural diversity, substance abuse, and ethics. In addition to her teaching and research, she serves as associate editor of the *Journal of Rehabilitation Administration*.

BETH KAMINOW is currently completing a Ph.D. in the Human Sciences Program at George Washington University. Her research has focused on Generation X and permanent body adornment, and she has presented papers on these topics at the Anthropology Round Table at American University and Dis/Connections at George Washington University, Washington, DC.

ERMA JEAN LAWSON is an assistant professor of sociology at the University of North Texas. She received her Ph.D. in medical sociology from the University of Kentucky, Lexington. She has practiced as a registered nurse and investigated stress and infant outcomes in Zimbabwe, Africa, and Lexington, Kentucky. Her research interests include behavioral aspects of reproductive health, social and cultural aspects of health and illness, the impact of racism on health status, and family sociology. She co-authored, with Aaron Thompson, *Shattered Marriages: Black Men and Divorce*.

KIMBERLY PORTER MARTIN is an associate professor and chair of anthropology at the University of La Verne, California. She received her Ph.D. in anthropology from the University of California at Riverside. Her most recent research has focused on the trauma, depression, and anger in Vietnamese immigrants to the United States. In addition to her teaching and research, she conducts multicultural workshops for educators and social service organizations.

PATRICK JAMES MCQUILLAN is an assistant professor in the School of Education at the University of Colorado, Boulder. Prior to assuming his present position, he was co-director of a long-term ethnographic study of the Coalition of Essential Schools, a national secondary school reform initiative based at Brown University. He is the co-author of *Reform and Resistance in Schools and Classrooms: An Ethnographic View of the Coalition of Essential Schools* and authored *Educational Opportunity in an Urban American High School: A Cultural Analysis*. His current research focuses on school reform, with an emphasis on the role played by culture in efforts to restructure secondary school.

RENEE A. MIDDLETON is Director of Human Resources and Outreach in the College of Education and assistant professor in the Department of Counseling and Counseling Psychology at Auburn University. She received her Ph.D. in re-habilitation administration from Auburn University, Alabama. Her interests include disability policy issues, multicultural competencies, and racial identity develop-ment. She conducts multicultural workshops for rehabilitation and human service organizations.

LARRY L. NAYLOR is a professor of anthropology, Institute of Anthropology, University of North Texas. He formerly served as the chair of anthropology and director of the Cultural Research and Training Center at the University of North Texas. He received his Ph.D. in anthropology from Southern Illinois University, Carbondale. While with the University of Alaska at Fairbanks, he did impact studies on the trans-Alaskan oil pipeline and proposed gas pipelines, and other topics. Over his career, he has undertaken culture change studies and applied anthropology projects in Alaska, New Guinea, and Latin America. Among his many publications, he is the author of *Culture and Change: An Introduction* (Bergin & Garvey 1996), and *American Culture: Myth and Reality of A Culture of*

Diversity (Bergin & Garvey 1998), edited *Cultural Diversity in the United States* (Bergin & Garvey 1997), and co-authored *Eskimos, Reindeer and Land.*

VIJAYAN PILLAI is an associate professor of sociology at the University of North Texas. He received his Ph.D. from the University of Iowa. Specializing in demography, he has research interests in social policy, reproductive rights, development, and fertility in developing countries. He is currently looking at the problems of primary school education in Kenya. He co-edited, with Lyle Shannon, *Developing Areas: A Book of Readings and Research,* and with Thomas Barton, *Welfare as We Know It: A Family-Level Analysis of AFDC Receipt.*

CAROLYN W. ROLLINS is an assistant professor of rehabilitation at Florida State University. She received her Rh.D. in rehabilitation from Southern Illinois University, Carbondale. Her primary research interests center on ethical practices, cultural diversity, and professional development. She also regularly conducts staff development workshops for both rehabilitation and human service organizations.

DANNY M. WILCOX is an adjunct professor of anthropology at the University of North Texas. He received his Ph.D. from Southern Methodist University. While his specific specialty is in linguistic anthropology, he has worked extensively with recovering alcoholics and others involved with drug use. He is the author of *Alcoholic Thinking: Language, Culture, and Belief in Alcoholics Anonymous* (Praeger 1998).

NORMA WILLIAMS is a professor of sociology, University of Texas, Arlington. She was formerly a professor of sociology at the University of North Texas where she also served as the assistant vice president for multicultural affairs and director of the Center for Cultural Diversity. She received her Ph.D. in sociology from the University of Texas. Most of her work has focused on the Mexican-American community in the United States. She is the author of *The Mexican American Family: Tradition and Change.*

ISBN 0-89789-615-7

HARDCOVER BAR CODE